SOCIOLOGY AND THE SACRED

An Introduction to Philip Rieff's Theory of Culture

T0341605

The acclaimed American sociologist and cultural philosopher Philip Rieff gained great academic prestige with his thesis on the emergence of 'Psychological Man' in western culture and with his classic book, *Freud: The Mind of the Moralist*, published in 1959. In this work and in *The Triumph of the Therapeutic* (1966), he not only offered a highly original interpretation of the work of Sigmund Freud, but critically evaluated the enormous influence of psychotherapeutic thinking on Western culture. However, Rieff's later work on the theory of culture did not garner the same attention, and his most recent writings have received very little critical engagement. In *Sociology and the Sacred*, Antonius A.W. Zondervan sets out to remedy this neglect, arguing that Rieff's work is ripe for intellectual reconsideration.

Zondervan begins by presenting an outline of Rieff's entire body of work, focusing on his theory of culture and explaining how the sacred is a key notion, pivotal to the overall understanding of Rieff's work. The author argues that the present upsurge in religion, in many varieties throughout the world, cannot be explained by the classical secularization thesis, making Rieff's theory of sacred order in culture an essential contribution to a new social theory of religion.

Including material from personal interviews with Rieff that enabled Zondervan to clarify important aspects of his work, *Sociology and the Sacred* is an essential contribution to the understanding of contemporary culture's maintenance of its ties to religion.

ANTONIUS A.W. ZONDERVAN is an assistant professor in the Faculty of Education at Windesheim University of Applied Sciences in Zwolle, The Netherlands.

Sociology and the Sacred

An Introduction to Philip Rieff's Theory of Culture

Antonius A.W. Zondervan

UNIVERSITY OF TORONTO PRESS
Toronto Buffalo London

Toronto Buffalo London
www.utppublishing.com
Printed and bound by CPI Group (UK) Ltd, Croydon, CR0 4YY

Reprinted in paperback 2016

ISBN 978-0-8020-8018-9 (cloth) ISBN 978-1-4875-2066-3 (paper)

♾ Printed on acid-free, 100% post-consumer recycled paper.

Library and Archives Canada Cataloguing in Publication

Zondervan, Antonius A. W.
Sociology and the sacred : an introduction to Philip Rieff's theory of culture / Antonius A.W. Zondervan.

Includes bibliographical references and index.
ISBN 978-0-8020-8018-9 (bound). – ISBN 978-1-4875-2066-3 (paperback)

1. Rieff, Philip, 1922–. 2. Culture – Philosophy. I. Title.

BD450.Z65 2005 128 C2004-906131-3

This book was published with help from a grant from the Netherlands Organization for Scientific Research (NWO).

University of Toronto Press acknowledges the financial assistance to its publishing program of the Canada Council for the Arts and the Ontario Arts Council, an agency of the Government of Ontario.

Funded by the Government of Canada
Financé par le gouvernement du Canada

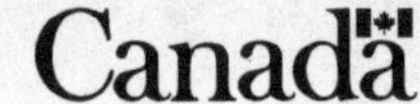

Contents

Acknowledgments vii

Introduction 3

1 A Bird's-Eye View on Rieff's Life and Work 12

2 Rieff's Reading of Freudian Metapsychology 25

3 The Emergence of Psychological Man in Western Culture 43

4 Blueprint for a Theory of Culture 67

5 The Limits of Modernity 90

6 Late Modernity as Second Culture Camp 119

7 Rieff: Prophet of a Post-secular Culture 140

Notes 167

References 195

Index 203

Acknowledgments

I am grateful for the subsidies I received for this book from the Netherlands Organization for Scientific Research (Nederlandse Organisatie voor Wetenschappelijk Onderzoek) and for the hospitality of the Department of Sociology of the University of Pennsylvania, which enabled me to work in Philadelphia to collect data needed for this book. I thank Professor Rieff and his wife for their cooperation and hospitality and Jonathan Imber for his information and fruitful discussions. Thanks also go to the editors at University of Toronto Press and to James McConica. I am particularly grateful to Raymond DeVries and Reinier Leushuis, who taught me that friendship is an essential part of academic work. Their encouragement, together with that of other friends, is the mortar that binds this book.

SOCIOLOGY AND THE SACRED

Introduction

> Haven't you heard of that madman who in the bright morning lit a lantern and ran around the marketplace crying incessantly: 'I'm looking for God! I'm looking for God!' Since many of those who did not believe in God were standing around together just then, he caused a great laughter. 'Has he been lost, then?' asked one. 'Did he lose his way like a child?' asked another. 'Or is he hiding?' 'Is he afraid of us?' 'Has he gone to sea?' 'Emigrated?' – Thus they shouted and laughed, one interrupting the other. The madman jumped into their midst and pierced them with his eyes. 'Where is God?' he cried. 'I'll tell you! *we have killed him* – you and I! We are all his murderers. But how did we do this? ... Is there still an up and a down? Aren't we straying as though through an infinite nothing? ... God is dead. God remains dead. And we have killed him! ... Do we not ourselves have to become gods merely to appear worthy of it?' ... Here the madman fell silent and looked again at his listeners: they too were silent and looked at him disconcertedly. Finally he threw his lantern on the ground so that it broke into pieces and went out. 'I come too early,' he then said. 'My time is not yet ... This deed is still more remote to them than the remotest stars and *yet they have done it themselves!*' It is still recounted how on the same day the madman forced his way into several churches and there started singing his *requiem aeternam deo.* Led out and called to account, he is said to have replied nothing but, 'What then are these churches now if not the tombs and sepulchres of God?'[1]

With these passionate words delivered well over a hundred years ago Nietzsche announced the death of God. Furthermore, this announcement was assumed to imply the end of religion itself in Western culture; however, that assumption proves to be mistaken. Indeed, we are witnessing a resurgence of religion, in various forms, throughout the entire world. This 'desecularization of the world,' as Peter L. Berger puts it,[2] has led to vehement criticism of the secularization thesis in the social sciences, philosophy, and theology. We are in need of an adequate theory of new forms of religion, and we must therefore examine anew the relations between culture and religion.

A singular and very useful contribution to this field of research has been developed by the American sociologist and cultural philosopher Philip Rieff. In the 1960s, Rieff acquired great academic prestige as an interpreter of the work of Sigmund Freud and as a cultural philosopher. Rieff's theory of 'the emergence of psychological man' was a provocative contribution to the theories of modernity and secularization (which he would elaborate upon in later writings). Yet, because of a change in style towards esotericism and a dramatic decline in the number of his publications since the 1970s, today Rieff is found only at the margins of the academic canon. What knowledge of Rieff's work does remain in the social sciences and theology is incomplete and stereotypical. In particular, his theory of sacred order (presented in his later works) is hardly known. In this book I offer an integral reading of Rieff's published work in its entirety, with the explicit aim of introducing the reader to Rieff's 'sociology of the sacred.' This introductory aspect of my undertaking includes a thematic focus whereby I examine Rieff's conceptualization of religion to demonstrate his contribution to our understanding of secularization and new religion at the turn of the millennium.

Philip Rieff's 'Sociology of the Sacred'

The fundamental changes in many aspects of life that modernity engenders make us witnesses to the emergence of a totally new *Weltanschauung*. Philip Rieff is fascinated by the vast transitions caused by the modernization of Western culture, and he suggests that the social sciences have (as yet) not matured enough to be able to formulate an encompassing theory of modernity.[3] A key problem is the inadequacy in conceptualizing transcendence and its role in social and cultural processes. Modern sociology is unable to analyse this problem because, says Rieff, modern sociology is based on the assumption that transcendence, or the 'super empirical,' no longer has relevance as a category for social theory. In his 1979 article 'The Return of the Sacred,' Bryan Wilson identifies this striking contradiction in modern sociology.[4] Evaluating the works of the founding fathers of the discipline – Comte, Marx,

Weber, and Durkheim – Wilson reminds us that in their interpretation of social development they all accorded a central place to religion. However, they also all shared the idea that the importance of religion was declining in modern societies: 'Whatever differences there were among the classical sociologists, an assumption common to almost all of them was that society could no longer rest on foundations provided by intimations of the super empirical.'[4] In other words, in its investigations of religious phenomena, sociology itself assumes a fundamentally secularizing position. In view of the upsurge of religion, in various forms, throughout the world, Wilson's criticism of a quarter century ago has become a very important theoretical issue.

Rieff, too, criticizes the inner contradiction in modern sociology. In his last published essay (1993)[5] Rieff calls his own work 'sacred sociology,' and he adheres to the classical sociological position that accords a central position to religion in social development. No culture can exist without transcendental undergirding. According to Rieff, the very essence of modernity consists in breaking away from this idea. Modern culture tries to establish itself without any reference to a transcendental order of existence, and sociology must be considered part of this enterprise. Rieff's polemical answer to this is his thesis that every culture that tries to establish its social order without reference to a sacred order must be called an *anti-culture.*

Basic Ideas of Rieff's Theory of Culture

The sacred is a main category of Rieff's sociological theory of culture. Every culture originates in ideals which belong to a sacred order of existence. Therefore, a sociological theory of culture must be able to comprehend conceptually the transcendental aspects of existence, otherwise it will fail to grasp the dynamics of culture. The shaping of the profane out of sacred prototypes is mediated by culture. We barely understand how culture performs this complex task, despite modern 'deconstructive' attempts to do so, such as Freud's theory of religion. Vital to theoretical progress in this matter is acceptance of the sacred as a theoretical category and acknowledgment that we will never be able fully to separate the profane from the sacred aspects of existence. In many mysterious ways the sacred is hidden in immanent reality. Our search for the sacred is a hermeneutical task never fully to be accomplished.

Beside this dialectic between the sacred and the profane is a second line in Rieff's thinking about culture, and that is the dialectic between the individual and community. Modern social theory tends to consider a human being primarily as a discrete individual and only secondarily as part of a community. To Rieff this is a false dualism. The individual and the community can never be conceived as separate entities: 'Culture is another name for a design of motives directing the self outward, toward those communal purposes in which alone the self can be realized and satisfied.'[6]

How culture performs its tasks can never be comprehensively assessed since these processes can only work unconsciously. In describing this idea theoretically Rieff uses the term 'primary cultural process,' to call attention to the unseen processes with which and through which culture does its work. As soon as we verbalize, write down, or put into images our view of this primary cultural process and how it works, we find ourselves on the level of what Rieff calls 'the secondary cultural process.'[7] With regard to the essence of this latter process we must remain ever aware that we cannot perceive culture empirically as we can perceive other objects that we might turn our attention to. As soon as we perceive culture as an 'object' we are engaged in a form of 'cultural expression,' and what we are in fact perceiving is the secondary cultural process. Cultural expressions must always be symbolic for they always refer to another, hidden, dimension of existence which we call 'existential.' Culture, according to Rieff, is the human *habitus*: it is typically human to create particular symbolic worlds to help us in our striving for a meaningful life in a world so hostile to our needs.

Rieff postulates that a cultural crisis emerges when a culture is unable adequately to serve in the creation and maintenance of these symbolic worlds. Modernity is such a crisis. The great modern artists and scholars help make visible and analyse this crisis. Psychoanalysis, Marxism, existentialism, paintings, and novels all express aspects of modernization, yet so far we have no comprehensive understanding of modernity. All of these cultural forms are symbolic worlds, as is religion. Each represents in its own ways some elements of the primary processes of modern Western culture. Our striving towards a meaningful life works in fundamentally different ways in premodern symbolic worlds and modern ones, and Rieff distinguishes sharply between the two.

Rieff's Interpretation of Freud

Sigmund Freud succeeded in formulating the most profound insights into the cultural crisis caused by modernization, according to Rieff, who considers Freud to be the greatest theoretical figure among social scientists of the twentieth century. In reading the Freudian text, Rieff distinguishes between Freud the psychotherapist and Freud the theorist: As a theory of the modern person, who is a person experiencing both high intrapsychic and social tension, psychoanalysis is an important contribution towards a cultural theory of modernity.[8]

How does Rieff build up his theory of psychoanalysis as a 'proto-theory' of modern culture? The point of departure for Rieff is his cultural-theoretical interpretation of Freud's ideas about neurosis as a typically modern disease. The essential point of Freud's diagnostic of neurosis, in Rieff's view, is the idea of the faltering processes of identification in 'directing the self outward, toward those communal purposes in which the self alone can be realized and satisfied.' The modern individual has tremendous difficulty in identifying the credible ideals and ideal-figures that help give direction to life. Furthermore, the mechanisms that enable these identifications no longer function sufficiently well. From such an interpretation of the concept of neurosis, Rieff asserts that Freud's basic concern is authority. The efficacy of authority functions through these identification processes, and this efficacy has been deteriorating. Thus, in turn, human desires seek other – neurotic – forms of expression. Freud, according to Rieff, considered the psychological symptoms that he examined to be symptoms of this crisis of culture.

Rieff asserts that, with his psychoanalytic therapy (Freud's remedy for the injurious consequences of the cultural crisis), Freud tried to intervene in these faltering identification mechanisms. Deeply interwoven with Freud's psychotherapeutic ideas was his profoundly atheistic view of modern culture. To Freud these faltering mechanisms were the heritage of a gradually deteriorating Christianity. Although this view implicitly grounded Freud's early writings, Rieff sees it formulated more explicitly in the later work, where Freud expressly asserted that the cultural tasks performed by Christianity could be taken over by science. But, Rieff concludes, Freud remained ambivalent on this point, because Freud also had his doubts about the abilities of science to perform in this cultural realm. In Rieff's view this ambivalence is only an example of a more fundamental ambivalence that occurs in many other forms in Freud's theories. Rieff suggests that, explored in a proper way, this ambivalence could be very fruitful for theory building. As Rieff believed that this exploration had not yet been done, in the 1950s he set about designing his own method for interpreting Freud's work, thus making a cultural-theoretical interpretation of it. Although in the pages that follow I will describe this interpretation, an evaluation of Rieff's interpretation of the work of Freud is beyond the scope of this book. The task I have set myself here is to identify and examine Rieff's main theoretical concepts and their relevance for research on secularization and new religion.

Freud felt keenly the essence of modernity, says Rieff, and suggested that in considering the end of Christianity we should look at another cultural phenomenon: the end of metaphysics. Rieff asserts that Freud taught us, more adequately than did Marx, that modernity is typically anti-metaphysical or anti-sacral. The modern individual needs – finally – to abandon identification with exalted ideals because these demand more of a renunciation of the desire for self-expression than is good for the individual. Psychoanalysis very clearly shows us, on a symbolic level, how the modern human being attempts to become free of such authority and its religious roots.

From a cultural-theoretical perspective, says Rieff, this aspiration to liberate themselves from authority is identified most clearly in Freud's theory of sublimation, which summarizes Freud's positions on the interaction between the individual and the social order, or culture. The two are at war. Each demands more of the other than it is willing to give. Still, the individual always has to accept being forced to renounce part of his or her desires to make communal life possible. Identification with the ideals of the communities one lives in is required. When that identification is successful, it will enable the individual to sublimate part of his or her instinctual desires. From this perspective, Freud's theory of sublimation can be considered a theory of the origin and dynamics of culture, says Rieff. But Freud developed this theory of sublimation in fragments, never systematically. Rieff thinks that these fragments ought to be esteemed as valuable points of departure for a theory of culture, but otherwise criticizes them severely. Rieff asserts that Freud imagined sublimation too one-sidedly, because he departed from human desire, that is, from his libido theory, and in doing so underexposed the importance of authority. Sublimation theories will not be of much help for our inquiries into the nature of modernity, because they render invisible the consequences of the crisis of authority for the modern human being and for the culture of modernity.

Towards a Theory of Culture

Freud had a keen sense of the essence of modernity, says Rieff. Therefore Freud's psychoanalytic therapy was exactly what modern beings needed in their search for liberation from oppressive structures and a means of free self-expression. Psychoanalysis, as a practice and as a theory, deeply influenced twentieth-century Western culture. In psychoanalysis we find the best clues for a typological image of modern man, which Rieff called 'psychological man.' In the concluding chapter of his first book – on Freud – Rieff advances his thesis on the emergence of the new character-ideal. In subsequent books Rieff refines his typological sketch of psychological man.

Rieff places modernization in a broad, cultural-historical context. Modernity is not the first crisis to assault Western culture's system of symbols. The way in which the individual and the social order mutually engender each other through culture endured radical transformations before modernity. Nevertheless, especially in his early writings, Rieff tends to consider modernity a radical rupture in the history of Western culture, because never before did people try so systematically to develop a culture on an entirely secular basis. This striving is fully expressed in the way modernity attempts to deconstruct authority in all its cultural forms. To Rieff then, the problem of modernity is one of authority. Authority is the central theme around which pivots Rieff's whole theory of culture.

In his later writings Rieff changes his mind regarding the radically discontinuous character of modern culture. The idea of rupture in Western culture is offset by a second central concept. No culture, says Rieff, can exist as a completely secular entity. Despite all of our attempts to destroy it, sacred order will never cease to exist. The feature typical of modernity is the attempt to deny the importance of sacred order in culture. As no culture can survive on this basis, Rieff asserts, modern culture must itself cease to exist: that is the cultural situation we find ourselves in at the beginning of the twenty-first century. Modernity gradually loses its grip on the Western imagination and gives way to a situation in which several competing worldviews must vie for priority of position in organizing the personality of Western man. This struggle Rieff calls the 'second culture camp,' a successor to the nineteenth-century German Kulturkampf.

In the arduous striving for a completely secular culture, Rieff perceives a concealed search for an 'ultimate foundation' of existence. In his analysis of the philosophical premises of modern social theory, Kieff exposes this theory's contention that access to the psychological and social order of human life is to be gained through an exploration of man's erotic capacities. Eros is conceived as 'the infinite possibilities of the self.' Therefore, because authority imposes limitations on the self, eros must be the antagonist of authority. Rieff criticizes this modern view of eros and authority, finding that it inverts life's foundations. According to Rieff, a philosophy of the foundations of life ought to centre around a theory of authority, and not around a theory of eros or of the self.

This Book in Outline

Chapter 1 is a short sketch of Rieff's life and academic career. In the succeeding five chapters I will present my reading of Rieff's published work, along two main lines. The first is an 'archeological' one, where we follow the development of the conceptual structure of Rieff's theory of culture. This begins in Chapter 2 with Rieff's exegesis of Freud's metapsychology (as expounded in Rieff's first book) and continues until Chapter 6, in which Rieff's last published work is discussed. The second, thematic, line is intertwined with the archeological line throughout the book and deals with Rieff's three basic themes: authority, sublimation, and sacrality.

Authority as an issue emerges from the question of how the individual might adjust desires propelled by instinct to the demands imposed by living in communities. Such a philosophy of authority is closely related to a philosophy of eros, the force that compels the self to long for the not-self (the Other). According to Rieff, modern man is obsessed with eros while shutting his eyes to authority. Rieff finds major support for this thesis in his reading of Freud.

In the psychoanalytic theory of culture a central concern is how to bring into balance eros and authority, self-expression and the curbing of one's desires. This dynamic is the foundation of culture. The balanced life has been discussed ever since the birth of Western philosophy, but Rieff asserts that Freud added an original contribution with his theory of sublimation. Rieff does go on to criticize Freud on this point, together with other scholars and artists whose works contain an interesting view on sublimation. In doing so, Rieff unfolds his own theory of authority and sublimation.

Rieff finds that Freud's theories typify modern thinking: Psychoanalysis is modernity's most typical artefact. The key to psychoanalysis, and to modern culture in general, is its anti-transcendental character. Beginning with this idea, Rieff developed his own theory of culture in which sacrality holds a central position. Rieff tries to move social theory 'beyond modernity.' I shall make clear how Rieff proposes a way back, a search for contact with the sacred order from which Western culture took its vital energies until the modern era. Rieff's fundamental assertion is that real cultural progress can be attained only through a renewal of contact with sacred order.

In the concluding chapter I will summarize the basic conceptual categories that emerged in my reading of Rieff's works. Using these categories I will demonstrate how Rieff describes religion and how his work relates to current debates on secularization and new religion in the sociology of religion, theology, and philosophy. I hope to convince the reader that Rieff's work is far from obsolete and is deserving of renewed attention.

1

A Bird's-Eye View of Rieff's Life and Work

Youth and Education

In 1921 Rieff's parents crossed the Atlantic on the steamer *Europa*.[1] They were Lithuanian-Jewish emigrants about to try their luck in the New World. Their son Philip was born in December 1922 in Chicago, about a year after his parents moved to that city. He grew up in a poor neighbourhood, where his father worked as a butcher. Rieff's parents took their young son to the synagogue regularly, where he underwent the Bar Mitzvah ritual. For the service he had had to learn the Hebrew liturgy by heart, although its meaning was not explained to him. When out playing, the children in the neighbourhood used their fists to make clear what the surrounding world thought of Jews. Rieff looks back on these years of his youth in Chicago with horror. As a young teenager he 'plundered' the local library every week, and in his later teens his talents were recognized. When he was old enough, grants enabled him to study political science at the Mecca of his teenage years: the University of Chicago.

The Second World War interrupted his study and deeply changed his future life. He decided to join the American army as a volunteer and was enrolled in the Air Force in 1943 as a pilot trainee. It did not take his superiors very long to see that young Rieff's talents could be put to better use somewhere other than behind the controls of an airplane. He was made assistant to Brigadier General O'Neil. Rieff recalls: 'I was his library, as it were, the Jew in the backroom ... [He] took me everywhere, and I would brief him. It probably saved my life. I probably would have died in an aircrash. I was certainly the worst navigator in the history of the American Air Force.' Rieff added to this that he would have been sent to Europe to fight had he been a better pilot. As it was, he remained in the United States. He lost, however, a number of European relatives who were murdered by the Nazis.

Rieff's interest in communism was another reason why he did not leave the United States during the war. He developed this interest during his secondary school years, when he was a member of a Jewish youth movement. During one of its summer camps he met Edward Fitzdale, who taught at the University of Chicago and was one of the leading figures of the Communist Party in Chicago. Rieff became fascinated by this man, who had fought in the war against the Fascists in Spain. The following anecdote makes clear that the Spanish Civil War appealed strongly to young Rieff's imagination. It is 1936. One fine day young Rieff makes a tough decision; he will go to Spain to join the battle against the Fascists. He tells his mother about this, who has no interest in politics at all. She replies: 'Very well, Philip. You may go fight in the Lincoln Brigade in the Civil War in Spain.' She spelled it all out, as if it were a legal contract. There was a pause and then she said: 'So long as you're home for dinner every night at six o'clock.'

Despite relentless attempts, Fitzdale and other communists did not succeed in recruiting Rieff to the Communist Party. Made suspicious by political scheming such as Stalin's purging of the Russian Communist Party and the banishment of Trotsky in 1929, Rieff was unwilling to believe the Stalinists' rhetoric about the blessings of communism. Rieff became enmeshed in contemporary debates on communism: 'My interest in Freud developed slowly. My first interest was in Marxism, simply because in the middle thirties Marxists were very active ... I was keenly aware of the differences between Marxism as an academic doctrine and Stalinism as it was practised, although the connections were quite clear.' Rieff got more interested in the Trotskyites and to become better informed about their ideas he attended several meetings of a Trotskyite group in Chicago. Several years later this was used against him, when he was interrogated by intelligence agents of the army (G2) and the Federal Bureau of Investigation. They suspected him of having communist sympathies, so during one of those interrogations they asked him why he read Russian literature, for example, the books of 'Doostooijeevskai' (the interrogator's pronunciation). Thus, Rieff discovered that intelligence agents had been watching him, for example, through checking the lending files of the municipal library of Chicago where he had borrowed so many books in his youth. These 'false steps' had far-reaching consequences, because Rieff was considered a person with sympathies that might be harmful to the nation. He was not allowed to leave the country during the war.

When the war was over, Rieff resumed his studies at the University of Chicago. At that time Robert Maynard Hutchins was the rector of the university, where the highly influential Chicago School in the social sciences developed. Rieff's tutor was the great Edward Shils, who supervised Rieff's master's thesis on Samuel Taylor Coleridge. Rieff's subject was Coleridge's thesis of the 'clerisy,' a neologism coined by Coleridge. Rieff asserted that Coleridge foresaw the later institutional failure of the English church and clergy as a cultural elite. As a cultural vanguard they had dominated English intellectual life for a long time, and Coleridge maintained that a new cultural elite had to come into existence to replace them. Here we see that Rieff's thesis and his interest in Freud were closely related: 'I wrote my master's thesis on Coleridge's theory of the clerisy, which was his neologism for a new culture elite, *Kulturträger,* which has always interested me essentially. That's what the Freudian elite became in America.'

The Early Period: 1959–1966[2]

In the 1950s Freud was omnipresent in the United States. Rieff said that his interest in Freud really developed out of a sense that the Freudian doctrine could be detected in some form or other everywhere around him, among the young and middle-aged intellectuals at the University of Chicago, for example, or in the school of education: 'To me, Freudianism, in some form or another, appeared to become the dominant form of ideation among American intellectuals ... whether they knew it or not.' Parallel to this development Rieff sensed a decline in Marxism's influence on the American intelligentsia. Rieff's interest in Freud determined the two following steps in his academic career. In 1954 he finished a doctoral dissertation with the title *Freud's Contribution to Political Philosophy* for the Department of Political Science of the University of Chicago. Thereupon Rieff acquired a grant for post-doctoral research, in the course of which he revised his thesis into a book. Rieff published this first monograph, *Freud: The Mind of the Moralist,* in 1959. In this book he analysed the Freudian text from a cultural-theoretical perspective, presenting Freud as one of the founding fathers of a new cultural elite. This elite embodied and propagated a new cultural ideology in which political, economic, or religious modes of explanation are superseded by psychological ones.[3] The general title for his ambitious thesis, which made him famous in the 1960s in both the United States and Europe, is 'the emergence of psychological man.'

Rieff was not the only one to launch a new cultural-ideal type in that period. His personality typology was one of many that were formulated by scholars working in social and cultural theory in the second half of the twentieth century. The most famous of these are the following: 'marketing personality' (Erich Fromm), 'neurotic personality' (Karen Horney), 'other-directed type' (David Riesman), 'one-dimensional man' (Herbert Marcuse), 'protean man' (Robert Lifton), and 'narcissistic personality' (Christopher Lasch). The historian R.H. King (1976) situates Rieff's ideal type like this: 'A charter member of Riesman's "lonely crowd" and close to Erich Fromm's "marketing personality," Rieff's projected figure was also an important anticipation, though more clearly nuanced, of Marcuse's "one-dimensional man."'[4] According to the literary theorist E. Goodheart (1978), Rieff's concept of the psychological man 'has affinities with Robert Lifton's Protean Man, but Rieff's elaboration of psychological man is intellectually more substantial and suggestive.'[5]

In general, critics received Rieff's first book positively.[6] It established his name as an important interpreter of the work of Freud. Like other leading figures in this field, such as Herbert Marcuse, Erik Erikson, and Norman Brown, Rieff proposed a very idiosyncratic way of interpreting Freud. They all criticized the prevailing interpretations of Freud as a social and cultural theorist dominating the contemporary Anglo-American journals in the social sciences. In the 1950s Freud was considered a predominantly conservative theorist by almost an entire generation of intellectuals, very often on account of stereotypical and oversimplifying interpretations of his work.[7] In *Freud: The Mind of the Moralist*, which comprises an analysis of the reception of Freud's work in the Anglo-American social sciences, Rieff demonstrates how crucial notions of Freud's thinking were obscured because of such oversimplifying interpretations. Persistent stereotypical ideas circulated about Freud's ideas about libido and authority. Moreover, many people did not grasp the theoretical and hermeneutical character of Freudian concepts. And, finally, psychoanalysis was too narrowly construed as a psychological theory, which blinded people to the enormous importance of Freud's thinking for cultural philosophy, the social sciences, the humanities, and theology.

In the 1950s, 1960s, and early 1970s, Rieff had a very succesful academic career.[8] While writing his dissertation, he became assistant professor of sociology at Brandeis University and chief consulting editor of Beacon Press. He held both these positions until 1958, when he became associate professor of sociology at the University of California and associate editor of the *American Sociological Review.* During the academic year 1959–60, he was visiting associate professor at Harvard and Fulbright professor at the University of Munich. In 1961 the University of Pennsylvania awarded Rieff tenure as a professor of sociology. There he occupied a special chair as University Professor from 1963. In the same faculty he was appointed Benjamin Franklin Professor of Sociology in 1967. He retained these appointments until his retirement in 1992. In the 1970s Rieff was a visiting fellow at All Souls College in Oxford. He also delivered prestigious lectures such as the Terry Lectures at Yale, the Gauss Lectures at Princeton, and the President's Lecture at St Michael's College, University of Toronto.[9]

This is an impressive career. Speaking about his only son, David, Rieff remarks: 'I was the editor of the student newspaper and expected to have a career as a foreign correspondent, which in fact is the career my son has chosen to follow, even when he was born to be an academic ... He is in fact a professional journalist. He is doing exactly what I in my boyhood thought I would do in life, although we never talked about it.' David Rieff is the son from Philip Rieff's first marriage, in the 1950s, to Susan Sontag; he is a renowned journalist and has published, for example, a book about the role of U.N. troops in Bosnia.[10] In 1963 Philip Rieff married Alison Knox, a lawyer.

Rieff's first book awarded him so much recognition that the American publishing house Collier-Macmillan approached him for an important project in the early 1960s: overseeing the American edition of an English translation of a series of smaller works by Freud. Collier-Macmillan's plans for this series, to be published with the title *The Collected Papers of Sigmund Freud,*[11] were remarkable for two reasons. First, a similar series already existed at that time, with the same title and exactly the same contents. It was issued in Europe by the British house Hogarth Press (first edition 1924) and appeared in an American edition for the first time in 1959.[12] Second, an integral English translation of Freud's published work, a project initiated in 1952, was almost finished (*The Complete Psychological Works of Sigmund Freud, Standard Edition* (London, 1961)). However, Macmillan expected an immense market for a publication like this, because of Freud's huge influence on the American intelligentsia and academic teachers and also because of the great number of academic institutions in the United States. The motives for Macmillan's project were purely commercial. They wanted to issue a cheap edition of the *Collected Papers* that would be easily available. Rieff was to introduce each volume and was also allowed to make his own grouping of Freud's works in the separate volumes. This project became very successful indeed; hundreds of thousands of copies have been sold over the years.

About the introductions he wrote for this series, Rieff says: 'I realized that the triumph of Freudianism in America was already secure before I published the ten volumes, but one thing I could do especially in the introductory volume was to introduce the reader to the perpetual struggle, all but invisible to the ordinary reader, between world theories, worldviews, *Weltanschauungen.*'

In the 1960s, the debates between Freudianism and Marxism were still high on the agenda of the social sciences, and renewed attempts were being undertaken to form a synthesis between the two. However, before matters could go that far, the reception of Freud's work had to change fundamentally. According to Sheldon Pollack (1984), Herbert Marcuse's *Eros and Civilization* (1955) dispelled the dominant image of Freud.[13] The book was a breakthrough in a development that had its roots in the activities of the theorists of the Institut für Sozialforschung in Frankfurt, Germany. People like Theodor Adorno, Max Horkheimer, Erich Fromm, and Wilhelm Reich sought to use psychoanalytic concepts in their studies of the family, politics, and culture. Very radical criticism of social processes developed with the aid of 'freudo-marxist' theory. Pollack's statement about the importance of Marcuse's book for the acceptance of Freud's work in the canon of the social sciences probably applies mainly to the Frankfurter Schule and its adherents in Europe. In the United States Rieff's *Freud: The Mind of the Moralist* played an important role, too.[14]

Marcuse and the Frankfurter Schule became increasingly popular in the 1960s among people of the American New Left.[15] At the end of this decade a small part of it, the 'Freudian Left,' had developed into an important theoretical movement. These 'left Freudians' considered Freud an important advocate for the liberation of repression and neurosis, the modern cultural equivalents of Marx's alienation.[16] Therefore, Freud must not be considered a conservative social theorist, but a 'full-blooded revolutionary.' Rieff developed a very controversial contribution to these debates, in his second book *The Triumph of the Therapeutic: Uses of Faith after Freud* (1966). Foremost, Rieff rejects the attempts by the Frankfurter School to make a synthesis between the theories of

Marx and Freud. He asserts that Freudianism is a much more vital intellectual movement than Marxism, because in Freudianism we find a far more thorough appreciation of the cultural implications of the modernization of Western culture. Therefore Freudianism has much more to offer for a theory of cultural change than does Marxism. Second, Rieff turns against the mode of Freud interpretation developed by the 'left Freudians.' According to Rieff, they did no justice to the complexity of Freud's thinking, in general, and especially to his theory of culture. Rieff asserts that Freud is not the conservative that the neo-Freudians made of him. He also contradicts the radical interpretations of Freud's texts by the 'left Freudians.' Mainly because of this criticism of the radical Freudians, Rieff was put in the right wing of the Freud interpreters, who were far less popular than their more radical colleagues.

At other points, Rieff's second book did belong to the public and intellectual mainstream. Around 1970 interest in cultural and moral issues, foreign politics, and economic issues became widespread. Intellectuals took a different approach to this from that of the politicians, who 'tended to think of the problem in terms of "moral decay," while the intellectuals are more concerned with alienation, the "cultural crisis" and the crisis of the university.'[17] Apparently, Rieff succeeded very well in bringing this problem to the fore in a recognizable way, because the book was nominated for a National Book Award.[18]

In *The Triumph of the Therapeutic*, Rieff is very critical about the impact of the emergence of psychological man on Western culture. This opinion ran counter to the optimistic spirit of the times, as Rieff was very well aware. Therefore, he wrapped his message in irony. Using a very dense language with many poetic overtones, he developed very abstract theoretical insights that presuppose a lot of knowledge on the part of his readers. Rieff's method in this book is very interdisciplinary, which is mirrored in its reception. In the citation indexes we find citations by authors in many fields of the social sciences, humanities, and theology. Some authors misunderstand Rieff's irony. They criticize him for being the herald of the triumph of psychological man, who praises this triumph. With such an interpretation, however, they have missed the point of the book completely.

The Middle Period: 1967–1972

The 1960s had an enormous impact on Rieff. He had great difficulties with the protest movements of this period, their theoretical undergirding, and their influence on academic teaching and on society in general. His third book, *Fellow Teachers of Culture and its Second Death* (1972), bears witness to this.[19] According to Kenneth Piver (1994), a former student of Rieff's, the influence of the counterculture on Rieff was so strong that an inner conversion took place.[20] The character of Rieff's work changed indeed, and this made Nietzsche's influence on him more clearly visible. In *Fellow Teachers*, the academic style of Rieff's early period is replaced by a very cryptic, aphoristic, and openly polemical style, which at the same time is much more personal.[21] He mentions his Jewish background much more explicitly than in his earlier books and refers to the killing of family members by the Nazis. As for the stature of *Fellow Teachers*, George Steiner compared the book with Julien Benda's *La Trahison des Clercs* (1927) and Martin Heidegger's essays on technological culture (1962). Steiner reviewed the book in 1975 and denounced the lack of interest in it.[22]

Like Georges Bataille, Rieff tends towards the point of view that poetry is the only means left in modern culture to write about the sacred. Tendencies towards 'scientific poetry' were already present in his early works, but in *Fellow Teachers* they became dominant. That turned Rieff into a very esoteric author. He moulds his readers in the same process as the one he aimed at in his academic teaching – acquiring hermeneutic skills. He calls this method 'unpacking.' Jonathan Imber,[23] another former student of Rieff's, writes about this notion: 'I arrived at his first seminar prepared to take course notes and to study social theory in earnest. I had no idea that we were going to begin reading Friedrich Nietzsche's "Beyond Good and Evil" or that I and others were to "unpack" its first question: "Supposing truth is a woman – what then?" Within weeks I discovered a small group of fellow students who were able to feel and see where and how such words and sentences took us into the present shapes of our social order. We unpacked for hours on end, ignoring the clock. Doing theory in this way, we read realities suddenly there before us.'[24]

In *Fellow Teachers* Rieff elaborates on his thesis of the emergence of psychological man. He puts it in the context of contemporary debates, which were dominated by existentialism and critical theory. All of this is enveloped in a severe polemic against trends in theory and policy at the universities. The 1960s brought great turmoil to the universities and to society. In the beginning of the 1970s the radicalization of the universities abated.[25] Academics reconsidered the role of the university in the new societal context in which the democratic and functional character of academic education had been broadly accepted. Rieff's book was a vigorous contribution to this reflection.

The changes in the universities mirrored the more encompassing movement of the counterculture. Rieff asserted that this cultural movement most strikingly expressed the paradigm shift of modernity. In *Fellow Teachers* Rieff polemicizes against theorists who help to undergird the political struggles for emancipation of the countercultural movements. For this criticism and his critical evaluation of modern culture in general, Rieff developed a set of conceptions by confronting his psychoanalytically based cultural theory with other theories of modernity like those of Max Weber and Soren Kierkegaard. Thus, Rieff developed a 'philosophy of transgression,' with which he indicated in more detailed ways the destructive implications of the modernization of Western culture. In this cultural criticism a positive view was hidden as well. Rieff maintained that cultural innovation was possible when the influence of modernity could be countered. *Fellow Teachers* can be read as an investigation of this process of cultural restoration. Viewed from this perspective the book is the starting point of a strand in Rieff's thinking that we may tentatively call his philosophy of postmodernity.

Fellow Teachers originated in an invitation by Robert Boyers and Robert Orrill for a public debate at Skidmore College about the theoretical chapters of *The Triumph of the Therapeutic.* Both were editors of the journal *Salmagundi* and admirers of Rieff's work.[26] They wanted to raise interest in it by printing the transcript of the debate in an issue of *Salmagundi.* But Rieff was not satisfied with the transcript and refused to give permission for its publication. In a prefatory note to *Fellow Teachers* he writes: 'My doubts about public interviews led me to begin this book, explaining how I felt about such occasions as part of the larger effort to meet expressed interest in the direction of my work.' An agreement was made that an early version of the book could be published in *Salmagundi.*[27] Rieff then reworked the manuscript into a book, tripling its size.

The book begins with this statement: 'Is it possible that my invitation to come to Skidmore ... was based upon a happy misunderstanding? Did you imagine that I am a herald of the therapeutic? I am neither for nor against my ideal type.'[28] Boyers and Orrill reply to this in the foreword of a book about Rieff's work from 1975[29]: 'It is our conviction that Rieff's writings, presently studied in detail by only a few, eventually will find acceptance as the single most penetrating effort of cultural analysis produced by an American in recent times ... We only hope that this book supplies a context in which the study of that work can begin.'[30]

The Later Period: 1973–Today

Fellow Teachers indicated a profound change in Rieff's career. In *The Triumph,* he still writes that the book is not primarily aimed at fellow theorists, 'but at those troubled readers in whose minds and hearts one culture is dying while no other gains enough power to be born.'[31] *Fellow Teachers* is explicitly aimed at his fellow theorists. In the course of the 1970s Rieff's reputation with a wider audience declined, because he refused to comply with the dictum that ruled the academic world; 'publish or perish.' Christopher Lasch (1991) points at the causal relation between the decrease in number of Rieff's publications and his disgust at the enormous increase in academic publications, very often of a dubious quality: 'The concept of the public became indistinguishable from the phenomenon of publicity. Under these circumstances, Rieff's decision to write less, to publish with university presses and scholarly journals, and to devote his energies to "strengthening our enclaves" can hardly be condemned. Still, he has paid a certain price for his strategic withdrawal.'[32] Rieff is almost ignored in a standard work about the American intellectual elite of the 1950s, 1960s, and 1970s.[33] He paid a high price for his ideas about the social role of intellectuals.

In this period, Rieff delivered the prestigious lectures mentioned above. In the course of time he started to rework the texts of these and other lectures into a manuscript for a new book, with the provisional title *The Return of the Sacred.*[34] He worked on it for years, but did not get as far as publishing it, for in the course of writing the plan kept growing. In the 1980s, the intended publication even reached the size of a trilogy, intended to become his magnum opus. The very few texts that he published in the 1980s are steps towards this trilogy. In the beginning of the 1990s, it was scheduled to be published,[35] but Rieff decided not to because he was still not satisfied with the manuscript. In that period two long articles, supposed to be summaries of the trilogy, were published. Both have very peculiar titles: 'The Newer Noises of War in the Second Culture Camp: Notes on Professor Burt's Legal Fictions' (1991) and 'Worlds at War: Illustrations of an Aesthetics in Authority; or Numbered Notes towards a Trilogy, of which the General Title is "Sacred Order / Social Order"' (1993).

In the same period a collection of selected writings was published, called *The Feeling Intellect* (1990), comprised of formerly published works from 1957 to 1987. This book, edited by Jonathan Imber, was intended to bridge the gap between Rieff's last book (from 1972) and the magnum opus to be published in the 1990s. It consists of reviews, articles, and essays that are more accessible to a broader audience. They deal with the main issues that dominated intellectual life in the United States in those decades, such as the struggle with communism, domestic reform, racism, and civil rights. The book also contains essays about important figures such as Oscar Wilde, Benjamin Disraeli, and George Orwell.

In 1992, the board of the Department of Sociology of the University of Pennsylvania used its formal right to force Rieff to retire. The Department of Psychiatry of the Medical College of Pennsylvania then invited Rieff to take a teaching position. There he taught for a few years more and worked on his manuscript for the magnum opus as much as his declining health allowed him to.

In the Rieff archive at Wellesley College in Boston, I found a copy of an application form for a one-year Fellowship of the National Endowment of the Humanities, to fund working on his magnum opus. Very succinctly Rieff describes the aim of this immense and ambitious project:

> I shall finish the writing agenda of my scholarly lifework. My lines of thought, in the trilogy, continue the work published earlier ... The *leitmotif* is the long cultural revolution that is transforming Western civilization. This transformation is called, in my historical typology, 'late second culture.' By 'second culture' I intend the complex order of compelling symbols and compulsive symptoms ... of Western social conduct under the increasing threat by intellectual and moral currents of thought and feeling representing by what I address, typologically as 'third culture.' The steady object of my lifework has been and remains what was first titled in Bismarckian Germany '*Kulturkampf*.'

Rieff, who is an ardent art collector, writes this about the style:

> The work will be published in three volumes – or, conceivably, four, with a few hundred illustrations. The text will weave around the illustrations, each of which will be fully examined in the theoretical context of the text ... Throughout each volume there are uses of poetry, philosophy, history, theology, music, psychology, art history and other disciplines ... My concluding work is synoptic ... The manuscript is broken, like the culture it examines, into a jumble of fragments that I have locked in, one to another, so to unify late 'second culture' thought in the humanities and social sciences. Call

> the style *bricolage*. If these books do their job, the humanities and the social sciences should be, in some signifying degree, reunited. I intend a unifying theory and praxis. Finally, my purpose is to supply a mode of thought that will revive 'second culture.'

A very telling detail is his answer to the question for intended travelling during the fellowship: 'If I travel, my journey will be to Auschwitz.'

The fellowship was not assigned. Rieff stopped working on the manuscript and appointed Kenneth Piver as the editor to finish the magnum opus. Piver has been working on it since 1996.

The Reception of Rieff's Work

Rieff's first book and the *Collected Papers* brought him fame as an interpreter of Freud. Next to this, his second book made him known as a provocative thinker about the 'psychologizing of Western culture.' In the 1960s Rieff was a well-known intellectual. In the 1970s this public reputation eroded. In the beginning of the twenty-first century, the image prevails that Rieff was an important social theorist in the 1960s and 1970s, whose work, however, is not relevant anymore for contemporary scientific debates. There is no 'Rieff school' of scholars who study his work thoroughly and try to 'translate' his very abstract ideas into useful concepts.

Still, a short survey of the digital citation indexes, carried out in the summer of 1999, proved that Rieff has not been totally forgotten. In the *Social Science Citation Index* (SSCI) and the *Arts and Humanities Citation Index* (*AHCI*) I found 256 references for the previous eleven years, in a great variety of disciplines. Three-quarters of these references are to works of Rieff's early period. In the American Theological Library Association (ATLA) *Religion Index* I only found ten references for the past forty years. This confirms that Rieff's later works are not very well known, in particular the articles of the 1990s. Apparently theologians are not very interested in Rieff's work. These conclusions cannot be more than preliminary. A further study of the reception of Rieff's work demands more elaborate research of the literature, which is beyond the scope of this book. A second consideration about Rieff's reputation is that he has been called a 'writer's writer' or a 'father figure for some of the best American intellectuals'.[36] Rieff's reputation as a public intellectual may have declined, his work still exerts a strong influence on some intellectuals who do have a great public reputation, such as Christopher

Lasch and Alisdair MacIntyre. And also in the sociological bestseller *Habits of the Heart* (1985) we find references to Rieff's early works.

As yet no overall study of Rieff's work has been published. This book is a more rigorous attempt than that by Robert Boyers[37] to supply a context in which the study of Rieff's work can be taken up again and includes Rieff's later works, in which his thinking develops towards a very interesting theory of 'the second culture camp.'

2

Rieff's Reading of Freudian Metapsychology

Psychoanalysis was the first real psychological discipline, says Rieff, and its founder, of course, was the Viennese neurologist and psychiatrist Sigmund Freud (1856–1939). Freud's theory and technique fostered a vast propagation of psychology. Psychological modes of approaching problems became increasingly widespread in twentieth-century Western culture. Therefore, a cultural theory of modernity must necessarily assess the meaning of psychoanalysis to Western culture. That is Rieff's aim in *Freud: The Mind of the Moralist.* He shows that psychoanalysis can be interpreted as a philosophy of culture that became an influential cultural factor itself. To see and understand this we must learn to consider Freud anew, because contemporary readings have blurred and even distorted many aspects of Freud's thinking that are essential to a cultural-theoretical interpretation of his texts.

The Theoretical Foundations of Psychoanalysis

Freud was the greatest social theorist of the twentieth century, Rieff asserts, because he gave us the theory of psychoanalysis. Although Freud himself never systematized his theoretical writings into one closely reasoned theory – apparently finding that to be abhorrent dogmatism – Rieff maintains that there are a few concepts that one can take as fundamental to Freud's thinking. The best place within the whole Freudian canon to start a search for these fundamental concepts is, according to Rieff, *The History of the Psychoanalytic Movement* (1914). Hence this is the first volume of Freud's *Collected Papers,* which were edited by Rieff. In its introduction Rieff points out that scientific theory is never developed in a vacuum: 'Intellectual questions soon shade off into questions of organization.'[1]

He reminds us of how, in his 'lonesome years' until 1902, Freud would brood about the intellectual questions upon which psychoanalysis is based. In the following period (1902 to 1910), a number of strong and bright personalities, including Ernest Jones (1879–1958), Karl Abraham (1877–1925), and Carl Gustav Jung (1875–1961) gathered around Freud.[2] Gradually, the psychoanalytic movement formed. Ardent debates were commonplace, with some leading to schisms, as did the famous rupture between Freud and Jung. Rieff suggests that these debates forced Freud to formulate the particular starting points of his own theory more explicitly and understandably.[3] In this way Freud made clear to the outside world what may be considered psychoanalysis and what may not – among the latter, for example, the theories of Jung and of Alfred Adler (1870–1937), another former 'disciple' of Freud. Rieff calls *The History of the Psychoanalytic Movement* a masterpiece of polemic.

Psychoanalysis as a New Scientific Discipline

The phenomenon of what was then called hysteria confronted medical science in the second half of the nineteenth century with huge therapeutic and theoretical implications. In 1895, together with neurologist Joseph Breuer, Freud published *Studies on Hysteria.* In this book they describe the spectacular therapeutic results they were able to achieve using hypnosis in the treatment of a patient with hysteria. Breuer had brought this patient under hypnosis so that she would talk; in listening to her, he discovered that her hysterical symptoms held meaning. Leading the hypnotized patient back to the traumatic scene in which the hysterical symptoms had originated aroused a vehement reaction from the patient – this was thought to be the draining of accumulated emotions, and the accumulation was considered the cause of the hysterical affliction. New possibilities seemed to announce themselves for developing a cure for this affliction. Similar experiments were carried out in France, by, among others, the neurologist and psychiatrist Jean-Martin Charcot. Freud worked in Paris with Charcot for some time and elaborated this therapeutic treatment with Breuer in Vienna, calling it 'the cathartic method.'

Gradually, however, a number of limitations of the cathartic method became apparent, and its development stagnated. From the perspective of this chapter the main point is as follows. Breuer clung to modes of explanation of hysteria that were mainly *physiological.* He tried to explain the mental dissociation that occurs in hysteria with the idea of a lack of communication between different psychic states. He developed a theory about 'hypnoid states' that penetrate into waking consciousness like 'unassimilated foreign bodies.'[4] Freud followed a different path in explaining this mental dissociation. He understood it as the effect of a rejection by the patient of an emotion that was considered improper. At first Freud called this 'defence,' and later on 'repression.' According to Freud, this repression does not come 'from without,' but is part of the complex and unconscious structure of human character. Thus, Freud tended more to a *psychological* explanation. The difference between these two approaches turned out to be so fundamental that it became inevitable that Freud and Breuer would grow apart theoretically. Freud went his way and developed the *analytic* therapeutic theory and technique. With his method, Freud tried to trace the causes for mental diseases that he saw as being deeply built into the structure of the character of his neurotic patients. According to Rieff, Freud made psychology into a real scientific discipline: 'It is only when psychic life is segregated conceptually from the rest of biological nature that psychology proper may be said to exist.'[5]

Disagreements on the Basic Concepts of Psychoanalysis

In his introduction to *The History of the Psychoanalytic Movement* Rieff identifies two other basic concepts that Freud describes in that book: the unconscious and the libido.[6] Both are related to repression. Rieff contends that the breaks between Freud and Jung and between Freud and Adler were also inevitable because of disagreement concerning basic concepts. These disagreements ran so deep that Freud wanted those who disagreed with him on these points to cease calling themselves psychoanalysts. We will stop here. This polemic, Rieff explains, is not relevant for us in the first place for its content: 'The first lesson to be learned from this book has little to do with the empirical content of the argument but rather with its theoretical form.'[7]

Rieff asserts that Jung and Adler did not attack only the *psychological* character of the cornerstones of psychoanalytic theory. Another danger appeared, because both Adler and Jung elaborated their theories into 'total systems.' According to Rieff, 'the major difference between Freud and the first schismatics is ... that Freud ardently desired to avoid having his insights locked up in a system. It is within the cosset of a symbol system that people can ease their minds in a security of spuriously complete explanation.'[8] That was precisely why Freud rejected metaphysics and religion, being eager to unmask the illusions of both, which he considered to be meaningless daydreams about an ultimate solution to the irreconcilable contradictions on which life is built. Freud maintained that science had proved such illusions untenable and that humanity had to wake up from these daydreams. Rieff describes the essence of Freud's debates with Jung and Adler like this: 'Adler and Jung sought, each in his own way, a cure, while Freud, the atheist, knowing there was no cure, sought an increase in human power over the most elusive rebel forces of all, those of the instinctual unconscious.'[9]

Rieff asserts that the theories of the unconscious of Jung and Adler cannot be reconciled with those of Freud. For the former the unconscious was not a critical principle of explanation as it was for Freud, but a 'total (ideological or religious) system.' Adler sought the causes of repression primarily in social processes instead of in the instinctual unconscious, says Rieff, and elaborated psychoanalytic theory into a social ideology. Jung came round 'to a version of the unconscious that really gave it the function of the ideal and eternal order, as in the older mode of theorizing. Without quite realizing what they were doing, both Adler and Jung rushed beyond Freud's doctrine of personal capacity into religious aspirations to understand man whole and cure him entire.'[10] In *The Triumph* Rieff uses the term 'doctrines of salvation' for the theories of Jung and Adler.

Thus, *The History of the Psychoanalytic Movement* is theoretically important for us because of the way Freud designated the specific character of his theory. Freud wanted to safeguard both the *psychological* and the *anti-metaphysical* character of psychoanalysis. Freud's metapsychological theory, which he developed more explicitly after 1914 as a theoretical foundation for psychoanalytic theory, was to serve mainly these two goals. Rieff considers this metapsychology as a totally new kind of theory in Western science. To account for this view he develops his own theory of theory.

Rieff's Theory of Theory

In his introduction to *The History of the Psychoanalytic Movement* Rieff places Freud's metapsychology in a broad cultural and historical perspective. Theories of the positivist sciences, including psychoanalysis, differ fundamentally from those of premodern sciences ('the older mode of theorizing'), says Rieff. He characterizes positivist theories like this: 'When psychoanalysis frees a patient from the tyranny of his inner compulsions, it gives him a power to choose that is not otherwise his. Thus the aim of psychoanalysis is the aim of science – power, in this case a transformative technology of the inner life. Where science is, there technology will be.'[11] This transformative character of modern positivist theory is the opposite of what Rieff calls the *conformative* character of premodern sciences.

The essential point regarding the differences between these two types of theory is that premodern science presupposed a totally different cosmology than modern science. Premodern science was based on the idea of the harmony of spheres. Reality was assumed to be a cosmos, consisting of a number of spheres all mirroring each other. The human being, for example, was considered a microcosmos, which mirrored the other spheres of the surrounding macrocosmos. For example, people thought that there were similarities between the four elements of the macrocosmos (air, water, fire, and earth) and the four human temperaments (the irascible, the indifferent, the passionate, and the melancholic). With such analogies relations between many different elements of reality were discerned. All these relationships in their entirety formed the order that God put into the cosmos when He created it. In this divine order all plants, animals, human beings, stars, planets, et cetera had their proper place and were interrelated through analogical similarities. This order is partly hidden from human perception. Thus it was the task of the premodern sciences to search for these similarities and interpret their meaning. From the knowledge obtained in this way, rules were inferred for living according to God's will. In this type of thinking 'description' and 'prescription,' in other words 'is' and 'ought,' are closely interwoven: 'Questions about how to live then smoothly passed into descriptions of human nature, of human physiology et cetera. Ethics consisted in offering a total view of reality and ideals which resulted from this of their own accord. One lived in a world where 'is' and 'ought' blended in a natural way.'[12]

In premodern theory it was assumed, says Rieff, that theorizing is the method with which 'what ought to be' – the normative ideal, establishes its hegemony over 'what is.' Truth and value are inseparable. 'Theory is the reflecting mirror of man's mind, catching glimpses of an order eternally right and good. In this first tradition of our culture, which persisted unbroken until well into the eighteenth century, there could be disagreement on the means of bringing mankind to conform to the eternal and stable order of things as they really are, but not on the ends. ... Theory is the way of understanding the ideal. In this theory of theory, knowledge finally emerges, at its highest level, as faith ... God is the final object of all classical theorizing, to know God in his natural order (or moral commandments) as the highest good.'[13]

Against this type of theory Rieff positions the second, more recent kind: transformative theory. This new form presupposes a different approach to reality. Transformative theory is silent about ultimate ends, and it arms us with the weapons for transforming reality. There is no longer room for the idea of conforming ourselves to a divine order. Punning on the Greek word for the New Testament (*eu-aggelion*), which means 'good news,' Rieff writes: 'In the absence of news about a stable and governing order anywhere, theory becomes more concerned with mitigating the daily miseries of living than with a therapy of commitment to some healing doctrine of the universe. In fact, the universe is neither accepted nor rejected; it is merely there for our use. In the second tradition, knowledge is not, at its highest reach, faith, but rather power.'[14] With this type of knowledge the 'autonomous individual' establishes his freedom to choose from the possibilities that proceed from the way theory imagines reality.

Implicit in Rieff's description of modern social scientific theory is a polemic against the way this type of theory usually conceives of itself. Positivist theory asserts that it is morally neutral. It 'merely recovers reality as it is,' rejecting the premodern idea of theory as an imposition of a religious worldview on reality. Rieff rejects this neutrality, simply because it does not exist. He asserts that the attempt of modern theory to supersede premodern theory is a clash of worldviews. For modern theory to attain a victory in this struggle it has to try to disarm the older, religious, worldview. Thus, in Rieff's opinion, modernization is not just a matter of substituting one type of theory for another. The new type of theory 'arose both as a response to the death of the gods and also as a weapon for killing off those surviving, somehow, in our moral unconscious and cultural conscience.'[15] This weapon must help the modern individual to acquire a real autonomy. The way to reach this goal is to learn to approach reality with a resolutely analytical attitude towards it.

According to Rieff, Kant's philosophy catalyzed the process in which this new type of theory came into being, because Kant shifted the way of recovering truth from the analysis of objective reality to an inspection of the structure of cognitive experience. For Kant 'man is not a passive beholder of the cosmic spectacle. Only the matter of reality is given; its form is dictated by the mind. Reality is actively organized by the *a priori* concepts that are anchored in the mind, as the "analogies of experience." Kant was certain that his critical philosophy had effected "a Copernican revolution."'[16] Rieff refers to Kant because Freud also frequently used the epistemological concept 'analogy.' In the next section I will show more elaborately what Rieff has in mind here. For now the point of Rieff's comparison of Kant and Freud is that the latter indeed used a concept that was also used in premodern theory, but Freud, like Kant, endowed it with a totally new meaning in his theory of the unconscious. With that concept Freud developed an entirely new theory of knowledge and rationality. Freud was certain, like Copernicus and Kant before him, that his theory was revolutionary. Psychoanalysis was a severe blow to human self-love in asserting that man is not his own master, because man is not governed by his rational ego but by his unconscious. Freud called this 'the *psychological* blow to man's narcissism and compared it with the *biological* blow delivered by the theory of descent and the earlier *cosmological* blow aimed at it by the discovery of Copernicus ... Freud's analogical discoveries were equally a destruction of metaphysics and a critique of knowledge as a pre-established harmony of nature and mind.'[17]

By invoking Kant in this way, Rieff establishes a relation between his own interpretation of psychoanalysis – as an anti-metaphysical theory – and the modern problem of 'the end of metaphysics.' Rieff asserts that Freud tried to make clear with his metapsychology how 'modern nervous diseases' came forth from the cultural crisis proceeding from the decline of Christian religion. Neurotic symptoms, according to Freud, are 'compromise formations,' which arise from a tension between instinctual desires and a psychic agency ('internalized morality') that rejects those desires for moral reasons. Neurotic symptoms revealed that traditional morality, based on Christianity, was eroding severely. It became less deeply anchored in the human mind, and thus it was less able to control the instinctual desires. Freud sought the cause of neurosis in the influence of this declining religion, still lingering in our unconscious. The solution to neurosis was to be found in a technique that helped modern man to get rid of this lingering influence and thus learn to live autonomously, without religion. Freud believed, although with ambivalence, that this technique would enable the individual to manage his or her instinctual life in a prudent and rational way.

This leads us towards a basic question of sociological theory. Every society faces the question of how to regulate the relationships between the individual and the community. The mechanisms that connect the individual and the social order are called 'therapy' in Rieff's work.[18] He asserts that the antimetaphysical ideal that characterizes Freud's theory is typical for almost all modern social theory, because it proceeds from the cultural crisis that I described in the previous paragraph. In sociological theory Rieff discerns two, related, major motifs: 'First, theory was developed as an ideological response to the problem of social order after the fall of the *ancien regime*; second, theory was developed as a source of ideals calculated to replace those fatally called into question during the period of middle-class political and social revolution.'[19] The founding fathers of sociology, like Comte, Saint-Simon, and Fourier, developed new theories of social structure and of the individual's place in it. This new, transformative, type of theory was meant to help emancipate the individual towards autonomy.

As I indicated in the introduction, the question of regulating the relationships between the individual and the community invokes the problem of authority. Rieff formulates the question like this: 'By what processes of signification does a social order breed moods of acceptance?'[20] The modern answer to this question is that an analytical attitude towards tradition and authority must be taught, in order to build up new social structures and mould people into critical individuals. This became an integral part of the modern processes of signification. According to Rieff, the great reformist theorists of modern pedagogy contributed to this development. Rieff criticizes them thus: 'The great reforming theorists [of pedagogy] have been misled by their conception of it as an instrument with which to alter the structure of authority in society.'[21] Rieff evaluates Freud's opinion of the social meaning of psychoanalysis under the same heading. Freud thought that one major task of the psychoanalytic movement was to propagate psychoanalysis as much as possible in science, education, and other cultural spheres, precisely to help alter fundamentally the structure and function of authority in society. Rieff calls this 'the Freudian pedagogy' and criticizes this ideal severely, mainly in his later works.

Basic Features of Freud's Metapsychology

We have seen so far how Rieff argued that Freud's theory was the first true psychology and that this theory belongs to a totally new type of scientific theory. We saw how Rieff undergirded this with a theory of theory. This is a theoretical instrument with which he laid bare the most fundamental disagreements between Freud, on the one hand, and Jung and Adler, on the other. From the vantage point of historical distance Rieff shows how Freud fought for the truly psychological and truly analytic character of psychoanalysis. Psychoanalysis, however, is more than psychology. Freud was deeply interested in the interaction between social processes and psychic processes. Therefore psychoanalysis must be considered a social science as well, says Rieff.[22] This interdisciplinary character of psychoanalysis was blurred in the later reception of Freud's texts, as was its moral nature. Dissecting Freud's Anglo-American reception in *Freud: The Mind of the Moralist*, Rieff develops his own view on the particular character of psychoanalysis and of the roles of its basic concepts. In this book Rieff undertakes a very broad exegesis of Freud's work. For the sake of brevity we have to confine our focus to the issues that are important for Rieff's theory of culture.

Psychological, Sociological, and Moral Aspects of Psychoanalysis

The first chapter of *Mind of the Moralist*, is entitled 'Science and Moral Psychology.' Here Rieff elaborates the specific character of psychoanalysis as a new, psychological discipline. He refers to the revision of Freud's theory by Franz Alexander: 'perhaps the most cogent among the revisionist attempts within the psychoanalytic movement is that of "psychosomatic" medicine which has grown up, under the leadership of Franz Alexander, at the Institute for Psychoanalysis in Chicago.'[23] In this psychoanalytic school a lot of work was done on the complex problem of the interrelations of body and mind. It disputed the alleged division in somatic and psychic diseases. Alexander sought to introduce a consistent division in neuroses with a psychic etiology ('conversion neuroses') and those with a physiological etiology ('organic neuroses').

According to Rieff, this theoretical work is very important because it recognizes the mind-body relationship as a fundamental problem and raises it in an adequate way. In addition, however, Rieff points to a serious difficulty that it ignores. Alexander does not recognize that the psychological and physiological criteria he uses in the classification of neuroses belong to two different fields of logical inquiry, neither of which alone is capable of engrossing the entire problem of disease. While possibly the most cogent attempt among the revisionist efforts to im-prove Freudian theory, it remains unable to solve a more basic problem which Rieff describes like this: 'Mind may be studied in purely physiological terms. Or it can be treated, in Dewey's words, as "the body of organized meaning by which events of the present have significance for us." Each method studies from an equivalent metaphoric distance, a different subject; no choice between them is necessary.'[24]

Rieff applies his criticism of Alexander's theory also to theories of later post-Freudians such as Karen Horney, Erich Fromm, and David Riesman, who revised Freud's theory. In *Mind of the Moralist* Rieff asserts that the unification of biologizing and sociologizing tendencies in depth psychology poses a problem which as yet has not even been stated clearly, let alone solved. Rieff's general criticism of the post-Freudians is that they do not recognize this theoretical problem adequately. Rieff is always looking for 'a third way,' by approving the points of criticism of the revisionists that he finds valid, while at the same time pointing to the shortcomings of their revisions, as can be seen in this passage: 'History changes the expression of neurosis even if it does not change its underlying mechanisms. If Freud may be accused of biologizing the ambivalences by which all societies are constituted, the post-Freudians may sociologize them too much.'[25] This problem, too, has not yet been solved, and in *Mind of the Moralist* Rieff contributes to a solution.

The specific problem refers to a more general problem, says Rieff, which is the relations between the social sciences and the physical or natural sciences. In psychoanalytic theory, Freud successfully combined both realms and was thereby able to penetrate more deeply into the problem of psychopathology than could medicine before that. According to Rieff, typically Freud aimed at the contents of the individual mind in his psychodynamic explanation and not at general categories. Freud wished to restore the neurotic patient's capacity for decision, and that is what makes psychoanalysis a moral science as well. Rieff pits this therapeutic aim of psychoanalysis against the goals of the natural sciences: repeatability and precision.[26] The price these sciences must pay in attaining those goals is to remain at a greater distance from the complexities and history of human reality. Freud tried to combine both scientific methods, in joining the 'distanced' positivist sciences that study human beings with the hermeneutical (psychological) concepts with which the social and moral behaviour of human beings can be studied more closely.

Freud was thoroughly educated in mechanistic psychology, and he had learned how to use mechanistic concepts like 'force' and 'psychic energy.' He kept on using these concepts, says Rieff, but their meanings for Freud became gradually more metaphoric. Freud realized that to develop his analytic theory he should not quantify and measure, but rather use his intuition and interpret and evaluate existing theories. This was required by the object of Freud's science, for 'the passions with which Freud concerned himself display such elusive modulations and reversals, express themselves so ingeniously, and are at the same time ... so gross, so morally fraught, so unwieldly, that experimental science cannot encompass them.'[27] Thus, for his psychoanalytic theory Freud employed concepts borrowed from various existing disciplines and also developed new ones. To grasp the meaning of all those concepts correctly, we have to be aware both of their functions in Freudian discourse and of the intuitions that Freud tried to think out in using them.

It is from this perspective that Rieff throws new light on the specific metaphorical cast of psychoanalysis. Freud's use of metaphors shows that he aimed at combining the methods of the natural and the social sciences, in order to optimize the goals of both. Probably Freud's most famous model is the one that he devised (and over the years refined) to describe the development of libido. In its most general form, the libido model consists of oral, anal, and genital stages of human development. Freud used 'anal stage,' for example, as a positivist concept, turning the experiences of particular people into a general law of libidinal development. Freud also, however, used 'anal stage' in searching for the etiology of psychological symptoms of a patient in individual cases. How did a particular patient learn to deal with certain desires and to control them? What meanings were passed on in this process? How were sanctions conveyed? 'Anal stage,' thus, denotes a cluster of known desires as well as the basic form in which this particular patient – in the particular constellation of his physical and mental constitution, his family, and his social and cultural circumstances – learned to deal with these desires.

Rieff believes that to have a psychology at all presupposes a conception of the mind in terms of social and moral behaviour. Neither the primitive notion of the soul (*anima*) as the principle of the preservation and locomotion of the body, nor the modern physiologist's dispassionate model of the brain as an intricate communications switchboard is a psychological conception: 'It is only when psychic life is segregated conceptually from the rest of biological nature that psychology proper may be said to exist, and that the individual can become, as it was for Freud, the unit of analysis.'[28] But Freud's psychological theory is essentially ambivalent. Freud sought to introduce new concepts into the vocabulary characteristic of late nineteenth-century materialist science that would make it feasible to examine human nature as distinct from the rest of nature. Freud also, however, wanted to share in the prestige of the positivist sciences, which dissolve the individual into the larger natural reality. In the next sections I will point out the consequences of this for Rieff's analysis of the basis concepts of psychoanalysis.

Instinct Theory

How can we discern the ambivalence described above in Freud's theory of instinct? According to Rieff, Freud assumes that the deepest motives of human behaviour are instinctual and believes that these instinctual desires are 'egoistic' by nature. The human being, however, must learn to live in social relations, too, and this requires a curbing of instinctual desires. For Freud the human character is the battlefield between instinctual desires and social inhibiting forces. According to Rieff, Freud builds a double dialectic into his conceptualization of this mental conflict by suggesting that the forces inhibiting instinctual desires do come not only from without, but also from within. The cause of neurotic symptoms 'can be traced not merely to social rigidities (as Dewey would have it) but farther back – to the ambivalent structure of instinct itself, which continually prepares the ground for conflicts.'[29] This brings Rieff to the conclusion that 'simple natural expressivity' is not possible because the very structure of instinct is ambivalent. I will return to this problem in more detail in the next chapter.

Rieff points out that this notion of the inner dialectical (intrapsychic) structure of libido is lost in neo-Freudian revisions of Freud's work. He puts Horney and Fromm, who followed Dewey, together with Adler in the single category of 'liberal revisors of Freud' who all stress 'individual growth.' Their conception of the antagonism between desires and inhibition is the struggle of the individual human being, striving for growth, against the cultural precepts that protect the interests of society. For them the inhibition of individual desires only comes from without.

The Theory of the Unconscious

Freud thought that psychoanalysis had to stand up to metaphysics and religion. Rieff gives the following polemical response: 'Philosophy cannot do without god-terms ... The unconscious functions for Freud as a "god-term" ... it is Freud's conceptual ultimate, a First Cause, to be believed in precisely because it is both fundamental and inaccessible to experience.'[30] Rieff asserts that Freud, in his theory of the unconscious, goes against the traditions of modern, empirical science even more radically than in the theory of instinct (libido). Rieff demonstrates this by evaluating Freud's notion of the unconscious from the perspective of the previous history of the concept (see below). Here Freud veers away from the tradition of classical ontology, where the 'conceptual ultimate' always invokes a notion of form or structure, from which one is led to infer that every form must form 'something.' Thus, secondarily, a fundamental substrate is imagined. In Freud's theory it is the other way around. First, Freud imagines a primary substrate – unconscious desires – which are shaped and controlled by a secondary agency. This puts Freud's version of the unconscious closer to the more recent notion of the creative eruption and subsequent repression of German idealism. Rieff is cryptic here. The central point seems to be that in Freud's thinking, as in German idealism, the forming and controlling agency is conceived of as secondary: 'Freud's concept is another version of the idea of primitive Chaos that supplied Romanticism with its first cause and last resort.'[31]

The concept of the unconscious had gone through a long evolution of meaning from Leibniz to German idealism: 'Leibniz used it to describe the appetitive intention of a transcendental nature installed in the self. But later philosophers – Fichte, Schelling, Hegel, Schopenhauer, von Hartmannn and Nietzsche – broached the meaning Freud was to give to the term, by seeing the unconscious as blind natural will.'[32] In these psychologizing philosophies 'will' is not the actual will, but metaphorical. It implies desires of which the conscious mind is ignorant or which it rejects. Like the mainspring in a watch, the potency of the mind lies coiled up within the self and unwinds inexorably in the course of time: 'Thus, from being a locus of subjective intention, the unconscious, in the psychologizing philosophies of the nineteenth century, became the expression of an objective force, of fixed contents and developments.'[33] In this latter citation Rieff plays with the notions 'subjective' and 'objective.' Leibniz held that a transcendental nature exists, which has been installed in the self from without, whereas in the psychologizing philosophies this nature comes forth entirely from the mind itself and thus has an immanent origin. We would call the former 'objective' and the latter 'subjective,' but Rieff turns this around. I interpret this ironic reversal as an implicit criticism of the idea that the origin of that which is beyond individual consciousness and at the same time the core of individual identity, or subjectivity, is imagined as wholly immanent. We will see in later chapters that this is an important idea for Rieff's theory of culture.

In this way, Freud radically psychologized the nineteenth-century philosophy of the will. For him the unconscious was an objective force, with a fixed content and a fixed pattern of development. As for the content, Rieff refers to Freud's *Interpretation of Dreams*, where the dream is called the *via regia*, the royal road, to the unconscious: every dream is, in a concealed form, a wish fulfilment. As for the developmental aspect, Rieff refers to Freud's model of character development with its fixed stages as an example of Freud's idea of the immutability of the development of unconscious, instinctual desires.

Freud added a second notion to the unconscious as conceptualized by German idealism, which Rieff describes as 'duality.' There is a deep and dormant unhappiness in our lives that is so far out of the reach of consciousness, contends Rieff, that Freud thought it must be lodged – metaphorically – in another part of the psyche. The revisionists were not satisfied with this diminishing of consciousness. Beginning with Adler, they altered the notion of the unconscious in such a way that it lost its critical acumen: 'The idea of the unconscious, which forms the cornerstone of Freud's historical conception of sickness, must be got out of the way before the situational or contextual control of sickness, given its most subtle formulation by Dewey and now dominant, in adulterated form, in American social and individual psychology, can prevail.'[34]

The Theory of Repression

The third basic concept of psychoanalysis is repression, and this has been subjected to a lot of discussion and revision as well. The idea of repression is closely related to the former two concepts and is crucial for the way Freud imagined neurosis and its symptoms. According to Rieff, the central point is as follows. The Freudian unconscious is not simply a reservoir of repressed experiences and desires, of which we are at the moment unaware; rather, it contains our 'forgotten origins' that still influence our life.[35] Repression cannot only be ascribed to the influence upon our inner lives of historically and culturally dependant moral ideas internalized in what Freud called the superego. The psyche itself also has various defence mechanisms to avert undesirable instinctual energies, and Freud discovered mechanisms in the unconscious part of the psyche that cause the repression of instinctual desires. Therefore a substantial part of the structure of the psyche remains unconscious. Freud formulated this metaphorically in his metapsychological idea that the ego is partly unconscious.

By defining his concepts dualistically, Freud endowed them with greater explanatory power than other existing psychological concepts. To illustrate this, Rieff explains how Freud's definition of repression presupposes another conception of memory than does mechanistic psychology. In treatments using the cathartic method the hysterical patient's symptoms would only vanish temporarily. Freud explained that was because consciousness is ruled out by hypnosis. Therefore what went unrecognized is that the causes of the hysterical affliction – the repressive forces that Freud metaphorically called the superego – were part and parcel of the structure of the patient's character. For Freud, real therapeutic success could only be attained by making the patient aware of this. Thus a much longer and more complicated process of investigation of the patient's character is required, with his or her conscious cooperation, than is possible using the cathartic method. Memory, for Freud, was not merely a reservoir of repressed experiences to be accessed through the right technique and thus withdrawn from repression. Freud held that repression can never be undone. Repression can only be approached via the symptomatic behaviour of patients, and then doctor and patient can try to understand how it works.

While Freud maintained that repression can never be abolished, he was also convinced that the work of therapy enables the patient to become at least partly aware of how repression is working in his or her case and thereby reduce its pathological effects. Freud's thinking oscillates with ambivalence between these two positions.

Geneticism and Ambivalence

Freud developed a historical outlook on the etiology of neurosis. Causes for neurotic diseases originated in the particular life history of the patient, in the experience of specific traumatic events. Freud considers 'all traumas ... prefigurative of later experience.'[36] That is the basis for Freud's use of transference (the patient's emotional response to the authority of the analyst). Diagnostically, the transference relationship is used to retrace the events experienced as traumatic. This has a therapeutic effect. Through psychoanalytic investigation the patient can become aware of her neurosis and enabled to practice other types of feelings and behaviour in the transference relationship.

In his later works, Freud developed a social psychology that incorporated the idea of the prototype. He took up the ideas of Jean-Baptiste Lamarck (1744–1829) whose theory of evolution had considerable influence. Lamarck assumed that in the group, as in the individual, unconscious memories of the past live on. That is how he explained the influence of the past on the present. Based on this assumption, Freud developed the idea of the transference – through tradition – of 'primal experiences,' for example, killing the primal father, to later generations, and the Oedipus complex is thus the psychological counterpart of this unconscious inheritance from the past.

In using these prototypical concepts analogically, Freud connected individual history with social and cultural history. He used the theory of the stages of development of libido as an analogy to the development of culture. Indeed, 'Freud's law of erotic development follows the familiar positivist sequence: the evolution of human conceptions of the universe, from animistic, through metaphysical or religious, to scientific.'[37] Rieff argues that Freud's deployment of these models is evidence of the strong influence that positivism had on him. But there is also an important difference. Whereas the positivists had gone 'from the social to the individual,' Freud's progression was the other way around. From the history of individuals' stages of mental development Freud postulated the levels of social-historical development.[38] According to Freud, 'the animistic phase would correspond to narcissism both chronologically and in its contents; the religious phase would correspond to the stage of object-choice of which the characteristic is a child's attachment to his parents; while the scientific phase would have an exact counterpart in the stage at which an individual has reached maturity, has renounced the pleasure principle, adjusted himself to reality and turned to the external world for the object of his desires.'[39]

The power of the past, as expressed by Freud in his theory of prototypes, is so strong that it is virtually impossible to break from it. This is why many have considered Freud to be a pessimist. But, according to Rieff, Freud's pessimism is persistently counterbalanced by his thinking in terms of development which always implies the possibility of attaining a higher stage. Development also entails a higher degree of integration of one's antagonistic psychic energies. Nevertheless, Rieff warns us not to get carried away by the one-sided, and optimistic, view of neo-Freudians concerning the possibilities for human growth. Freud's thinking in terms of development is never to be separated from his pessimism grounded in a biological theory of the duality of the instincts: 'Freud's "instinctualism" or "biologism" is his way of expressing the more fundamental idea, sacrificed by his revisors, of human behaviour conceived as conflict.'[40]

Rieff argues that Freud's concept of 'conflict' is related to Freud's contention that the modern individual finds himself in social and intrapyschic tension. In that way Freud connects his etiology of psychopathology to a cultural-historical development: modernity. However, for Freud the concepts of 'ambivalence' was even more fundamental than that, Rieff submits, because ambivalence also implies a solution to the modern individual's neurotic conflicts, and that is therapy: 'The untragic promise in Freudianism is this curative use of the ideal of scientific neutrality, embodied in the ostensibly amoral knowledge of the ego.'[41]

Psychoanalysis and Culture

For an adequate understanding of Rieff's attitude towards Freud, we must keep in mind the distinction that Rieff makes between Freud the theorist and Freud the therapist. Rieff finds unresolved tensions in Freud's ideas about culture, because Freud thinks about culture from both positions. As a therapist, Freud is convinced that the most radical solution to neurosis is for the individual to replace traditional, cultural, religiously based, mechanisms of repression with new cultural mechanisms in which that individual takes a more 'honest' attitude towards his or her 'natural needs.' Freud has a 'shrewd feeling ... for the incompatibility of the modern sense of self with our historic legacy ... Christianity was now nothing more than a painful "historical residue" of those valuable "repression-like processes which took place in antiquity" ... Freud viewed himself as treating specific cases of the mental suffering produced during the interregnum between the failure of one system of moral authority and the establishment of another.'[42] From this perspective Freud takes a 'psychologistic' position, according to Rieff, because he studies culture only from psychological perspectives. As a theorist, Freud concedes that the maintenance of the social order and culture demands a certain degree of repression of instinctual energies. From this perspective, Freud does have an eye for the legitimacy of the demands of culture. Thus we see a 'vacillation between a reductionist (to the psychological level) theory of culture and one in which culture is a phenomenon *sui generis.* This vacillation he never resolved. But there is everything still to be gained, I think, from using Freudian models in further developing a theory of culture.'[43]

In Rieff's work Freud is the pre-eminent interpreter of the cultural crisis created by modernity. Psychoanalysis, because of this crisis, is a 'theory of the modern individual that finds himself in high intrapsychic and social tension.' In Rieff's thinking, however, psychoanalysis is not only a theory and a technique, but also a cultural phenomenon with tremendous influence. In his early works Rieff argued that the psychological modes of explanation have become so vastly influential and penetrating that we have been witnesses to the emergence of a new ideology that now dominates Western culture. The psychological has superseded political, economic, and religious modes of explanation. Through a meticulous and critical study of psychoanalysis we can learn a lot about ourselves and about our worldview.

Rieff himself is ambivalent towards Freud. In his early works he tends to the idea that Freud ought to be remembered as a 'saving culture critic,' rather than a damning one. At the same time Rieff is severely critical about the emergence of 'psychological man,' for which he holds Freud almost entirely responsible. In Rieff's later works this criticism takes the upper hand, and Rieff is far more negative towards Freud, although never without ambivalence. Gerry Watson contends that this ambivalence hindered Rieff in fully developing his own theory of culture.[44] I think Watson underestimates the theoretical importance of Freud for Rieff. As I will demonstrate in the next chapters, Freud never ceases to be important to Rieff, in various ways, most of all as a critical anchor point. Again and again Rieff returns to Freud, to develop his own criticism of culture and modern social theory, always starting from Freudian ideas.

3

The Emergence of Psychological Man in Western Culture

> Psychology has become a way of asking and dealing with new types of fundamental questions, those of psychological man: time again has produced a type specially adapted to endure its time. A new discipline was needed to fit the introversion of interest. Freudian psychology with its ingenious interpretations of politics, religion, and culture in terms of the inner life of the individual and his immediate family experiences exactly filled the bill.
>
> Rieff, *Freud: The Mind of the Moralist*[1]

Rieff acquired great academic prestige with his theory of the emergence of psychological man in Western culture. About the theoretical goal he wanted to attain he wrote this: 'I have tried to say something about the consequences of psychological man for Western society – but not everything, for I do not consider the advance of the social sciences toward a theory of culture yet sure enough to convey such an attempt. Nevertheless my assessment of these consequences has led me nearer the task of helping to develop an adequate sociological theory of culture ... that theoretical problem which I consider the central one in sociology.'[2]

Unlike Freud, Rieff never attempted to describe the theoretical foundations of his theory systematically. This chapter is a sketch of Rieff's 'metasociology.' I will describe the basic concepts of his early theory of culture, including their relation to psychoanalysis, starting from a description of Rieff's thesis of the emergence of psychological man.

Western Cultural History According to Rieff

In his early works Rieff postulates that until modernity three character-ideals successively dominated Western civilization. First is:

> the ideal of *political man*, formed and handed down to us from classical antiquity. Plato was the greatest psychologist of political man and his most persuasive teacher. From Plato we first learned systematically to divide human nature into higher and lower energies. ... in Plato, the health and stability of a person is analogous to – and moreover, dependent upon – the health and stability of the political order: that is, a proper subordination of passions to intellect will follow from the subordination of the uneducated classes to the educated. Elaborated as a doctrine of human nature, Greek political philosophy was also, at the same time, Greek psychology.

The second character ideal is *religious man*:

> The second dominant character ideal of Western civilization borrowed the Platonic dichotomy between higher and lower energies and adapted it for different cultural purposes, chiefly religious. Although originally a naive and straightforward, even ecstatic faith, Christianity could not resist going to the Greek philosophical schools. As a result, the *religious man* that Christianity formed and handed down to us shows certain recognizable Greek traits. The Christian doctrine of human nature grafted faith onto the place once occupied by the idea of life as a continuing intellectual and moral reeducation ... Adapting Greek intellectualism to his own purposes, the main Christian institution developed a Western personality type that organized itself around the expectation of achieving faith, asserting it as superior to reason, which could, at best, merely support and confirm the religious gift.

The third character ideal is that of *economic man*:

> 'one who could rationally cultivate his very own garden, meanwhile solacing himself with the assumption that by thus attending to his own lower needs a general satisfaction of the higher needs would occur. A moral revolution was the result: what had been lower in the established hierarchy of human interests was asserted to be higher. But economic man, as I have suggested in *Freud: The Mind of the Moralist,* turned out to be a transitional type, with the shortest life-expectancy of all; when this typical character of

the enlightenment showed a faltering belief in his own superiority to his predecessors, a successor began to emerge – the *psychological man* of the twentieth century.

However intellectually sophisticated that psychological man is, he is anti-intellectual. However church-going still, he has reason to be dubious about the therapeutic efficacy of faith – which he believes to be the main purpose and function of his religion. However much involved in getting and having things, psychological man knows that the satisfactions he wishes to own, as his property, carry no certain price tag. For these reasons he is profoundly skeptical of the received hierarchy of values to which even his immediate predecessors assented. Yet psychological man cannot completely shake off his past. He has in fact the nervous habits of his father, economic man: he is anti-heroic, shrewd, studying unprofitable commitments as the sins most to be avoided, carefully keeping a balance of his satisfactions and dissatisfactions, but without the genial confidence of his immediate ancestor that the sum will mount to something meaningful and justify his entire life. He lives by the ideal of insight – practical, experimental, and leading to the mastery of his own personality.[3]

Basic Concepts of Rieff's Early Theory of Culture

Rieff's thesis on psychological man is very ambitious. Maybe that is why he used a very rhetorical style to launch it. Some years later, after having established his fame as a social theorist, he is much more careful, as can be seen in this passage from *The Triumph*:

> All this may be too ephemeral, as yet, to lay out the psychological man for an anatomy lesson as economic man has been laid out – his anxious Protestant heart, his open Enlightment eyes, his democratic accents dissected and probed now by every student doctor of the social sciences. It may be too early to squeeze my fragile conception dry between the cover of a book. I am merely announcing his presence, fluttering in all of us, a response to the absent God. ... That a new myth of man is developing, at least among the educated classes, seems evident to me. It is a response to the divisiveness and destruction without and to the chaos within. But we are ourselves involved in the creation of this new myth and cannot be expected to see the type in clear perspective.'[4]

The thesis of the emergence of psychological man refers to the history of worldviews or to 'Western psychohistory' as Rieff calls it. This term 'psychohistory' is a neologism for which I provisionally give this definition: a vision of Western cultural history in which the successive phases are marked by a radical change in the understanding of the interaction between the individual and the social order. Rieff describes these changes as changes of the 'character-ideal' of a culture. These two key concepts of his early works, 'character-ideal' and 'psychohistory,' are complex amalgams of existing social-theoretical and philosophical notions and are closely related to Rieff's ideas about the social role of myths. In the following we will explore these three topics – the role of myths, the character-ideal, and the concept of psychohistory – and their relation to psychoanalysis.

A very important thing we have to keep in mind is that Rieff, like Freud, is interested in *dynamics*. Essentially he explores how culture 'works' sociologically. Rieff's contribution to a sociological theory of culture is that he strives to discover 'prototypical cultural processes.' Not even as much as Freud did he develop an encompassing theory of culture. His work contains 'depth-explorations' of crucial issues for a sociological theory of cultural dynamics. In this chapter we will focus on these dynamics. We will have to resist the temptation to explore the contents of Rieff's imaginative descriptions of the character-ideals of Western cultural history.

A New Myth of Man

Gabriel (1982) criticizes Rieff's theory of psychological man because he thinks that 'in and of itself psychological man is a wish-fulfilling fiction which could never materialize within the given sociopolitical conditions or any conditions that would allow society to function as a cohesive whole.'[5] In the course of this book I will show that that is precisely what Rieff thinks, too. For now the crucial point here is that Rieff's theory is not a 'description of reality,' but a theory of ideation, dealing with character-ideals that were or are used to form human identities. This focus on ideation is crucial for Rieff's interpretation of psychoanalysis as well and is, according to Browning (1973), well in line with the best studies of Freud proceeding from Ricoeur and Lacan.[6] In *Freud and Philosophy* Ricoeur writes that in Freud's texts 'it is not desires as such that are placed at the center of the analysis, but rather their language ... the "vicissitudes of instincts," to use one of Freud's expressions, can be attained only in the vicissitudes of meaning ... How do desires achieve speech?'[7] This idea can, too, be transposed to Rieff's theory of culture. Rieff's basic question is: how are cultural ideas expressed in individual and social behaviour?

Freud's 'technology of the emotions' helped us to acquire a totally new kind of awareness of ourselves, of our fellow men, and of the world, argues Rieff.[8] This thesis presupposes a number of conceptions of how we are influenced by cultural ideas and how we have influence on them. We are always born in a specific cultural situation with a specific set of ideas and convictions. However, they can never be assessed as abstract cultural entities. These ideas and convictions always operate in individual minds and in human relations. Furthermore, our behaviour constantly changes those cultural ideas and convictions. Rieff's usage of the term 'myth' alludes to this problem, which was also elaborated upon in symbolic interactionism. (Rieff probably took cognizance of this theory as a student, because it was developed in the so-called Chicago school in the social sciences.)

How does Rieff use the term 'myth'? At first glance the commonplace meaning of the term 'myth' is helpful. When we use it in our normal conversations, we refer to a story which we know does not literally correspond to reality. But we believe that myths do tell us something in a symbolic way about fundamental aspects of the realities we live in. Myths always have a moral, as well. Through our belief myths have an impact on the way in which we perceive ourselves and the world we live in, as well as on our behaviour. Myths about, for example, femininity and masculinity or about how the world came into existence have great influence on our thoughts and acts. Rieff's usage of the term is close to that commonplace meaning.

For Rieff myths do not only belong to 'non-rational' realms of culture like art and religion. Referring to an old philosophical debate, he asserts that myths have an important function in the sciences as well. Rational knowledge is always based on starting points that cannot be traced back to a rational origin. Every scientific theory has its 'temporarily authoritative consensus of received interpretations' that Rieff calls 'dogmas.'[9] These interpretations are based on 'terms, without which nothing greatly significant can be conceived to follow; these I call "god-terms."'[10] So, every science has its own myths, based on its 'dogmas' and 'god-terms' (or 'conceptual ultimates' as Rieff calls them elsewhere).

Rieff's usage of words like 'god-term' or 'dogma' in the context of social theory is, of course, very provocative. I assume that Rieff deliberately uses them for methodological reasons. First, because they refer to religion and theology, thus invoking the problem of interdisciplinarity.

Rieff comes to the conclusion, just like Freud in his own way and own scientific context, that existing social theories are not sufficient for development of his theory. Religion plays an important role in cultural dynamics, and modern social theory is not adequately equipped to explore the relation between culture and religion. Second, Rieff thinks that contemporary social theories cannot do justice to the complexity of the interaction between personality and culture, which he demonstrates with analyses on the level of the starting points or 'god-terms' of these theories. As for this second point, Rieff elaborates the theoretical lines set out by Norbert Elias (1897–1990) in his book *The Civilizing Process*, in which Elias asserts that contemporary sociology is blind to long-term transformations of societal structures and, correlatively, of personality structures.[11] In this double methodological sense a great deal of Rieff's work is theoretical sociology; he evaluates existing theories from meta-theoretical perspectives and searches for adequate notions for a sociological theory of culture.

After this short methodological excursion we must return to the main theme of this section, the role of myth as mediator between ideation and reality. Ricoeur described two functions of myth that are useful here, the expressive and the heuristic.[12] When used expressively, myths generalize human experience into univeral concepts or paradigms, as in the myths of Prometheus, Anthropos, or Adam and Eve. These symbolic narrations about 'human prototypes' teach us how people think about the *condition humaine* and about human destination. Apart from that, myths also have a heuristic value, because they confer 'universality, temporality and ontological meaning unto our self-awareness.'[13] This is the opposite of expression: we receive something 'from without' that helps forming our images of ourselves, our fellow men, and the world.

This description helps us get a clearer picture of Rieff's thesis of psychological man as a new 'myth of man.' Rieff seems to refer to the heuristic function of myths when he asserts that Freud created psychoanalysis as a means of survival in a period of severe metaphysical crisis in Western culture. Because of this crisis Western culture was not able anymore to confer 'universality, temporality, and ontological meaning' on the individual in a way that helped this individual to come to terms with the big existential questions of life. According to Freud, the most fundamental cause of neurosis was to be sought precisely in this lingering influence of the traditional metaphysical systems on the modern individual. Psychoanalysis was meant to liberate man from this influence and to teach him how to manage his life rationally, without seeking recourse to religion or metaphysics and their myths.

An important example of this is Freud's usage of the Oedipus complex. Freud maintained that everybody has to come to terms with the Oedipus complex, the situation in which the young child has to establish ways of dealing with the father and mother as the first prototypes of authority. Freud suggested a totally new solution in order to come to terms with the complex problems the young child faces. Here the relation to religion and myths and their heuristic function is evident. Traditionally people in Western society learned to accept the authority of the father, which was legitimized with references to religious myths like the story of creation. Adam was the first man and Eve was created from one of his ribs (in one of the versions of the myth of creation, at least). This symbolized the subjection of women to men.

Freud lived in an era in which the patriarchal structure of society was attacked. Apart from the question of how patriarchal Freud was, the main point here is that Freud advocated analytic awareness of how we are influenced by myths like that of the story of creation from Genesis. Rieff interprets psychoanalysis as 'a critique of those archaic and instinctual images – the prototypes – around which our roles and perceptions of roles are organized.'[14] Freud wanted to map this process because it was *terra incognita* to a great extent. On this abstract level Rieff demonstrates how Freud's scientific theory embodies a new Weltanschauung, in which man develops a totally new awareness of himself and his relations to his fellow men and the world.

Freud's Weltanschauung has become very influential in Western culture. With Paul Ricoeur we can say that the psychoanalytic myth about man has become an important myth with which modern man confers 'universality, temporality, and ontological meaning' onto his self-awareness. But we have to be careful, because the heuristic function of psychoanalytic myths differs radically from those of existing religious and ideological myths. As an ardent anti-metaphysician Freud wanted to settle accounts with the irrational influence of those myths on modern man. So, viewed from a premodern perspective, we ought to call the Weltanschauung of psychoanalysis in fact an 'anti-myth.'

Rieff recounts, in bits and pieces, the story of psychological man, the new prototype or character-ideal around which we organize our roles and perceptions of roles. Viewed from premodern cultural perspectives this ideal must be called an 'anti-character-ideal.' A basic motif of the myth of psychological man is its anti-metaphysical character: 'Modern scientific myths are not myths of transcendence but myths of revolt against transcendence ... Scientific myths, in contrast to religious myths, are designed to free individuals from their psychological thralldom to primal forms.'[15] This concept of primal form is an aesthetic concept that Rieff uses to designate the influence of culturally accepted values and ideas on the individual. One example is the aforementioned pattern of gender-related roles that a culture provides for individuals to develop their gender identity.[16] A second central motif of modern myths is their individualizing character: 'The essentially secular aim is to wean away the ego from either a heroic or a compliant attitude to the community.'[17] Individual autonomy is the highest goal to be attained. According to Rieff, it had never occurred before in Western culture that these two motifs were elaborated so systematically. Therefore Rieff tends to call the emergence of psychological man a rupture in Western cultural history.

A New Character-Ideal

In the former section a central issue was the mediating functions of myth. This is an important issue for a theory of cultural dynamics. Rieff's ideas about this have crystallized around the concept 'character-ideal.' In this section I will sketch how it is based on Freud's ideas about the Oedipus complex, which Rieff calls 'the core complex' of Freudian theory.

According to Rieff, it is evident that Freud wanted to explain how myths influence the human mind. Freud had to work with a new set of concepts that were not fully elaborated, which caused a number of theoretical inconsistencies. In general, however, we can say that in Freudian theory myths are the bearers of the 'primal forms' of social structure. These myths exert their influence through identification processes in which belief in myths helps the individual to identify with an (inner image of) one or more authoritative persons. One fine example is pop-star Madonna. In building up her image she uses many elements from existing myths, beginning with her name. This appeal to myths gave her a powerful image that made her an identification figure for many young people. She helped change the images of gender in Western societies. Thus the prototypical structures of the social order in a given period, embodied by the mythical *exempla* and mediated through identification figures, are as it were replicated in the psychic structure or character of individuals. Freud, using mythical constructs like the Oedipus complex and the primal murder of the father, analysed the causal relations between the human character and the structure of the social order. Rieff's analysis on this point makes clear that Freud discovered what I would call 'cultural DNA.' Here, by the way, we encounter a paradoxical feature of psychoanalysis: it uses myths to demythologize.

Rieff holds that psychoanalysis teaches us that the 'cultural DNA' of the Western world is thoroughly mutated by modernization. The two central motifs of modern social theory, liberation of the individual from primal forms of culture and autonomy of the individual towards the community, are pre-eminently expressed in psychoanalysis. The best example to illustrate this is Rieff's evaluation of the meaning of Freud's ideas on the Oedipus complex for a theory of culture. In this evaluation we encounter the three main themes of Rieff's cultural-theoretical interpetation of Freud's work: (1) identification and authority, (2) repression, and (3) the double dialectic of nature and culture. I will deal with a few relevant passages from *Freud: The Mind of a Moralist* in which these themes occur, interwoven with each other.

Rieff summarizes his opinion on the importance of the Oedipus complex in *Mind of the Moralist* in a passage on the essence of psychoanalytic therapy. To achieve psychological freedom, he says, the patient is invited to adopt a retrospective position. This 'retrospection is focussed, more than upon any other point in the patient's past, on the Oedipus complex, that nuclear configuration of sexual desire, repression, and identification with a parent-figure which all persons experience ... Authority is Freud's basic problem, neurosis the occasion for examining its vicissitudes; his therapy attempts to erode the childhood laws by which obedience is maintained.'[18]

Through the Oedipus complex the child learns to express erotic impulses by letting them assume culturally accepted forms, which at the same time control these impulses. Thus the child learns to be obedient to the law. The prohibition of incest that dams up (or represses) the incestuous love for the mother is the first, prototypical taboo that structures the process in which the child learns to build its first social relations. The term 'taboo' refers to the *unconscious* character of this process. Rieff puts this in the following general formula; 'all repression is of natural impulse.'[19] This formulation is ambiguous, because of the double meaning of the genitive 'of.' Rieff says that in every repression natural or instinctual impulses are being repressed. At the same time the sentence can be read as a characterization of repression as 'natural.'

Nature and culture are closely interwoven, because the 'natural repression' of a part of the 'natural impulses' is a precondition for social and cultural life.

Rieff finds this an adequate reply to the criticism of Malinovski, who maintained that what Freud called 'natural' (like the Oedipus complex) is just a part of a cultural process: 'Freud's subtler point is that in "nature" there exist already the two essential elements of culture. The Oedipus complex, which expresses the tension between sexual assertion and submission to the parents, is not a pre-cultural formation but carries within it the dualistic dynamic of culture. It is this erotic dualism which accounts for the characteristic tension between order and rebelliousness present in every culture.'[20]

Freud was very ambivalent about the function of authority, says Rieff. On the one hand, Freud points at the inevitability of authority, in the form of unconscious controls, as a precondition for normal psychic and social life. On the other hand, he maintained that the cause of neurosis must be sought exactly in the unconscious identifications with authority figures. Freud used transference as a therapeutic instrument to have the old prototype(s) with which the patient forms his social relations gradually replaced by news ways of learning how to relate to people. According to Rieff, this implies a fundamentally new sort of relation to authority as well. The influence of the first figures of authority, operative through the repressed resolution of the Oedipus complex, is undone. When the therapy is successful, authority is brought under rational control of the patient as much as possible.

Based on his analysis of the importance of the Oedipus complex for a theory of culture, Rieff draws the following conclusions conforming to the three main themes:

- *Identification and authority.* In many different ways modern man learns that he has to become an autonomous individual by unlearning to identify unconsciously with traditional figures of authority and build up his identity around the ideals they embody. The new ideal, which is in fact an 'anti-ideal,' presupposes a totally new relationship to authority, in which the individual chooses for himself in a rational way his exemplary authority figures. The individual's independent and rational power of judgment becomes the highest authority.
- *Repression.* Psychoanalysis demonstrates clearly that repression is the basis of culture. Eros, or the human instinctual life, cannot be separated from authority as it is formed by the cultural ideas we use to

express our instinctual life and which curb or control our instinctual life in this process. Thus repression is part and parcel of our instinctual life, which accounts for the dual structure of the instincts.

- *The double dialectic of nature and culture.* Repression is the dynamic link between nature and culture. Rieff extrapolates Freud's dualistic conception of the instincts to culture. Culture itself is dualistic, suspended between the poles of order and rebellion. The Oedipus complex is a cultural formation that expresses the dualistic form of the psychic, social, and cultural order.

Rieff's thesis of the emergence of psychological man is built up around these three psychoanalytic themes. In Western culture man learns to identify with a totally new character-ideal. Because of this ideal, modern man loses sight of his divided inner life and his split relation to the social and cultural order. The self is conceived of as an 'authentic core' and social and cultural demands alienate man from this inner core. Development of the self, as an unfolding of this inner core, demands the abolition of this alienation, caused by the 'unnatural' effects of repression. Rieff criticizes this ideal, because it oversimplifies the operation of authority.[21]

This may all sound very abstract. Rieff's style is very dense. Therefore I insert an interlude here, in which Rieff's interpretation of Freud is compared with that of two other great and innovating interpreters of Freud. Through that comparison we will get a better view of the three main themes in Rieff's interpretation of Freud. At the same time the connections to sublimation theory, which is very important for a psychoanalytic theory of culture, will become clear.

Cultural Theory and Sublimation: Rieff versus Counterculture

Freud initiated new ways to explore the relation between the individual and the social order. In the psychoanalytic theories that were formed after Freud this was worked out in very different ways, because there were great divergences of opinion on how Freud's cultural-theoretical notions must be elaborated. On this point it is useful to compare Rieff's Freud exegesis in *Mind of the Moralist* with that of Herbert Marcuse in his *Eros and Civilization* (1955) and Norman Brown in his *Life against Death* (1959). These three books mark a new phase in the reception of Freud's work in the Anglo-American social sciences. Rieff considered the works of the other two authors as representative of counterculture, against which he polemicized forcefully. This polemic is interesting for us because it hinges on the theme of sublimation.

In sublimation theory the question of how the individual and the social order interact is put most acutely. To have social and cultural life at all, our instinctive impulses must be adapted. Put in psychoanalytic terms, libido has to be desexualized. But what does this process of adaptation imply for our libidinous lives? How does it contribute to the formation of culture? And how are culture and sexuality formed in this process? These questions arise when we confront Rieff's theory with the theories of Brown and Marcuse. There are fundamental differences in their theories, but as for the cultural-theoretical interpretation of Freud's texts they agree on some important issues too. I will sum up these agreements first and then stake out the differences.[22]

Brown and Marcuse fully agree with Rieff that Freud's theory is essentially *social* theory, characterized by fundamental dualisms. In this theory the deepest dichotomy between social and antisocial impulses is localized ín the human being itself: in the unconscious, to be precise. The unconscious contains immutable, instinctive, and egoistic desires as well as mechanisms regulating these desires. These mechanisms, that curb the satisfaction of the desires, and thus deflect libidinal energy towards other goals, are the results of the deep influence of culture. (All three reject the neo-Freudian revisions which localize the most essential dichotomy outside the individual, between the individual and the social order.) This regulation and curbing of libidinal energy is a precondition for social order. Brown and Marcuse argue forcibly, as does Rieff, that this is an essentially unstable structure, which can only hold together with the aid of social myths.

These myths are created and maintained in a culture as part of the belief system. In these myths it is proposed, in various forms, that a particular control or deflection of libidinal energies is to be followed in the name of a 'reality principle.' This principle, which is based on the demands of the social order, poses that these demands are 'more real' than the egoistic instinctual desires of the individual himself or herself Rieff points to this mechanism in his description of political man, where he says that Plato taught us to divide nature systematically into higher and lower energies. In the Platonic myth reason was connected to the higher energies that are morally more outstanding than the lower energies. The principle that says that man always ought to pursue the higher principles in a rational way would coincide with the idea of the reality principle. Thus, 'identifying individual functioning and well-being with fulfilling the values and functions of the group is the anchor which keeps the individual tied to a life path of activity devoid of much of its erotic appeal.'[23]

Brown and Marcuse criticize Freud for his reductionist view of the relation of the individual and the social order, which they also consider ahistoric. They think that his view implies an unnecessarily conservative theory of culture. They assert that Freud's cultural theory has a strong ascetic tendency, because Freud thought that a lot of unruly libidinal energy had to be desexualized to maintain culture. Freud was blind to the fact that the ongoing industrialization of Western culture, aided by science and technology, led to an explosion of possibilities that could be helpful in forming and maintaining culture.[24] These cultural processes require less deflection of libidinal energy than in the pre-industrial era, which makes possible a less ascetic lifestyle. To achieve this goal, libido first needs to be liberated from the routinelike processes that modern technological culture imposes on modern man. Brown and Marcuse considered counterculture a struggle against these modern, repressive mechanisms that led to alienation.

The liberation advocated by Marcuse and Brown as a 'cure' for alienation boils down to the idea of breaking open culturally determined patterns of deflection or sublimation of libidinal energy. At this point they attack Freud, too, because Freud was very pessimistic about the possibilities of interfering with our libidinal economy. Freud asserts that our acculturation draws deep furrows in the human mind and forms our character and the correlative libidinal economy. Sensible rational management of our inner lives was the most that we could hope for. Interfering with libidinal life itself was a bridge too far for Freud: 'What he could not envision, in fact, is that the progression from mobile to quiescent cathexes [of libido] ... can be reversed to create a form of social life that is therapy against the belief in culture.'[25] Here Brown and Marcuse revise Freud's theory by pointing at the inconsistency that, on the one hand, Freud (as a theorist) was very pessimistic about the possibilities of interfering with our 'libidinal economy' itself, but, on the other hand, Freud (as a therapist) had to assume its possibility because the effectiveness of psychoanalytic therapy depends on it. In sum, Brown and Marcuse radicalize Freud's therapeutic ideas and apply them, combined with Marxist theory, to modern culture.

This revision of Freud's cultural-theoretical notions has led us far from Rieff's ideas on those notions. Rieff finds the same sort of ambivalences in Freud's theory as Brown and Marcuse do, and he agrees with them on the ahistorical character of it, but draws totally different conclusions. Rieff does not think that a cure for alienation can be distilled from Freud's theory. For him Freud remains a highly ambivalent figure, in whose work we find an implicit defence of (the demands of) culture, too. Freud never resolved the vacillation between these two positions. Rieff advocates detailed analysis of this problem, because it is fertile ground for a theory of culture. As I demonstrated above, the problem of sublimation is central here.

Before taking a closer look, I must mention that Rieff hardly ever uses the term 'sublimation.' In the first editions of *Mind of the Moralist* it occurs only a few times and in *The Triumph of the Therapeutic: Uses of Faith after Freud* just once, which is remarkable for a term so central to a psychoanalytic theory of culture. The epilogue of the third edition of *Mind of the Moralist* (1979) may provide a clue for this. There we find passages where Rieff goes deeper into the problem of sublimation theory, but he always puts the term between quotation marks. From a critical remark in a text two years later[26] I infer that Rieff does not want to use the meaning bequeathed to the term in psychoanalytic discourse, because he does not agree with it theoretically. Still, the problem cannot be eluded because of its theoretical importance, so when Rieff uses the term 'sublimation theory' he demonstrates his disagreement by putting it between quotation marks.

The most essential difference between the way Rieff extrapolates Freudian cultural-theoretical notions and the approaches of Brown and Marcuse has to do with sublimation theory. The latter hold that it is possible to create new forms of social life that are less alienating, because those forms liberate the individual from oppressive cultural forms and their ascetic moral implications. They assert that, viewed metapsychologically, libidinal energies can be liberated from these cultural forms and that the individual can himself determine how to express his or her erotic energies. In this approach sexuality and sublimation are conceived of as antagonists. For Rieff it is impossible to agree with this, because it presupposes a totally different view of sexuality. Rieff transposes the idea of the duality of the instincts into sexuality. Sexuality itself is a dual and unstable construct, built on an ambivalent relation to authority. The crucial point for a theory of culture is that the most essential polarity is not that of sexuality versus sublimation, but that of sexuality versus authority.

This implies that the idea of 'liberation of libido from oppressive structures or forms' is futile. Rieff concedes that sexuality and culture to some extent have an antagonistic relationship, because libidinal energies have to be deflected or desexualized to make social life possible. The culturally determined regulation of that process is built into sexuality itself, however. Sexuality cannot be thought of apart from formative or structuring principles. Sexual liberation, one of the core ideas of counterculture, is an illusion. More fundamental for a theory of culture, says Rieff, is the Oedipus complex, which refers to both the dual form of sexuality and the dual form of culture.

Now we know globally what Rieff means with his thesis of psychological man as a new character-ideal around which a new myth of man took its form. It is time to explore more thoroughly what view of history is presupposed in this theory of the history of Western culture (Western 'psychohistory').

The Place of Psychoanalysis in Western Cultural History

Rieff holds that the way Freud situated psychoanalysis in Western cultural history betrays his awareness that his striving to restructure the cultural mechanism of authority was historically unique. Freud summarized Western cultural history as a sequence of different types of repression, which Rieff describes like this: 'Freud developed his sense of the times and of the place psychoanalysis had in them from the crude positivist chronology. History had moved to the last of the three stages from (1) cohesive societies of primitive man, a system of repression implemented by taboos; to (2) religious cohesions, a culture of repression upheld by theologies; to (3) modern culture, an era in which the old repressions are being loosened but not yet superseded.'[27] Psychoanalysis was meant to help modern man in doing away with the old repressions and, instead of that, teach him a 'technology of the emotions.'

What conception of history is presupposed here? This question brings us to a topic that may be surprising: religion. We usually remember Freud as an ardent atheist, but what is ignored in this vulgar image of Freud is that he was deeply fascinated by religion. An impressive demonstration of this is his working like a madman in the last months of his life, while severely suffering from cancer, to finish his last book, which is about Moses. For Rieff's theory of culture *Moses and Monotheism* (1939) is important. I will show how it helped Rieff in developing his psychohistorical model and how Freud made him aware of the importance of the category of the transcendent for a theory of culture.

Freud passionately denied that his theory contained a Weltanschauung, because it was strictly analytical and therefore it could never be labelled a 'new religion or ideology.' In other words, Freud took great pains to show that psychoanalysis could not be considered a new system of repression that was to take turns with the old, religious system of repression, because psychoanalysis was based on a totally new conception of the relation of the individual to the social and cultural order. According to Rieff, *Moses and Monotheism* is Freud's final and ambivalent effort to solve this question once and for all. The main thesis of this book is an 'experiment in psychohistory'[28] that was novel and daring. Its main value, however, lies in its polemical focus: because in this book Freud demonstrates a vision of the relation between individual/psychological and collective/historical experience that differed radically from the then-dominant model of Hegel and Marx. To be able to explain Rieff's thesis on this, I must first summarize the contents of Freud's last book and briefly put it in its historical context.

Moses and Monotheism is an unruly book, the place of which in the canon of Freud's texts is hard to determine. The interpretation of the book is difficult because it is full of profound ambivalences, both in style and content. Beyond that, it is hard to recognize the book's theoretical import because most of the historical, anthropological, theological, sociological, and psychological material Freud used in it is not new in comparison to contemporary literature.[29] The book is significant because of the way Freud deals with these materials and because of the contemporary historical context. In a time when the persecution of the Jews in Austria was such that Freud had to flee from Vienna to London, he published a book in which the main thesis is that Moses, the 'father' of the Jewish people and their religion, was not a Jew but an Egyptian. In a time when the Nazi's worked out their *Endlösung,* Freud put a bomb under the foundations of Jewish identity.

Through all of his life, Freud was fascinated by great leaders and by religion. In his lifelong fascination with the figure of Moses these two topics meet. *Moses and Monotheism* is, among other things, a study of the origin of the special character of the Jewish people, which is formed to such a great extent by its religion. Freud tries to bring to light Moses' influence on the Jews by applying the prototypical concept of the primal murder of the father (from *Totem and Taboo*) to the Jewish tradition. By ordering the materials in ingenious ways he claimed to have proven that the Jews killed Moses, the great lawgiver and leader of the people. Thus 'the sons of Moses' tried to elude the constraining influence of the

Mosaic law. The law that forces the Jews to repress instinctual desires is repressed itself. But according to Freud, the repressed always returns: guilt-ridden, the Jews decided to stick to the Mosaic law and its correlated cult, to atone for their murdered father. Thus Moses, who was an Egyptian himself according to Freud, became the founding father of the Jewish people and their religion.

Freud maintains that from a cultural-historical point of view the roots of Christianity are at stake here, too. He describes the relation between Judaism and Christianity with a psychoanalytic scheme in which he calls the Jewish religion a 'father-religion' and Christianity a 'son-religion.' In their relation the motif of the primal murder of the father plays a central role. The schism between the two religions was not a divorce in which the common household was neatly divided, but an attempted total takeover of power from the father (Judaism) by the sons (Christianity). This attempt is doomed to failure, because the repressed always returns. In Western cultural history, says Freud, the murder of Moses and the subsequent return of the repressed is prototypical. In *Moses and Monotheism* he suggests that Christ is the 'resurrected Moses and the returned primeval father.'[30] The dynamic which underlies the Jewish religion is set forth in the Christian religion, which in its turn underlies Western civilization.

After this précis of *Moses and Monotheism* we can take a closer look at Freud's conception of the relation between individual/psychic experience and the collective/historical experience that we find in tradition. Rieff points out that Freud needed the Lamarckian hypothesis about the relation between the individual and tradition.[31] Lamarck asserted that in the group, just as in the individual, memories of past events live in a collective unconscious and influence the present. According to Freud, we find in traditions the prototypical contents of this collective unconscious. Every individual interiorizes these forms in his unconscious and is, literally, formed by them. By applying the prototypical myth of the murder of the father to religion, says Rieff, Freud tried to prove that religion was merely a psychological need. This need was rooted in the trauma of the murder of the father in the primal horde, repeated in the murder of Moses and, later on, of Jesus. Freud tried to show how we can discern a neurotic and repetitive pattern behind the complex and multiform reality of religion and culture, which could be halted by a thorough psychoanalytic re-education of Western man. Thus Freud reduced religion to a psychological, neurotic phenomenon that needs psychoanalysis as an antidote.

Rieff thinks that a fundamental problem is at stake here: 'By his enticing analogy between individual neurotic behavior and that of whole groups, and by the related reading of "primitive" motives into present actions, Freud suggests a way out of the inclusiveness of historical study.'[32] Behind the apparent complexity of social acts, the 'manifest layer of historical facts,' lies the more fundamental content of the latent psychological motif. For Freud the private and psychological is definitive for the public and social, says Rieff. He pits this position of Freud against Hegel's view of the relation between the latent psychological and manifest historical. Rieff asserts that in Hegel's theory meaning hinges on the public historical contexts, which are autonomous and supreme as systems of social causation. For Hegel the world spirit has its own immanent purposes, to which private psychological constellations are secondary. Therefore the Hegelian position excluded the psychologistic view. Rieff asserts that Marx followed Hegel in his anti-psychological orientation.[33]

By pitting these two positions against one another Rieff wants to show how the Freudian and Marxist positions correct each other. According to Marx, historical processes are characterized by change, whereas Freud tended to depreciate the possibility of change. From a historical perspective the essence of Freud's prototypical method and his concept of the return of the repressed is that only a few immutable motifs return in different forms throughout history. Thus Marx corrects Freud. But Freud also corrected an important shortcoming in the Marxist conception of history, which tended to subordinate (human) nature to history and make the individual invisible. Freud rehabilitates the importance of human nature, in the form of repressed and returning unconscious motifs. For Freud, unconcious experiences, however collective they may be, can only exist in individual unconscious processes. Thus he restored the role of the individual in historical processes.[34]

Here we see another example of Rieff's thesis that Freud gave a new impetus to dialectical thinking. In Freudian thinking the individual/psychic and collective/historical are not simply antagonists, but presuppose each other and are dynamically interrelated. So we have a double dialectic here, too. Of course the individual and the historical are dialectically related, but Freud teaches us that both history and the individual are internally divided as well. The historical cannot exist except in the form of individual histories. And the individual cannot express himself except in historical forms. According to Rieff, repression is the dynamic link between the individual and the historical. Furthermore, cultural dynamics cannot change fundamentally except in their mechanisms of repression. That makes Freud's psychohistorical scheme of Western cultural history an important basis for Rieff's own psychohistorical model.

That Rieff builds up his interpretation of Freudian psychohistory around the concept of 'repression' must of course be viewed in the light of his wish to draw our attention to a neglected topic in the reception of Freud's work, the important role of authority (as a limitation of human possibility). According to Rieff, the role attributed to authority by Freud is an important corrective to the social theory of Freud's contemporaries, which was far less dialectical than was Freud's. But at the same time Rieff points to a fundamental shortcoming of Freud's thinking: 'Freud never articulated a truly social psychology. Against the main drift of contemporary social science, his concern remains the individual and his instincts[35] ... From his therapeutic concern for the individual we can evaluate Freud's pejorative analysis of the state, of the mass, of the crowd, of the antheap of culture measured against the lonely private intelligence.'[36]

This is an example of Rieff's ambivalence towards Freud in his early works. He holds that Freud's thinking about culture vaccillates between a reductionist (to the psychological level) theory of culture and one in which culture is a phenomenon sui generis. Rieff thinks that this ambivalence is a very rich one and 'there is everything still to be gained from using Freudian models in further developing a theory of culture.' Let us see what there is to be learned from Rieff's analysis of *Moses and Monotheism* for the transcendent or sui generis character of culture.

Freud was highly ambivalent about religion. As a theorist he respected it. In premodern culture, theologies provided social orders with religious cohesions. Religion was the vehicle for the prototypes or primal forms of the social order that put their repressive imprint on the individuals in the acculturation process. In this way religion was useful because 'without the illusion of a divine order the social order would disintegrate into barbarism.'[37] But Freud the therapist could not accept this sociological defence of religion. Freud the therapist conceived of modernity as 'an era in which the old repressions are being loosened but not yet superseded.' This is another way of saying that the cultural force of religion was waning. As an ardent atheist Freud did not regret this, because modern science had shown that more efficient ways of installing repressions were possible. Freud held that modern men needed psychoanalytic re-education, to acquire rational control of their unruly instinctual lives.

Rieff asserts that Freud's aversion to religion made him blind to theoretical inconsistencies in his theory of religion. An important shortcoming is that religion is conceived of as an instrument of maintaining social order. According to Rieff, Freud's opinion is exemplary for modern social theory: 'All sociology, and now psychology as well, has been repeating Kant's mistake in regarding religion as the apprehension of our moral duties as divine commands. Religion provides that "solemn air of sanctity" which has been the established way of pledging allegiance to the laws of culture. It is on this original identity of religion and authority that Freud's rejection of religion is based.'[38] Rieff's Kierkegaardian criticism is that this kind of theory is blind to the sacral or transcendent aspect of religion.

In Freud's treatment of religion we encounter the same paradox as in his treatment of myth. Freud studied religion intensively, but only in order to be able to settle accounts with it. Rieff suggests that we profit from Freud's fascination with religion, because it helps us to explore the complex relations of culture and religion. Rieff proposes several important revisions, to correct psychologistic and atheist preoccupations that cause reductionist views of culture and religion. To avoid this reductionism, Rieff weaves in a dialectic between a cultural order, on the one hand, and the social and individual order, on the other. In the following section I will describe how Rieff proceeds on this point.

The Double Dialectic in Rieff's Theory of Culture

In the introduction to *Triumph of the Therapeutic* Rieff introduces his two most important metasociological concepts, the primary and secondary cultural process. He does not explain their theoretical foundation. From Freud's metapsychology we know that Freud undergirded his libido theory with a very complex theory of the primary and secondary (psychic) processes. Rieff does not give any hint about the connection with Freudian theory, but I assume that the resemblance of his basic metasociological concepts to those of Freud's metapsychology is no coincidence. A more detailed analysis of this assumption, for which I had to interview Rieff personally, turned out to be an important contribution to my investigation into the Freudian basis of Rieff's theory of culture.

Freud circumscribes the primary process as the entirety of psychic mechanisms that the unconscious uses in its striving for satisfaction of its desires. This process is regulated by the 'pleasure principle,' as Freud calls it in *Beyond the Pleasure Principle* (1920). The secondary process consists of the psychic mechanisms in which the collision is regulated between unconscious desires and the demands of reality, under the aegis of 'the reality principle.' The distinction of these two processes and the hypothesis that the psyche operates differently in them 'are among the most fundamental of Freud's concepts.'[39] We have to keep in mind that we are dealing with theoretical *postulates* here.[40] I follow Ricoeur, who says that these metapsychological terms were important for Freud as critical-hermeneutical principles. What Freud wanted to make clear with his ideas about the mutual relations between the primary and secondary process 'is the indestructibility of the primary system.'[41] We came across this idea before in another form, the concept of 'the return of the repressed.' Thus, what is at stake in this section is the *theoretical function* of the concepts 'primary process' and 'secondary process.'

With these theoretical postulates Freud tried to conceive of how the human imagination works and how it is driven by instinctual desires. Imagination belongs to the unconscious which cannot be empirically perceived in a direct way. Therefore Freud says that the only way of empirically perceiving the unconscious is through its outward expressions. When thus 'desire achieves speech,' the distorting mechanisms of the secondary process have already done their work. Psychoanalysis was intended as a hermeneutical method to decipher these expressions and thus trace them back to their instinctual roots. According to Rieff, an important connection can be made between Freud's one-sided focus on the individual instinct in his theory of culture and the way he imagined the primary processes. Rieff says that 'in Freud, the primary process is patently pre-cultural. It is his version of chaos theory ... In Freudian theory, or any other major theory of culture, whether it be Herder or Cassirer at the two ends of the great philosophies of culture in Europe, there can be no instinctual life in culture ... Instinct is always pre-cultural. Therefore for Freud, sexuality as such, if one can imagine such a thing, is really a doctrine of primordiality. Upon primordial inexpressible sexuality there are superimposed modes of expression which are culturally, that is, historically determined.'[42]

The major problem for Rieff's metasociology is Freud's conception of the primary process as pre-cultural. This idea leads to a theoretical deadlock which Rieff describes like this:

> The theory of the unconscious is unthinkable without the theory of the primary process. But I must add to that, that the theory of the primary

> process is an ordered theory of chaos, at the level that precedes, predates and continues into the conscious. And it is very important to recognize that there is an inseparable relation between [the conscious and][43] the unconscious, which is the repressed part that also represses and organizes. Since every repression must, according to Freudian theory, have its expression, no repression can remain repressed. On the other hand, the primary process is not itself an outcome, a result of repression. It precedes repression in mental history. But then the question arises; what is the primary process? How to describe it? And at this point we are stuck, because Freud cannot describe a process that does not have a procession, that is not ordered. This [primary process] is a function of disorder and can appear at any time.[44]

When Freud's theory of culture ends up in a deadlock as described above, it ceases to be theory, says Rieff. 'There appears no way of thinking about disorder that doesn't immediately discover order about disorder. I don't understand chaos theory. I don't see how you can have a theory of chaos. "Theoria" is literally a vision of the highest.'[45] Or, as he puts it in *Fellow Teachers*: 'All disciplines of theory, are visions of the highest formalities.'[46]

Freud's theory of the unconscious has no answer to the question where to find the origin of order in mental processes. According to Rieff, it is tautological to refer to the unconscious as Freud does. That is no theory, because theory is by nature ordering and the essence of the operation of the unconscious is that it has its own logic that eludes our theories. To create a way out of this theoretical deadlock, Rieff suggests this: 'Suppose it is from the superior level of the cultural system that organizing (and disorganizing) higher principles thrust into the social structure. That thrust of higher (cultural) principles into the myriad activities of men ... would then establish the modalities[47] of societal integration and disintegration.'[48] Rieff calls the adaptation of instinctual desires to those higher cultural principles 'the primary cultural process.' As soon as these formative principles, which according to Rieff are essentially repressive, have penetrated the social order, they become part of the secondary cultural process. He circumscribes both processes like this: 'To adjust the expression of impulses to the controlling paragon, or character-ideal, defines the primary process in the shaping of our inherited culture; the arts and sciences define the secondary process, in which exemplary modes of action are extended further, into a moralizing experience, thus transforming individual into institutional action.'[49]

In the way Rieff defines his two central metasociological concepts, all revisions he suggested of Freudian theory were integrated. I will summarize them seriatim:

First, the primary cultural process is 'instinctual.' In this process our instinctual life, which is not directly knowable or perceivable, is adapted to ruling paragons (examples for behaviour) and thus becomes an observable phenomenon. The other side of this medal is that the same applies to cultural life. The cultural forms we inherited will only come alive when they contact our instinctual lives and are thus transformed into personal and social behaviour. In this way the 'primal forms' of a culture present themselves to us in historical forms. These primal forms are part of the superior level of the cultural system. Conceived like this, the primary process is not precultural, as it is for Freud, but it is part of culture itself.

Second, the 'regulative principle' of the primary cultural process is the character-ideal. Just like Freud's Oedipus complex, this Rieffian concept is a *dynamic* concept, aimed at cultural mechanisms. This principle regulates the operation of authority in a society, because it transforms individual instinctual impulses into socially accepted behaviour. This is really an inversion of the way Freud conceived of the primary and secondary processes. For Freud the adaptation of our instinctual lives to the demands of reality is regulated in the secondary process. The primary process, however, has its own dynamics and its influence on the individual cannot be destroyed. Rieff inverts this by conceiving of the adaptation of instinctual life to the demands of reality (or culture) as the primary process. The central theme for a psychoanalytic theory of culture is not that eros is indestructable, but that authority is indestructable. Repression is Rieff's most fundamental problem.

A second aspect of this reversal is that the primary and secondary process for Rieff mutually relate to each other in a different way than for Freud. For Rieff the secondary process supports the primary process, by extending exemplary modes of action. At this point, too, the duality of concepts which is so typical for Freud's theory is driven deeper by Rieff. He transposes the duality that Freud posited between the primary and secondary processes into the primary process.

With these revisions of Freud's most fundamental assumptions we can see now how Rieff provides his cultural theory with a double dialectic. First, Rieff defines his concepts in such a way that the relationship between the individual and the social order is dialectical. This is his answer to the 'reductionistic trend in modern social theory' that can only think about social order from the perspective of the individual and thus subordinate the interests of the social order to the interests of the individual. Second, Rieff replies to modern social theoretical thinking about culture which repeats 'Kant's mistake,' by perceiving cultural phenomena, like religion, as an undergirding of social phenomena. The relation between the social order and the cultural order is dialectical, says Rieff. Here I get ahead a little on themes that I will deal with more elaborately in the following chapters. In the passages from *Triumph of the Therapeutic* quoted above we do not yet find a dialectical approach. Here, the formative principles from the cultural order penetrate the social order, in a kind of 'one-way traffic.' In his later works Rieff corrects this one-sidedness in his theory of culture. It is evident that the problematic of 'sacred order' is already at stake here in an early form.[50]

4

Blueprint for a Theory of Culture

So far I have described the fundamental concepts of Rieff's theory of culture – the psychohistoric model, the character-ideal, the dialectic between the cultural and the social order, and the dialactic between the individual and the community and/or social order – and their relation to psychoanalysis. In this chapter I shall describe how Rieff refines this cultural theory in his book *The Triumph of the Therapeutic: Uses of Faith after Freud.*

In *Triumph,* Rieff develops a critical analysis of modernity from perspectives that are based on premodern cultural dynamics. A typical feature of Rieff's method is to use existing concepts, like 'commitment' or 'therapy,' in such a way that the reader of *Triumph,* while reading the book, gradually grasps a new meaning of the concepts. This is Rieff's way of criticizing common concepts. For example, the term 'therapy' in the modern sense refers to a psychotherapeutic situation in which the individual is temporarily exempted from social demands, in order to create room for psychotherapeutic processes. Rieff asserts that this is a reversal of the original, pre-modern meaning of the word. Then 'therapy' is the process that links the individual to the social order. Through identification with ideals or ideal figures individual instinctive energies are focused on shared purposes. This process is constitutive for both the self and social order. The reversal of meaning of the term 'therapy' is symptomatic of profound changes in Western culture, says Rieff: 'Now, contradicting all faiths, a culture of indifference is being attempted, lately using the rhetoric of "commitment" with which to enlarge the scope of its dynamism.'[1]

Modernity as Rupture in Western Cultural History

In the previous chapter we saw how Rieff postulates the existence of a cultural order which exists separately from the social order. From this cultural order formative principles penetrate into the social order. In the primary cultural process, for example, the expression of instinctual energies of the individual gets its form from the character-ideal and is regulated by it. The character-ideal is a formal and *dynamic* concept that refers to *processes.* On the level of *content* the character-ideal of a cultural era is embodied in cultural artefacts like myths, works of art, or music. In cultural traditions this is elaborated into complex wholes. Rieff defines the entire collection of these as the symbol system of a society, or of a group of societies that share a symbol system, like 'the Western world.'

Rieff's thesis on the emergence of psychological man refers to fundamental changes in what he calls 'the central symbolism of personal and corporate experience' of Western culture. Viewed from a cultural-sociological perspective it is typical for modernity that the conformative symbol system is attacked, says Rieff. The Christian symbol system, expressed in its most abstract form in the character-ideal of religious man, was typical for the premodern period until the Enlightenment. From then on a rupture occurs in the cultural traditions of the West. In the era of economic man, early modernity, the demolition of the cultural symbols that were based on Christianity begins. In late-modern culture this proceeds in high gear, and possibly is nearing completion: 'Now the dissolution of a unitary system of common belief, accompanied, as it must be, by a certain disorganization of personality, may have run its course. The long period of deconversion, which first broke the surface of political history at the time of the French Revolution, appears all but ended. The central symbolism of personal and corporate experience seems to me well on its way to being differently organized, with several systems of belief competing for primacy in the task of organizing personality in the West.'[2] Rieff's working hypothesis in his early works is that one winner seems to emerge in this competition – psychological man.

Cultus as the Organization of a Commitment Therapy

Psychological man's belief system differs radically from pre-modern belief systems. Premodern belief operated in a sacred cultural order, in which basic forms of culture ('primal forms' or 'higher cultural principles') structured, organized, and maintained the psychological and social order. These organizing processes were perpetrated in the cultus of a culture. According to Rieff, one main clue to the understanding of social organization is to be found in its symbolic of communal purpose. This symbolic operates through a social system enacting that symbolic in a way at once admonitory and consoling. Here, the character-ideals of political man and religious man resonate, because they belong to social systems in which the health of the individual was intimately connected with integration into the social order. In other words, 'the healthy individual was the healthy citizen.' When social structures change radically, in times of social crisis, we have to frame new integrative systems ('therapies'). Rieff says that Plato's philosophy, for example, can be read as a design of a new integrative system for contemporary Greek communal life.

Rieff's character-ideals always refer to such a social and cultural crisis. Political man came into existence during a crisis in classical Greek culture. The transition from the era of political man to that of religious man took place as a result of the crisis caused by the collapse of the Roman Empire. Rieff read the social contract theories of Rousseau, Locke, and Hobbes as new designs for integration of the individual in the changing social orders of early modernity (economic man). Freud's theory mirrors the crisis of late modernity (psychological man).

What does Rieff mean exactly by 'the cultus of culture'? The central symbolism of personal and corporate experience gives form and means of expression to human desire. In its most elementary forms this takes place in the 'cultus' of a culture. It is typical for premodern culture that the cultic formation of desire consisted 'mainly of ritual forms to elicit and produce stable responses of assurance to more or less fixed wants – fleshly and spiritual, as it used to be said.'[3] To attain this effect the 'sacred socializing agencies' drew from a 'standard range of expectations from which reassurance was elicited.'[4] This reassurance was mediated through consolation and, more importantly, through admonitions (this is what I described as Rieff's idea of 'primary cultural process' in the previous chapter). Thus the sacred socializing agencies composed a moral order.

Rieff's definition of therapy is closely connected to this: 'Each culture is its own order of therapy – a system of moralizing demands, including remissions that ease the pressures of communal purposes.'[5] Premodern faith was enacted in the regular acting out of mandatory therapies of commitment that were built into the charter of society. Western man 'once organized for himself modes of willing obedience, or faith, in which he found a sense of well-being and, also, his freedom from that single criterion.'[6] Rieff says that in modernity this premodern cultural dynamic is demolished. Therefore we face a historically unique situation: 'Culture without cultus appears, in almost all historical cases, a contradiction in terms.'[7]

The Task of a Cultural Elite

In premodern societies the shaping of cultural symbolism was the task of a cultural elite. Rieff's definition of the cultural elite reflects a polemic with counterculture that was so focused on 'the self': 'The test for the cultural elite has been its capacity to express ... the self-effacing moral demands.'[8] This symbolism was expressed in their ways of living, which were exemplary of how to relate personal and social life and the cultural order of ethically charged ideals to each other. Therefore Rieff calls the cultural elite the 'therapists of commitment' or 'therapeutic elite.'

Rieff thinks that the cultural elite does not have to be identical with the socially higher classes. It is true indeed that very often close ties develop between the cultural and social elite, but throughout history cultural classes have been ambivalently related to social classes. The upper social classes rarely preserve a strict system of moral demand. Rieff mentions the rise of the Puritans in the seventeenth century as a historical example of protest against this. This is one of the 'periods in history when a cultural elite, opposing refinement with aesthetically coarse moral demands, has risen in critical passion from both the lower social orders and from disaffected members of the higher.'[9]

Premodern therapeutic elites were predominantly supportive of culture as a system of moral demands, instead of being critical: 'Admonitions were the expectable predicates of consolation; that is, what is meant, nowadays, by "guilt" culture. When therapeutic elites grow predominantly critical then a cultural revolution may be said to be in progess.'[10]

Salvation of Desire

Significant for premodern Western cultural systems was that their primary processes were aimed at limiting impulses of independance or (individual) autonomy, says Rieff. In the culture that preceded ours the therapeutic order was embedded in a consensus of 'shalt nots.' Cultic commitment therapies never mounted a search for some new opening into experience. New experience, on the contrary, was not wanted and cultic therapy domesticated the wildness of experience. The apparently new was integrated into a restrictive and collective identity, by treating some novel stimulus or ambiguity of experience in the cult. Cultic therapies consisted, therefore, chiefly in participation mystiques severly limiting deviant initiatives. Individuals were trained, through ritual action, to express fixed wants, without receiving commensurate gratifications. On the contrary: 'The limitation of possibilities was the very design of salvation.'[11] Rieff's focusing on the limiting impact ('authority') of this dialectic probably is polemical, in an era that focuses on the 'expression of desire.'

The Soteriological Character-Ideal

With the concept 'salvation' Rieff specifies the idea that in the primary cultural process the cultural ideals frame the social structure and the personality structure. In the premodern era the Christian concept of salvation (based on the death on the cross and ressurrection of Jesus) structured the moral and social order: 'To the ironic question "And, being saved, how are we to behave?" Western culture long returned a painfully simple answer: "Behave like your Savior."'[12] Christian culture, like other organizations of moral demand, operated, however imperfectly, through the internalization of what Rieff calls a 'soteriological character-ideal.' He describes this as 'the highest level of controls and remissions' that 'experienced an historical and individualized incarnation.'[13] In other words; the ultimate incarnation of the divine, in Jesus the Saviour (in Greek: *sotèr*), expressed itself time and again as an ideal in the lives of those who, identifying with Jesus, became saints and examples. The soteriological character-ideal carried tremendous potentials for fresh intakes of communal energy. 'Such ... processes may have been indispensible for the vitality of the old culture.'[14]

Modernity as Cultural Revolution

With the cultural-sociological vocabulary described above, Rieff can formulate more precisely what determines the revolutionary character of modern culture: 'What is revolutionary in modern culture refers to releases from inherited doctrines of therapeutic deprivation; from a predicate of renunciatory control, enjoining releases from impulse need, our culture has shifted toward a predicate of impulse release.'[15] The premodern therapies aimed at limitation of impulselike needs, at an ascetic self-discipline of desire. He thinks that the central Christian symbolic was not ascetic in a crude way which would destroy any culture. Rieff refers to Scheler's notion of 'positive ascetism,' which had as its purpose not the total extirpation of natural drives, but their control and complete spiritualization. This form of asceticism is aimed at liberating the 'highest powers' of personality from blockage by the automatism of the lower drives. Rieff's comment on modern belief is this: what has to be liberated are not the instinctual impulses, but the higher powers that control those impulses.

The Analytic Attitude Versus Faith

Rieff aims at developing adequate sociological theory for analysis of cultural change. Notions of culture, religion, therapy, and morality have thus far been reviewed. Now we must take a closer look at how precisely Rieff describes these basic concepts and their interrelations sociologically in *Triumph of the Therapeutic.* He reacts against approaches in social theory in which, he thinks, our view of these interrelations is blurred. One main example is the reductive way religion is commonly thought of in social theory.

Religion presents jointly and in fusion two analytically discernible alternatives: either a therapeutic control of everyday life or a therapeutic respite from that very control.[16] 'On the one hand, faith is doctrinal, and that doctrine is internalized, thus becoming functionally anti-instinctual. On the other hand, faith is ecstatic or erotic; there is a relative absence of doctrinal internalization, and the religious mood covertly provides an opportunity for the instincts to express themselves more directly – for example, in orgiastic behavior, or in mystic states of mind which release the subject from traditional authority.'[17] Here, Rieff alludes to phenomena of the primary cultural process. In premodern belief systems methods were framed to curb human expressiveness, in order to attain emotional stability and social integration. Thus Rieff defines asceticism as the typical feature of premodern religious experience in cultural-sociological terms.

As for therapy, Rieff confronts the notion of therapy from premodern culture with that of later, psychologizing discourses. The definition of religion from the previous paragraph shows that Rieff gives purposely an ambiguous meaning to therapy. For Rieff therapy means both 'mutual tuning of the individual and social order' (as in premodern cultural dynamics) and 'temporary exemption from the demands of the social order for the individual.' Rieff has a strategic reason for making his concepts ambiguous, as I explained in the introduction of this chapter. We know that for modern therapy the idea of rational control of our psychic economy is crucial, as can be glimpsed from the psychotherapeutic situation. The comparison with premodern therapy leads Rieff to a definition which radically changes this notion. He says that historically various methods are known to exist for keeping up a sense of assurance, which may have had its origin in a state of ecstacy (as in orgiastic behaviour). These methods may fairly be called 'ascetic,' and Rieff gives examples such as forms of abstinence, control of breathing, and even semi-starvation. Such ascetic devices, if they are functional, prolong, and even regularize, the subjective feeling of security. To preserve this sense of ultimate security is thus the first function of all asceticism. 'History supplies enough examples of that deliberate emptying of consiousness, which may be the essential characteristic of all systems of therapy.'[18]

Rieff rejects the functionalist approach of religion and specifies religion's task in culture with a dialectical approach. On the one hand, religion belongs to the primary cultural process. Religion does not have influence on all aspects of everyday life, but on those aspects only that give an assurance of salvation, whatever that may mean in a specific cultural situation. That influence comes about in the primary cultural process, when the individual identifies unconsciously so very strongly with the dominant character-ideal that he or she expresses his or her instinctual desires with the forms the ideal provides for. This is the controlling mode of religion, which leads to emotional stability and social integration. This assurance of salvation is the basis for adequate moral behaviour. On the other hand, religion belongs to the secondary cultural process, too. When the therapeutic controls from the primary cultural process are succesful, they tend to spread in the entire social order. Everone is expected to have the right attitude in every activity of life and to conform these activities to the system of controls. As an example Rieff mentions the Chinese arts, in which the pentatonic scale was decreed as correct by Confucian doctrine.[19] This is how Rieff illustrates his thesis that the arts and sciences define the secondary process, in which exemplary modes of action are extended further, into a moralizing experience, thus transforming individual action into institutional action.

Implicit in this description of religion is Rieff's idea of cultural dynamism. Cultural principles stem from the 'upper part of the cultural system.' In the cultus of a culture these principles are preserved and transferred to its participants. In secondary cultural processes these principles are elaborated into modes of morally adequate behaviour. According to Rieff, this dynamism is blocked by modern cultural processes, and psychoanalysis is a representative example of this. In Rieff's reading of psychoanalysis, psychoanalytic therapy can be conceived of as a tracing back of the socio-and psychogenetic tracks of acculturation.[20] Put in Rieff's cultural-sociological terms: Freud strived to lay bare how the primary and secondary cultural processes have formed the character of a particular individual. Psychoanalytic therapy, he thought, must be aimed at resolving the transference in the psychotherapeutic relation. Thus the ultimate goal is to enable the patient to gain rational control over the most fundamental psychic levels of his personality. In this sense Freud's definition of psychic health is purely psycho*dynamic* and avoids prescription of (morally charged) contents, says Rieff.[21] From this perspective Rieff indicates how Freud radically reshaped the idea of therapy. In premodern culture therapy was always connected to faith, but for Freud 'the analytic attitude is an alternative to all religious ones.'[22]

The Symbolic Impoverishment of Western Culture

Rieff strives to develop *dynamic* explanations of processes of cultural change. He advocates the inclusion of transcendence in modern social theory, because without that concept we will not be able to develop an adequate theory of culture. Therefore he posits the existence of a transcendent cultural order, which operates in the primary cultural process. As such, culture works as a symbolic and cultural artefacts are conceived of as referring to this transcendent order. Modernization must be understood as a radical change in the interaction between a cultural symbolic and the social order. In *Triumph of the Therapeutic* Rieff analyses these changes, focusing on the transitions from premodern culture (of religious man) to early modern culture (of economic man) and from that to late-modern culture (of psychological man).

Symbolic Impoverishment and Participation Mystique

In *Triumph* Rieff uses the notion of 'participation mystique' to refer to the interaction between the social and the cultural order in premodern culture. Through participation in the cultus, premodern men internalized a symbolic representation of salvation, which was the basis for emotional stability and social integration. Such participation mystique is typical for what Rieff calls 'positive communities,' which are held by guilt. Here Rieff alludes to Freud's social psychological ideas. Freud

> supposed guilt the normal attitude of an individual toward authority, social as well individual. One of his favorite theses is that human beings have an ineradicable social heritage of guilt. The great religions are attempts to solve the problem of guilt; they are all 'reactions to the same great event,' the murder of the primal father, 'with which civilization began and which, since it occurred, has not allowed mankind a moment's rest.' ... Morality too stands under the sign of guilt. The best behavior of which we are capable is 'at bottom' an attempt 'to conciliate the injured father through subsequent obedience.' ... The sense of guilt is thus the pivot for Freud's conception of morality and religion.[23]

Rieff adopts this notion of Freud as far as the dynamics between the individual and (the symbolic representations of authority in) the social order is concerned. He rejects Freud's conception of authority and religion as identical, as we saw in the passages in the previous chapter on 'Kant's mistake.' Guilt, in its religious expressions, is not neurotic (as Freud thought religion to be) but, on the contrary, 'the normal attitude of an individual toward authority.' Guilt is also the motor of identification of the individual with the dominant character-ideal. In the positive communities of premodern Western culture, people believed that identifying with the soteriological character-ideal would lead to salvation.

The modernization of culture has rendered the formation of such communities impossible. In modern culture there is no fully operating symbol system anymore and no participation mystique. Social behaviour is acquired in totally new ways, in wholly new cultural dynamics. Guilt is no longer considered the basis of culture, but is culture's central problem and is conceived of as the neurotic influence of obsolete cultural norms and values. The basis for psychic health and for a new social order is sought in a liberation from this neurotic influence. Psychoanalysis is the symbolic mode of this analytic attitude. Individuals that live together in this mode form what Rieff calls 'negative communities.' The social cohesion thus attained does not rest on symbolic processes in which the individual identifies, mainly unconsciously, with the dominant character-ideal, but on a 'negative symbolic' which preaches an unlearning of this kind of identification.

The Ascetic Becomes the Therapeutic

The character-ideal coming into existence in modernity differs radically from its predecessors: 'The classical ideals were personifications of a release from a multitude of desires. Not only our Western system but every system of integrative moral demand, the generative principle of culture, expressed itself in positive deprivations – in a character-ideal that functioned to commit the individual to the group.'[24] The analytic attitude fully reverses this dynamic, because 'the analytic capacity demands a rare skill: to entertain multiple perspectives upon oneself and even upon beloved others ... so to soften the demands upon oneself in all the major situations of life – love, parenthood, friendship, work and citizenship.'[25]

Rieff traces back the origins of this analytic attitude in early modernity. Before I can go deeper into that I must pay attention to a change in Rieff's usage of the notion 'character-ideal.' In *Mind of the Moralist* and the article 'Psychological Man in America' (1960) there is an ambiguity in the use of the term 'character-ideal.' Rieff calls typologies like economic man the character-ideal of a cultural era, but he also uses the term in a broader sense to refer to the typological human being of that era itself. In *Triumph of the Therapeutic* he distinguishes between the typological human being and his character-ideal. So Rieff speaks of economic man with his character-ideal the ascetic, or of psychological man and his character-ideal the therapeutic.

Rieff traces the origins of the analytic attitude back to early modernity, the era of economic man with his character-ideal the ascetic. Typical for the ascetic is his practical attitude and orientation to the present: 'Once launched into some activity, conceiving of himself as an instrument of God's will, the ascetic did not stop to ask about the meaning of it all. On the contrary, the more furious his activity, the more the problem of what his activity meant receded from his mind. In time the Western ascetic ceased cultivating his doctrinal imagination.'[26] This 'cultivating his doctrinal imagination,' I think, alludes to the fact that in the nineteenth century societies changed rapidly and people did not succeed in keeping those new social orders connected with a religious view of life, nourished from religious traditions. The industrializing world became increasingly technological and became 'autonomous' from the religious sphere. 'Those remote areas [of religion] are brought up only in order to be put in their proper place, as dead events and motives rather than as the models for events and motives of the present life.'[27]

According to Rieff, the era of economic man was a transitional phase in Western culture. The quick absorption of psychoanalytic thinking in American culture indicated a new phase, which radicalized the previous one: 'The most congenial climate for the training of the therapeutic has been in a waning ascetic culture like that of Protestant America.'[28] In the primary cultural process of premodern Western culture the individual learned symbolically that his or her desires had to serve 'higher purposes' that gave him or her a guarantee of salvation. Modern man considers this cultural system as obsolete, which Rieff makes clear by indicating the profound change of definition that modern culture attributes to therapy.

Therapy is no longer a process which is in itself dialectical and in which can be distinguished a main function of mutually tuning the individual and social order and a secondary function of release of that tuning, which is also therapeutic. In modern therapy this secondary function is the most important one. The essence of modern therapy shows itself in the psychotherapeutic situation, in which the individual is temporarily exempted from social demands in order to create room for psychotherapeutic processes. Therapy becomes a technique in which man learns to create his own salvation by learning the analytic attitude, which increasingly takes over the function of the premodern symbolics. That is what Rieff means when he speaks of the symbolic impoverishment of Western culture. It started in early modernity and the triumph of psychological thinking, in various forms, in the twentieth century radicalized this process. Thus, we find ourselves in a new psychohistoric phase of culture: 'The ascetic becomes the therapeutic.'[29]

Cultural Alienation

The emergence of this new character-ideal shows itself most clearly when we compare the late modern cultural elite with the early modern one. The latter still considered the symbolic impoverishment caused by the loss of traditional religion's meaning to be a problem (think of Rieff's master's thesis on Coleridge). For the modern cultural elite this is not a problem anymore, because it has found functional equivalents for religion and morality in psychoanalysis and art. The democratic, anti-hierarchic, and anti-authoritarian features of modern Western culture brought about a totally new kind of cultural elite, which no longer mobilizes its spiritual energies by presenting itself as the bearer of new moral demands: 'Both American and Soviet cultures are essentially variants of the same belief in wealth as the functional equivalent of a high civilization.'[30] The cultural elite consists of bearers of a cultural symbolic of self-chosen life-styles: 'Western culture is changing already into a symbol system unprecedented in its plasticity and absorptive capacity. Nothing much can oppose it really, and it welcomes all criticism, for in a sense it stands for nothing.'[31]

This big change in the central cultural symbolic in the West is correlated with what I described in Chapter 2 as the transition from conformative to transformative theory. In the cultural eras of political man and religious man people believed that reality reflected an eternal order 'through the mediating myth that there were natural laws.'[32] Psychological man 'has discovered no natural harmony of goals, no hierarchy of value inscribed upon the universe.'[33] This had a profound influence on the way modern man envisions social order: 'The public world is constituted as one vast stranger, who appears at inconvenient times and makes demands viewed purely as external and therefore without the power to elicit a genuinely moral response.'[34]

At this point Rieff's distinction between the cultural and the social order is relevant again. As for the relationship between the individual and the world he lives in, modern therapy not only alienates him from the social order, but from the cultural order as well. I suggest that we call this 'cultural alienation.' In the previous chapter we saw how Rieff revised psychoanalytic cultural theory with the theory of the inner dualism of both the individual and culture. Modern man tends to lose sight of these inner dualities, because in modern therapy he learns that the self is an inner entity from which he is alienated by antagonistic cultural demands. Modern man believes that he has to acquire a conscious and pragmatic relation to culture in order to attain autonomy and authenticity through self-expression. This belief leads to a 'cultural alienation' which cannot be analysed with existing social theory.

Community and Therapy

In *Triumph of the Therapeutic* Rieff evaluates modern social theory and points out what is lacking for an adequate theory of modern culture. Rieff asserts that in all social theory, from Plato to de Tocqueville, the therapeutic implication was remarkably consistent: 'An individual can exercise his gifts and powers fully only by participating in the common life. This is the classical ideal. The healthy man is in fact the good citizen.'[35] In the Middle Ages this tradition was institutionalized in a church civilization in which the therapeutic functions were reserved to functionaries of the churches. The 'classical therapist' had to commit the 'patient' to the symbol system of the community, with all means provided for by culture and cultus. On the symbolic level the integrative functions were expressed in doctrines such as that of natural law. This kind of therapy is what Rieff calls 'commitment therapy': 'Behind shaman and priest, philosopher and physician, stands the great community as the ultimate corrective of personal disorders.'[36]

Yet, suppose there occurred some disorder so fundamental in nature as to destroy the therapeutic function of the community per se? Rieff asks rhetorically. Suppose, for a variety of reasons, that the community were no longer able to supply a system of symbolic integration? 'Here, then, in the destruction of all idealizations upon which traditional and classical communities were based, in theory and practice, is to be sought the origin of modernity.'[37]

Analytic Therapy versus Commitment Therapy

According to Rieff, nineteenth-century social theory met modern conditions in three different ways. The first is the classical position, defended by de Tocqueville against Rousseau: the individual's sense of well-being depends on full participation in the community. The second position is the early-modern one, formulated by Rousseau and, according to Rieff, generally accepted nowadays: men must free themselves from binding attachments to communal purposes in order to express more freely their individualities. The third position, based on the Marxist diagnosis, is that there is no positive community now in which the individual can merge himself therapeutically. Freud adheres to this tradition too, says Rieff: 'It may be said that Freud came on the scene not long after a new type of therapeutic effort became necessary, that is, one suitable for the development of individualist culture.'[38]

With the aid of Marxist theory Rieff lays bare another typical feature of modern analytic therapy for which Freud provided the model. Although they can be grouped together from the perspective described above, Marxist theory distinguishes itself from Freudian theory on the point of a utopian ideal of a new community. Marx's prophetic vision of a communist identity, which is the predicate of true individuality, combines both the conservative and the radical traditions. Marx created a new kind of commitment therapy with a return, on the symbolic level, to a new kind of community. 'Marxism is more than theory; at the same time it is a type of commitment therapy.'[39]

In *Triumph of the Therapeutic* Rieff asserts that Marx's theory is less adequate to analyse the situation of late modern Western culture, because it lacks a distinction that is essential for that analysis: the difference between *negative* and *positive* communities. Positive communities guarantee to the individual a certain salvation of the self, through the internalization of a soteriological character-ideal. Rieff specifies salvation as an experience that transforms all personal experiences by subordinating them to agreed communal purposes. Negative communities, which survive almost automatically by a self-sustaining technology, do not offer a type of collective salvation. Here the therapeutic experience is not *transformative* but *informative.*[40] Commitment therapies can only prove their full therapeutic efficacy in positive communities. So, what Marx cannot explain is that highly developed industrial communities are no longer 'culturally positive.'

The failure of the Marxist utopia is symptomatic for a cultural development in modern culture, says Rieff. No new forms of community have developed that functioned culturally in a way comparable with the communities of premodern culture. In those cultures therapeutic systems were operative that produced cultural mechanisms of control through transformative experience. Under late modern cultural conditions these mechanisms of control have to be established in different ways. 'The ways suitable to modern culture are generally classifiable as "informative," aiming at the strengtening of ego-controls over inner conflicts. As a result, there emerges a more purely therapeutic type, complete with doctrines intended to manage the strains of living as a communally detached individual.'[41] Analytic therapies are developed precisely in response to the need of the Western individual for a therapy that would not depend for its effect on a symbolic return to a positive community. Thus Freud and Marx meet back to back for Rieff.

By pitting analytic therapy against commitment therapy in this way Rieff introduces some more cultural-sociological concepts for his theory of modernity. Rieff asserts that ritual participation (as it takes place in the cultus) is an extreme form of commitment therapy. Reasoning analogically, he says that the function of ritual participation for the group is the same as what mysticism is for the individual. Mystical experience is always a form of unification with a 'saving agency.' Once the mystic unity with the saving symbol and with the community behind it is achieved, a climax of inner stability has been reached. Rieff specified this saving symbol for premodern Western culture as the soteriological character-ideal. Typical for modern culture is that it stimulates the opposite movement, towards alienation of the saving agency. That is what I proposed to call 'cultural alienation.' Rieff describes it like this: 'The tendency to inaction itself has a supportive value, for once ... a climax of inner stability has been reached, there is no place to go except further down, so to speak, toward alienation from the integrative god-term with which the mystic has been infused.'[42] I take this cryptic formulation to be an allusion to the ideal of depth psychology, which can be deduced from the spatial terminology Rieff uses here. In its therapeutic processes depth psychology strives after the sort of alienation Rieff hints at. It goes 'further down' into the human psyche to free the patient of unconscious ties that it considers causes of psychopathological behaviour. Herewith it strives to interfere at the level of the primary cultural process. It does not aim, however, at an inner unification with a 'saving agency,' but, opposite to that, at creating an inner distance of the symbolic representations that were internalized and that led to control of instinctual desires. This inner distance is considered salutary. From this perspective, Rieff's use of the term 'alienation' inverts the contemporary use of the term. For Rieff alienation is not a process in which the individual loses contact with an authentic and original core, the self, but rather a process in which the individual loses contact with an agency 'outside itself,' the culturally determined saving agency, which Rieff considers as equally authentic and original as individual character.

Rieff points out a very important aspect of the process of mystical union with the saving symbol or character-ideal. He refers to Roman Catholic doctrine to show that 'it is significant that ascetism ... is considered propaedeutic to a mystical commitment experience.'[43] Rieff asserts that in modern analytic therapy the process of generating commitment to communal purposes is flawed at this level. To describe this in the terms of his sociological theory Rieff introduces an auxiliary concept: 'the ecstatic.' With that he describes the process that inverts identification with the character-ideal. 'The ascetic would be as characteristic of symbol systems in which the therapeutic function would be that of control as the ecstatic would be characteristic of systems with releasing functions ... Ecstatics probably constituted the first therapeutic type, communicating ecstatically their sense of release from established patterns of control to others.'[44]

Then he gives a cultural-sociological definition of renewal of the belief system, in a way that reminds us of the psychogenetic explanations of religious dynamics by Freud in *Totem and Taboo* and *Moses and Monotheism.* Rieff says that when the ecstatic was the first religious leader, then the orgy was the first religious institution. This ecstatic phenomenon has a therapeutic function, because it temporarily relieves the pressure of symbolic integration. In a certain phase of the history of a culture such 'releasing' cultural functions may become dominant over the 'controlling' functions. That would be typical for cultural change on the most profound level. Until modernity such changes in Western cultural history always involved the development of a new system of symbolic integration. The original 'releasing' cultural functions are transformed into 'controlling' ones. From that perspective Rieff defines the renewal of belief systems: 'Faiths develop first as primary modes of release from earlier uses of faith, and then develop their own control functions.'[45] The ascetic would be as characteristic for symbol systerms in which the therapeutic function is controlling as the ecstatic is typical for systems with releasing functions. Typical for premodern Western culture, then, would be a dialectical tension between the ascetic and ecstatic, which was regulated in premodern therapies. This is a cultural-sociological elaboration of the previously mentioned idea that cultural dynamics essentially consist in a primary pole of controlling modes and a secondary one of release.[46]

Jung, Reich, and Lawrence: Prophets of a New Culture?

Rieff describes the central problematic of the second part of *Triumph of the Therapeutic* like this: 'The analytic attitude ... points towards a character-ideal that is in principle anti-ascetic and therefore revolutionary if viewed from perspectives formed in the inherited moral demand system.[47] ... From the point of view of commitment therapies, by which we are still influenced, the analytic attitude of detachment is itself a symptom of illness.'[48] Rieff asserts that Carl G. Jung, Wilhelm Reich, and David H. Lawrence were all, each in their different ways, susceptible to these pathological symptoms of modern Western culture. They were all former adherents of psychoanalysis, but turned into severe critics who developed alternative theories. In my reading of *Triumph* Rieff's analysis of their works reflects one common denominator: they all tried to combine the analytic attitude with pseudo-conformative theory, in order to develop new types of commitment therapy with which the modern individual could attain psychic integration. Rieff analyses these attempts critically in three very complex 'case studies,' in which he uses the theoretical concepts developed in the first part of the book. I can only give a few hints of the theoretical richness of these studies.

Rieff's choice of these three subjects must be viewed in the light of his ideas about the function of a cultural elite. These authors tried to develop a new type of commitment therapy under the cultural circumstances of late modernity. They all rejected the old ontological order based on Christianity and recreated new symbolics that they needed in order to develop their commitment therapies. In this sense Jung, Reich, and Lawrence belonged to the cultural elite that helped create new cultural symbolics for late-modern Western culture. According to the criteria that Rieff develops, however, they cannot be considered cultural innovators, because in their works they do not transcend modernity but rather radicalize it. Again, 'ambivalence' is a key word here. On the one hand, Rieff considers the attempts of these authors to 'work through' modernity very valuable for a theory of culture. On the other hand, he suggests that their attempts fail and that modern culture shows itself as *anti-culture* in their work. Rieff gives no definitive judgment about the value of their works.

Rieff's approach is *aesthetic*: he is interested in cultural *forms* that are used for expressing human desire and combines theories from many different disciplines.[49] Our inner lives cannot be expressed as such, but need modes of communication between what is inside of us and what is outside. In these processes the individual externalizes his or her inner life and thus becomes a social being: 'In the theory tentatively presented in the introduction of this volume, the religious problem is identical with the moral and the moral with the cultural. As systems of moral demands, every culture produces its communication modes, its aesthetic.'[50] In the case studies in the second part of *Triumph of the Therapeutic* Rieff wants to indicate how the communication modes of late-modern culture differ fundamentally from premodern ones.

Jung's Religious Psychology

The modern social sciences (psychology, sociology, anthropology) and art (e.g., naturalism) all 'avowed a panoramic and faithful reproduction of the particularity of human experience.'[51] It was thought that reality was nothing more than unordered particulars. Ideas in general (as a product of rational activity), and the idea of any single integration in particular, were considered an artificial and dangerous imposition. Thus modern science and art testify to the gradual breakdown of the ontological order that was based on Christianity. Carl G. Jung asserted that a very valuable substitute for this lost ontological order can be found in myths. Jung adhered to the Lamarckian hypothesis of the collective unconscious, the source of all individual and social life, which becomes manifest in myths. He maintained that modern man had cut himself off from this archaic source of life, from his 'creative impulse,' because he had overdeveloped his rational abilities. By opening himself up for what myths have to tell, modern man ought to create his own personal myth. In this way he could regain contact with his creative impulse.

Jung also believed that religious tradition could survive in this way: 'The representation of the archaic in modern situations, mainly internal to the person, was the mode in which tradition survived.'[52] Rieff criticizes Jung's treatment of religion as very ahistorical and uncritical, because he lifted the mythical materials from their historical and geographical context and gave them archetypal contents. These contents he called 'eternal,' because they occur in so many different cultures and throughout history. 'In Jung, psychology was transformed into an inventory of traditions, from which culture could borrow variety and relieve the boredom of an "unspiritual," although comfortable life.'[53]

Rieff asserts that Jung developed his libido theory into an integrative personal symbolism, a new kind of commitment therapy. When used in the proper way, the libidinous energies can be considered forces that propel us into a process of 'individuation.' In this process the eternal order replicates itself in a specific way in the individual. Jung disagreed with Freud on the function of reason in this process. Freud advocated 'rational management' of the unconscious energies, which Jung considered impossible. The creative impulse cannot operate except unconsciously. That is why Rieff thinks that Jung came round to a version of the unconscious that really gave it the function of the ideal and eternal order, as in the premodern mode of theorizing.[54]

The ideal character type thus produced by Jung's theory 'is neither mystic nor ascetic, but therapeutic – a person assessing even his own myth in terms of how much it contributes to his sense of personal well-being.'[55] Salvation in Jungian theory has nothing to do anymore with integration of an individual in a community through integration in a communal symbolic order. The symbolic order is adapted to the individual, in the search for symbols in the cultural storehouse that fit with the individual. Rieff asserts that, viewed meta-theoretically, this is an inversion of the idea of conformative theory, which makes Jung's theory 'pseudo-conformative.'

Another point of Rieff's criticism of Jung's use of symbolism is that 'Jung never analyzes the social structures within which all creative symbolisms occur. Indeed he seems unaware of social structure.'[56] Rieff accuses Jung of fully separating the social and symbolic orders and therewith the complexity of cultural dynamics. Salvation, which is the climax of social and psychic integration in Rieff's theory, is reduced to a non-institutional, psychological process in Jung's theory. We have seen in previous chapters that an important aspect of Rieff's theory of modernity is the link between social structure and that of the psyche. Thus Rieff concedes that Jung's theory contains important corrections of Freud's theory of religion, but at the same time it is reductionist. Rieff says that Jung's theory is not a critical analysis of modernity, but a polemical reaction to it.

According to Rieff, Jungian theory is an important premonition of what religion would develop into, outside the traditional institutional settings in Western culture. Therefore this theory is 'prophetic.' Rieff was proved right by the enormous growth of 'New Age' ideas, drawing heavily on Jungian concepts, since the 1960s. Rieff's analysis of Jung's theory illustrates how Rieff exerts himself to develop theoretical criteria to compare 'traditional religion' with these and other new forms of 'religiosity.' Rieff draws our attention to cultural and social aspects of religion that tend to be forgotten in those new forms because of their therapeutic character.

Reich's Religion of Energy

Wilhelm Reich (1897–1957) is now less known than Jung, but his work has been very influential, too. For example, the therapeutic method of bio-energetics is based on it. Reich believed that the 'natural sociality' of the instincts was hindered by cultural constraints and his credo was: 'abolish the repressions.' The way to achieve this was to break down social structures that hindered the biological or natural sociality of the instincts. He experimented with this by setting up new communes with a very free sex life and sex education. In his later works he turns away from changing societal structures and developes a cosmological theory, with the same goal; to protect the life-giving instinctual energies from countervailing forces. Reich developed a 'quasi-theological' theory about a divine life-giving cosmic energy that is threatened by a devilish deadly opponent. He believed that a cosmic struggle was going on between these two forces, in which man had to take sides with the life-giving energy, in order to attain his full humanity.

This may all sound very eccentric and esoteric, but according to Rieff it is relevant for us because it reflects a typical feature of modern religiosity. Reich confusedly mixed natural and moral notions. In a Reichian way modern religiosity focuses on the problem of expression of human desire, without paying attention to the problem of authority (as a control or curbing of human desire). How does this work in Reich's case?

As in Jung's theory, the concept of libido plays an important role in Reich's theory. Reich thought that Freud in his analyses had not gone 'deep' enough and had remained stuck in the perverse anti-social 'layer' of human character.[57] Reich posited a biological substrate of desire, which he considered man's 'natural sociality' that is 'adulterated by the repressions through which it must pass on the way to action.'[58] To make individuals and societies more healthy, Reich thought, the repressions had to be abolished. He radicalized Freudian theory with a Marxist criticism and vice versa. Real salvation could be attained when the super-ego, the repressions built into human character, could be destroyed. Then a real liberating revolution could take place, analogous to the Marxist thesis of destroying alienating political and social structures. This revolution would free man from his most fundamental alienation; that of his healthy, biological or instinctual impulses. This radicalized Freud's ideas, because for Freud the abolition of the super-ego was impossible. Reich maintained that he had radicalized Marxist theory as well, because Marxist eschatology was only formulated in terms of social theory and therefore was blind to Reich's idea of the more fundamental alienation of our biological impulses.

It is typical of Reich's early works that he tries to radicalize the analytic attitude, which implies a new type of commitment therapy. Commitment is conceived of as bringing man into free and non-repressive social circumstances, as in the communes he founded. Reich's experiments with communal life did not succeed and the focus of Reich's interests shifted. 'In his religiosity, Reich gave up trying to understand altogether. Finally, Reich offers the ecstatic attitude as superior to the analytic.'[59] Typical for the ecstatic experience is that it strives after a direct mystical union with the divine, without ecclesiastical mediation (through buildings, priests, rituals, etc.). To achieve this, the ecstatic strove after release from established patterns of control. According to Rieff, Reich elaborated a full blown pseudo-conformative theory. The therapeutic doctrine of his earlier works 'was fully elaborated into the scientific theological fantasia of Reich's last years.'[60]

Reich gradually developed a theory and practice that on first sight looks like a religion, with a new therapy of commitment and new forms of symbolic integration. But, as in the former case study, Rieff tries to demonstrate that Reich's system is a quasi-religion. It is based on the exaltation of the ecstatic, whereas according to Rieff's theoretical standards, a dialectical tension between the ascetic and the ecstatic is typical for religious systems. The tension between the moral (which limits the human instincts) and the natural or biological can never be resolved. Repression can never be abolished. Therefore an adequate theory of culture (and religion) should be based on real dialectical polarities, like *controls-remissions*, *ascetic-ecstatic*, and *positive community–negative community*. With concepts like that the dynamics of culture and religion can be studied without reducing their complexities.

Lawrence's Religious Art

David Herbert Lawrence (1885–1930) was fascinated by eroticism, which he considered the mysterious, primal power of life. Like Brown and Marcuse after him, Lawrence believed that 'the rationalizing of life by technological sciences'[61] alienated modern man from this divine source. The purpose of Lawrence's literary work is to permit an experience of the divine to be encountered anew, in a culture where the experience with the transcendent ('numinous') is not ordinarily available.[62] Lawrence thought that no living society was possible but one which was held by a great religious idea. 'But he rejected a culture dominated either by Agape or by Reason – by the Christian concept of love or by the Greco-Christian scientific *logos*.'[63] All these concepts alienated man from his divine passions.

Thus, says Rieff, Lawrence was aware that 'alienation was originally neither a Marxist nor a psychiatric tool of understanding the human condition, but theological and specifically Christian.'[64] Rieff asserts that Lawrence, unaware, resumes theological debates about 'the self'[65]: 'In the original version of the doctrine of alienation, man may cure imself only by accepting God's forgiveness, through Christ, and thus, in imitation of the divine mood, love not only his neighbours but also himself.'[66] This is what Rieff calls the identification with a soteriological character-ideal in the first part of the book. After the fall, man became alienated from God. He can only be reconciled with God through identification with a soteriological character-ideal. Rieff asserts that Lawrence had recognized this fundamental aspect of alienation. Lawrence thought that Western culture had not yet been able to solve this existential problem.

Lawrence's solution was to develop a 'language of sanctified sex'[67] with which he created literary work that aimed at offering the reader a religious experience. Lawrence, like Jung, wanted to restore the dynamic of religious forms and 'argues vigorously for each man steering straight toward his own sort of collision with the power of emotions; this Lawrence considers the very core of religious experience – an experience of self.'[68] This he called 'the old religious faculty.' He believed that our erotic nature, from which religious emotions grow, had to be liberated from attempts, like Freud's, of encompassing it within rational science.[69] 'Lawrence inveighs against all abstractions, including psychological ones.'[70]

Generally speaking, for Lawrence our passions had to be liberated from any cultural restraint, in order to be able to do their salutary work of bringing man in contact with the Other inside the self. This would save man from the isolation of the self that modern culture imposed on him through the analytic attitude. Lawrence took his origin from the powerful tradition of religious mysticism, both Christian and non-Christian. According to Rieff, Lawrence's work testifies to the working conception of the modern novel: 'The war of desire with the delicate and selective sentiments of civilization – which constitutes the working conception of modern depth psychology – has been long since the working conception of the novel. The modern novel has as its object to show the natural impulses of man breaking against the retaining walls of civilization.'[71]

Rieff thinks that Lawrence's diagnosis of modern culture is valuable for a sociological theory of culture, because he was very sensitive to cultural dynamics and the influence of modernization on it. As in the former two case studies, however, Rieff rejects Lawrence's solution as too one-sided. It is too much focused on the expression of human instinct, without paying adequate attention to the necessity of curbing and controlling human desire with cultural devices. Lawrence's faith is in the erotic mode, and therefore Rieff concludes that Lawrence cannot be considered a cultural innovator. Following his sociological principles, Rieff thinks that cultural innovation can only proceed from a total renewal of the system of cultural controls and remissions. Lawrence's theory therefore must be considered totally remissive because of its focus upon the liberation of human instinct. A real innovation of the 'old religious faculty' has to be conceived of dialectically, as a new dynamic between controlling and releasing modes of expressing human desire.

5

The Limits of Modernity

> There are moments in life when the question of knowing if one can think differently than one thinks, and perceive differently than one sees, is absolutely necessary if one is to go on looking and reflecting at all.
>
> Michel Foucault, *The Use of Pleasure*[1]

The status of the sacred is a key question for a sociological theory of culture, because it refers to the central dynamic of culture. Despite attempts to revive a religious outlook on life, late-modern culture cuts itself off from the sacred, says Rieff. The sacred cannot be conceived of with theories that focus too one-sidedly on (the expression of) human desire. According to Rieff, the sacred reveals itself primarily in the authoritative mode. Therefore the problem of the sacred refers to the problem of authority.

The problem of authority is the problem of curbing human desire, of limiting human possibilities. Repression is the central concept here. Rieff thinks that late-modern Western culture refuses to acknowledge the central importance of repression, because of this culture's anti-authoritarian or transgressive character. Rieff's cultural criticism can be read as an unmasking of transgressive attempts to destroy authority. He tries to deconstruct the method of these attempts that conceive of the role of authority inadequately. They cannot succeed, says Rieff, but what they do achieve is to mislead, or seduce, modern man to believe that he can be liberated from authority. Rieff's reply is that authority is indestructible. In Rieff's middle period we see the beginnings of a new line of thinking. In his earlier works he tends to conceptualize late modernity as a rupture or discontinuity in Western cultural history. Next to this line of thinking, in his middle period Rieff begins to think of possibilities of continuity. Our contact with the sacred can be reconstructed when we are able to reconstruct the working of authority.

We saw in previous chapters that in Rieff's theory repression is the dynamic link between the individual, the social, and the cultural. A central notion in Rieff's thinking is the idea of restoring a real dialectical approach to sociological thinking about the interrelations between the individual, social order, and the cultural/sacred order. In this chapter we will see how Rieff elaborates his metasociology, which was to become the foundation for the theory of the sacred in his later works.

The Interior Space of Culture

In the beginning of the 1970s the political radicalization of the universities abated. In the academic world people started thinking about the function of the university in the new societal context, in which democratization and the functionality of academic education have been broadly accepted. *Fellow Teachers* is a vigorous contribution to this reflection. Rieff had to accept that the academy had changed fundamentally, but he searched for new ways of thinking of its core function, training a cultural elite which can play a guiding role in the formation of culture.

In an earlier text, from 1959, Rieff had expounded his ideas about the function of academic teaching. In 'The Function of the Social Sciences,' he mentions two main goals of academic teaching. No student starts from scratch, asking 'first questions,' he says. Therefore 'the primary aim ought to be ... to teach the leading formulation of problems and the splendid variety of solutions thus far suggested in our intellectual trades.'[2] This ought to be done in such a way that a student acquires a basic knowledge of 'leading formulations of problems,' which he calls the 'dogmas' of a discipline, as well as the capacity to analyse them. The secondary goal is to teach the student how to integrate this basic insight in the dogmas of his or her discipline in his or her own personal and intellectual life. Both aims ought to contribute to personal reformulations of the acquired theory.

Writing on the same topic in *Fellow Teachers*, Rieff's tone is much more polemical, which makes more visible what meta-theoretical questions are at stake in 'The Function of the Social Sciences' implicitly. Rieff uses an aesthetic concept again to formulate this. The theories of the social sciences and humanities, mathematics, biology, the plastic arts, literature, and music are all aspects of our attempts to decipher 'the mystery of man and his culture,' he says. It is the task of the teacher to initiate students in these attempts. 'Plato, Haydn, Beethoven, Freud, Weber: all our greatest teachers are always dead. Yet God enlivens their minds in us. Except for us, their scores become too settled; they need constant performance in order to be realized. Our task is to perform them, in order to see what lives. When, prepared slowly enough, a student can make his own sudden plunge through the words, into the interior space shaped by those words, then he inherits his share in the living authority of our great predecessors.'[3]

Generally speaking, academic education is more than transferring (so-called) objective knowledge, put in neat definitions. It is a preparation for getting acquainted with 'interior spaces' that are shaped by our 'great predecessors.' This process requires a certain discipline. 'That discipline, the critical performance rightly transferred, is highly personal; it is also risky; however well disciplined, we risk failure. I see no way of reproducing a true interiority exactly from one time to another.'[4]

Here we see how Rieff describes his ideal of academic teaching from three interrelated perspectives: that of the task of the teacher, of the student's learning process, and of the sort of theory taught in the academy. Rieff's ideal is opposed to the ideal that managers try to impose on the academy, to train students to become 'problem-solvers.' Rieff considers this a betrayal of the task of the academy of educating a cultural elite.

In good academic education, says Rieff, the student acquires sensitivity for the principally aesthetic character of theory. This character he describes like this: 'Music, philosophy, the literature of human conduct in cases or fictions, mathematics, I suppose, all disciplines of theory are visions of the highest formalities.'[5] The relation between theory and reality is conceived of in modern science in a totally different way than in premodern science. In his early works Rieff called this the difference between transformative and conformative theory. Modern, transformative theory frames a new conception of reality, driven by emancipatory ideals. This conception is the rule of conduct for human action. The main function of theory is to solve concrete problems. Rieff rejects this oversimplification of the relation between theory and reality. The constructs devised in theory principally belong to another realm or order than that of reality itself. This distinction must not be blurred: 'The visionary disciplines are what we should require of our undergraduates; then, at least, they may acquire a becoming modesty about becoming "problem-solvers," dictating reality.'[6] Rieff calls it 'order-hopping' when this distinction between the order of theory and of reality is not respected.

In a type of academic education which is anti-authoritarian, politicized, and democratized, the preconditions which prepare students for an exploration of 'interior spaces' are lacking. Such education is not aimed at maintaining chains of critical interpretations in which the authority of the masters of theory can be transferred in renewed forms. This type of academic teaching rather aims at enhancing critical reflection, meant to break down such chains.[7] This overemphasis on critical reflection makes real academic education impossible, because this reflection ought to be preceded by a phase in which the student opens himself up for the theory of the grand masters of his discipline. Teaching social theory is not 'the taking of endlessly critical positions,' so-called 'reflexive sociology.' Rieff thinks that such theories are empty because they can draw no hermeneutic circles.[8] 'We teachers should produce nothing new, no breakthrough, until we produce, first in ourselves, those protections of older wisdom which may help stave off arrogant stupidities parading as originality, modernization, revolution – and, of course, "values."'[9] Without those protections, that which has to be controlled, the 'endless expressional quest' which critical students and teachers believe will lead to liberated thinking, gets the upper hand.[10]

In *Fellow Teachers* Rieff is more openly polemical than in his earlier works towards fellow theorists who take sides with counterculture and its striving after cultural change by breaking down authority. In previous chapters I proposed that authority was already a basic theme in Rieff's earlier works. He was aware that this was not a very popular theme in those days, and therefore he chose to raise the matter only in 'enveloped forms' such as his cultural theory of *Triumph of the Therapeutic.* In *Fellow Teachers* the problematic of authority is raised in full. Among many others, Rieff argues against Marcuse and Brown, whose theories he considers as 'symptomatic' of modern social theory. Like the theories of Jung, Reich, and Lawrence, their theories falter because of their one-sided attention to the expression of human desire. Therefore they do not adequately analyse the complex interactions with controlling mechanisms. In *Fellow Teachers* Rieff calls this 'the manipulation of super-ego symbolism.'[11] The essential role of authority became a 'repressed problematic' and the curbing of human desire became a taboo subject.[12]

This therapeutic motif of manipulation of superego symbolism is dominant not only in post-Freudian psychoanalytic theory and in modern social theory, says Rieff, but in all central realms of acculturation:

the arts, sciences, and education. These realms belong to what Rieff called 'the secondary cultural process' in *Triumph.* There the cultural principles that originate from the primary cultural process are elaborated in exemplary social forms of behaviour. In *Fellow Teachers* Rieff tries to show how important theorists, artists, and other leading figures try to change culture by transforming its heart: 'It is interior space that is first reshaped, preliminary to the reshaping of social order.'[13] The manipulation of superego symbolism must be considered an attempt to change culture at the core of its dynamic.

Repression, Interdicts, and Transgression

Rieff builds up his theory of culture around a theory of authority. He interprets modern culture as an attempt to change ('transform') the structure of authority and thus install a radically new type of cultural dynamic. In psychoanalysis this attempt shows itself in its most succint form. Let us see how Rieff 'works through' the psychoanalytic notions that are constitutive for a psychoanalytic theory of culture in writings from his middle and later period.

In *One Step Further* (1979)[14] Rieff resumes consideration of the problematic of the dual nature of our instinctual lives: the impulses or instincts 'cannot participate in any order of actual existence until they are transformed into that which limits them.'[15] Desire and limitation, eros and authority are intimately connected. The tension field between 'original desires' and the forms with which we express those desires is the realm of culture. This expression is never a perfect fit; in every expression desire retains something of its unruly nature that resists limitation. Thus in every expression there is a delicate balance between repression and the return of the repressed, which Rieff describes like this: 'The cunning cultivated in repression, commanding intelligences unrecognized in the distortions and distances that it registers between original desire and object, may facilitate the return, by negation, of what has been repressed.'[16] Rieff concedes that 'the repressed returns,' but stresses that concomitantly a necessary precondition for this return is the working of an invisible force, a sort of secret police, which changes the character of the repressed desires.

Rieff leads us to a crucial ambivalence in Freud's theory of the unconscious. He says that Freud's metapsychology teaches us, on the one hand, that this dialectic of expression and repression cannot operate but unconsciously. If we were to unmask 'the secret police' it could not do its work anymore. On the other hand, Freud had to maintain, for therapeutic reasons, that it was possible to bring authority under rational control. Rieff asserts that Freud was close to the point where he would have had to give up his therapeutic belief. In *The Ego and the Id* (1920) Freud explained that psychoanalysts concede that the unconscious does not coincide completely with the repressed. Everything that is repressed is unconscious, but not everything that is unconscious is repressed. Freud's therapeutic labour brought him to the idea that part of the ego may be unconscious, too. This unconscious part of the ego cannot be latent like the preconscious, for if it were it could not be activated without becoming conscious, and the process of making it conscious, through therapeutic labour, would not encounter such great difficulties. Thus theoretically there has to exist a part of the psyche that is neither preconscious nor repressed, which Freud calls 'the third unconscious.'[17]

Freud admitted that there is a fundamental problem here for psychoanalytic metapsychology. Repressed psychic materials are accessible for psychoanaltyic scrutiny, because they return in a different form, which Freud maintained psychoanalysis could decipher, tracing it back to the underlying, original desires. But the psychoanalytic method falls short of psychic phenomena that are not subject to repression and subsequent return. This realm of the psychic, which contains the deepest motives of our behaviour and thought, does not escape 'primal repression.'[18] Freud warns us, with theoretical honesty, 'to beware of ignoring this characteristic, for the property of being conscious or not is, in the last resort, our one beacon-light in the darkness of depth psychology.'[19]

Despite this theoretical honesty, says Rieff, Freud preferred 'cognitive avoidance' and never reflected on the implications of this discovery: 'He withdrew in his inveterate talent for repressing the repressive, lest this characteristic of being take over the life of his work.'[20] Here Rieff ironically applies Freud's ideas on negation on Freud himself. He maintains that Freud, negationally, discovered the importance of a repressive agency that cannot be made conscious. 'In the repressive unrepressed, Freud encountered the spiritual rule of life.'[21] Rieff calls this rule of life 'the repressive imperative.'

Rieff's definition of culture is based on this imperative: 'Culture is the achievement of its unconscious distancing devices made conscious, yet indirect, in a variety of visual, acoustical, and plastic registrations. In a word, culture is repressive.'[22] The essence of repression lies in a necessary turning away from direct and conscious expression of everything that is before praise and blame. Rieff asserts that in every expression, repression remains operative. Only thus is culture able to control 'the horrible' which is always present ín the cultivated expressions of instinctual desires.[23]

The Interdict

We saw how Rieff argues that repression is the dynamic force of culture that links the individual, the social, and culture. This leads us to a next critical question: what is the origin of repression? Rieff says that on this point, too, Freud's theory meets with a dead end. 'Freud tells us that as soon as an "idea which is fundamentally offensive exceeds a certain degree of strength, the [intrapsychic] conflict takes on actuality, and it is precisely activation of the idea that leads to its repression."'[24] Rieff thinks that this definition of repression is tautological. 'What gives an "idea" its fundamentally offensive character cannot be generated in the repression itself.'[25] Freud's definition presupposes something that is transgressed and which puts the repression into operation. This 'something' is what Rieff calls 'the interdict.' It is from the interdicts, says Rieff, that the repressions gather their energy; only then can repressions subserve interdicts.[26]

This revision of Freud's theory is in line with Rieff's criticism of psychoanalysis as a 'technology of the emotions.' The notion of 'technology' invites an ethical question, because technology, in all its forms, carries no interior controls.[27] Thus, rational control of intrapsychic conflicts, Freud's 'technical' solution to neurosis, is impossible. The curbing of instinctual desires always requires an 'entity' which is brought into the psychic system from without. This entity operates unconsciously, or it does not work at all. 'If we are aware of our repressions, then we are not repressed. If we are not obedient to the interdicts, then we are not cultured ... Interdicts are the primary forms of high culture.'[28] The interdict is the highest formal principle of limitation, says Rieff. This thesis probably is polemical against theories of culture that are developed in modern sociology and the humanities.[29] These theories, with their syntheses of science, art, and religion, obscure the fact that 'interdicts are the primary form of high culture, not the arts and sciences.'[30]

Rieff mentions ancient Israel as an example of a high culture. This, I think, can be read as a rejection of the idea that the degree of development of a culture is measured by its degree of technological development. For science and technology belong to the realm of the secondary cultural processes. The heart of culture is to be found in the primary cultural process, or in the 'interior space' as Rieff calls it in *Fellow Teachers.*

Transgression

In the previous chapter we saw how Rieff pits the premodern notion of therapy against the modern one. In the latter a refuge is created from social life, in which the operation of the interdicts is suspended. This refuge is an 'alternative space,' set apart from daily life. According to Rieff, this notion of suspension of the interdicts has spread itself widely, because of the great influence of psychological or therapeutic thinking in Western culture. Therefore so many interior spaces, 'within which humans get a different sense of themselves and others,' are opened up 'that even the least cultivated are aware of the vast emptiness inside: all our symbolics are manufactured for instant use; none are constraining ... The "Everything New" syndrome, an unconstraining spaciousness, however the space may be divisible and rearrangeable for multiple uses, is readymade for eternally youthful order-hoppers.'[31]

Here Rieff comments very ironically on the spread of a rhetoric of cultural change in the West in the 1960s and 1970s. In the interior space of culture, cultural controls or interdicts do their work, which is temporarily released by remissions that 'ease the pressures of communal purposes.' This dialectic has a historical dimension, too. To make cultural change possible the existing cultural forms have to be broken open. That is done by stressing the remissive functions that suspend the interdicts, which Rieff calls 'transgressive behavior.'[32] In Rieff's theory cultural innovation takes place when the original 'releasing' cultural functions are transformed into 'controlling' ones. Now, that does not happen in late modernity, because typical for that period is the 'prohibition to prohibit ... A displacement of right order by perversion occurs as transgressive behavior is praised as the enactment of a theory critical of all orders of authority.'[33]

Rieff's theoretical way of formulating the discontinuity of Western culture is asserting that transgression has become, literally, normal. Therefore late-modern Western man is unconscious of transgressiveness. This dissolving of transgressive consciousness presupposes another important modern phenomenon: the loss of historical consciousness. 'To be radically contemporaneous, to be sprung loose from every particular symbolic, is to achieve a conclusive, unanswerable failure of historical memory. This is the uniquely modern achievement.'[34]

A Casus: The End of the Road

In *Fellow Teachers* we find the same casuslike analyses of works of art or science as in *Triumph of the Therapeutic*, though not in separate paragraphs this time, but in passages spread throughout the book. As an illustration of the new theory expounded thus far in this chapter, I will summarize one of these analyses in which Rieff comments on the novella *The End of the Road* (1958) by John Barth. The main topics are: the operation of the interdicts, the effects of transgressive behaviour, and the mixing up of the orders of theory and of reality ('order-hopping').

I will first summarize the novella. The story is set in the 1950s. A man named Jake Horner gets a new teaching job at a college in a small town somewhere in the United States. Jake becomes a close friend of one of his colleagues and his wife, Joe and Rennie Morgan. At a certain moment Jake and Rennie start an affair. Jake is rather depressive, is in therapy, and undergoes the affair resignedly. At a certain moment Joe discovers it. He thinks it can go on, if only he and Rennie will be honest with each other. They discuss it endlessly and finally Rennie concedes that by analysing what is going on their marriage will deepen itself. Through the affair Rennie becomes more conscious of her ambivalent feelings about her marriage with Joe, who spends most of his free time writing his dissertation. After a while Rennie finds out that she is pregnant by her lover and the whole situation escalates. One act of despair follows the other, leading to a dramatic climax. The social codes of the town they live in are very strict. The affair had to be kept secret, but would be revealed if Rennie would not have an abortion. She cannot decide to do that and thinks of suicide as a 'way out.' When her lover discovers that, he becomes desperate and moves heaven and earth to persuade her to have an abortion. Finally she gives in, but then they cannot find a legal doctor for the abortion. In roundabout ways they end up with a quack, whose medical tinkering during the abortion causes Rennie's death.

Rieff treats the characters of the novella typologically. Apparently he considers the plot of the story less important, because he hardly gives information about it. From these characters Rieff describes certain features of the cultural type that dominates late-modern Western culture: the therapeutic. The end of the story seems to suggest Rieff's apocalyptic premonition of what may happen when this cultural ideal-type triumphs in a culture: 'You can see where existentialist decision-making, an activist ethic of honesty, leads our three actors – Joe deeper into his dissertation, Jake into permanent therapy, Rennie into death.'[35]

In the end, all three characters are victims of the central theme in Rieff's analysis; the inner struggle of each person in her or his own way, with the interdicts that are still operative in them to different extents. Rieff calls this 'the residual inwardness.' The struggle is most intense in the woman. Both she and her lover have transgressed the moral injunction against adultery, but significant in Rieff's eyes is the woman's preference for suicide over abortion. The interdict 'You shall not commit murder' (Exodus 20:13) seems to turn the scale for her. She is ambivalent about it, however, and despairingly lets herself be convinced by her lover. He considers himself not subject to this injunction and therefore of the three of them he has the most in common with the therapeutic. He goes to any lengths to override her. Rennie's husband gets no further than an analytic approach towards it all, by asking for explanations.

In his analysis of this novel Rieff wants to indicate how in this novella the transgressive behaviour of the three actors impedes the operation of the interdicts. That impediment releases a destructive force in the complex game of the relations between these three people that finally leads to the woman's death. The main cause for this impediment of the interdicts must be sought in the mixing up of theory and reality, says Rieff. Both men are scholars/teachers and the woman admires them almost unlimitedly. That admiration is the basis on which she builds her relationship with them and upon which she lets herself be seduced into certain choices, being ambivalent herself. Thus in both relationships the love-relation is mixed up with the master-student relation, each belonging to a different order. The love relation belongs to the social order and the master-student relation to the order of the arts and sciences.

Rieff asserts that the creative work of the order of the arts and sciences consists of questioning the existing cultural forms. That is possible because there are absolute systems of limitation in that order. That creative work cannot be transposed to another order: 'The endless expressional quest belongs to art, with its absolute systems of limit, unchallengable within the work itself. Because life cannot be made over into a work of art, the endless expressional quest can never belong to it. What destructiveness is implied in our desire to make life extraordinary.'[36] Rennie mixes up those two orders and lets herself be seduced to transgressive behaviour by breaking through the existing moral forms. Rieff refers to the philosophical discussion about the function of art like this: 'As moral forms, works of art (and behavorial science) help mount the assault of experience.'[37] In every aesthetic or erotic experience the horrible is concealed and in the cultural shaping of experience ('sublimation') this dimension is controlled. Rieff implies that 'desublimation' must lead to violence. That danger lies in wait when people seek the 'assault of experience' in the order of reality of a society in which the interdictory forms lose their function.

Rieff's Theory of 'Sublimation'

Rieff's ideas about the cultural importance of repression imply a theory of sublimation. *Fellow Teachers* contains passages in which Rieff discusses thoughts on this subject from Freud, as the typical figure for early modernity, and from Marcuse, who exemplifies late-modern thinking about this subject. From these passages important hints of Rieff's own theory of 'sublimation' can be deduced.

The Directions in Freud's Theory of Sublimation

Freud did not develop a univocal and systematic theory of sublimation. His ideas on this topic require a careful reading of his writings. When Rieff writes about Freud and sublimation he uses the same methodology as in *Mind of the Moralist*; he distinguishes Freud the theorist from Freud the therapist.

It is very significant for a theory of sublimation that for Freud the therapist the resolution of transference is the final goal of a psychoanalytic treatment, says Rieff. In the operation of transference, the patient dramatizes his relation with certain authority figures, in order to overcome certain psychopathological aspects of those relations. This is exactly the new possibility that psychoanalysis provides: 'the unique (verbal) freedoms and the accessibility of a final figure of authority.'[38] As a theorist, however, Freud never tires of pointing at the inevitability of authority. Therefore Rieff replies: 'The object of true transference is not its resolution.'[39] The therapeutic ideal of resolving transference makes invisible how, even after a psychoanalytic treatment, authority influences the individual. Typical for human relations is 'true transference,' which is that kind of transference that comes forth from the identification with ideals and ideal-figures that is necessary for social life. According to Rieff, such figures are always essentially interdictory figures. As such, authority is always a part of human relations.

This leads to an important connection between authority and sublimation in Rieff's theory. He points at a crucial aspect of Freud's theory of sublimation, where sublimation is 'the releasing activity that follows upon interdictory and repressive achievements.'[40] It is crucial here that repression precedes sublimation of libidinal energy, from which it follows that sublimation depends on repression. According to Rieff, repression depends on the interdict and that implies that both repression and subsequent sublimation are caused by the operation of the interdict.[41] We have already gone far beyond Freud. For him this idea is impossible, because of his tautological definition of repression. But if Freud did have an inkling that sublimation is preceded by repression, why did he not arrive at the same point as Rieff? Rieff's answer is that Freud imagines sublimation as one of the 'vicissitudes of instinct,' in which the instincts adapt successfully to the repressive social process.[42] Freud begins with the instincts and ends up with the curbing that is necessary for a healthy personal and social life. Rieff remarks critically: 'Freud got his directions reversed, I think mainly because his theory of authority remained, to the end of his life, attached to his therapy.'[43]

According to Rieff, the main flaw in Freud's theory of sublimation is that it is conceived of as libido theory, in which the instincts are the primary substrate that is being formed and controlled by secondary cultural principles. From a metapsychological point of view, therapy is essentially the search for repressed motifs from the primary substrate that become manifest as distorted desires in the form of psychopathological symptoms. For therapeutic reasons Freud kept on trying to fathom the mystery of authority, in order to bring it under rational control. Rieff rejects the metapsychological basis of Freud's theory of sublimation: 'Mind is not necessarily a reformed whore. I see no reason to call every risen possibility by its Freudian name, "sublimation."'[44] Rieff revises Freud's theory on this point by separating the question of authority from the therapeutic strain. He inverts the direction of thought by putting to the fore the interdict, the curbing of desire, as the primary object of thought. 'Sublimation is *from* the sublime, not *to* it,' is the essential point of his revision.[45] This parallels the idea, launched in *Triumph of the Therapeutic*, that 'it is from the superior level of the cultural system that organizing (and disorganizing) higher principles thrust into the social structure.'

Marcuse's Toothless Eros

In *Fellow Teachers* Rieff polemicizes openly with Marcuse, about whom he writes thus: 'Like others among our most progressive theorists, Marcuse is an ally of the technologic mystagogues.'[46] Rieff quotes one of Marcuse's formulations that are evidence of his therapeutical stance as a theorist: 'He has said that since the world is essentially as we know it to be, a place in which reason has barbarized sensuality and virtually eliminated the possibility of its authentic expression, what we need to establish is a kind of freedom from the established reality. This involves an aestheticization which in Marcuse's terms at least would make reality a thing of lightness and play. The reality would lose its seriousness.'[47] We have seen in Chapter 3 how Marcuse revises Freud's theory of sublimation. Marcuse thinks that Freud was too ascetic. Technology provides man with so many possibilities of preserving culture that fewer of our instinctual energies need be sublimated for this task. Theoretically there is more room for a more leisurely life that allows for more 'direct' gratification of our desires, but we still live under the yoke of the old culture. Based on Freud's theory Marcuse sketches new ways to reduce old culture's grip on our instinctual lives. A part of the libido that is petrified in old cultural forms has to be made fluid again, a process which he calls 'desublimation.' Marcuse's cultural ideal is a 'non-repressive sublimation' in which curbing and expression of our desires have found a new balance.[48]

Rieff comments on this attempt of Marcuse 'as a social theorist to elaborate the dubious Freudian dichotomy between the concepts of repression and sublimation'[49] like this: 'In his attack on repression, Marcuse must also attack sublimation – and certainly all idealizations. But authority cannot exist unless it is possessed in an idealization to which it is willing to submit, although never uncritically.'[50] In short, Marcuse's theory blots out the operation of real authority: 'In order to possess any truth, a theory must be of order – of authority and its descent. An "aestheticizing" theory treats reality as a game; such lightness and play cancels out the shadowed nature of authority, at least in the theory itself.'[51] Thus Rieff conceals his philosophical criticism of Marcuse's theory in a Platonic image he conjures with the term 'shadowed nature of authority.' Marcuse intends to develop theoretical perspectives with which the operation of authority can be deconstructed. What Marcuse does not recognize, according to Rieff, is that the origin of authority is to be found in the primary cultural process. That is the transcendent cultural order, a counterpart of Plato's world of ideas. The world we live in is an adumbration of this 'superior level of the cultural system.' We have no direct access to this world and therefore our transformative attempts to get the operation of authority under rational control can never succeed.[52]

Rieff criticizes Marcuse, whom he calls a 'technological mystagogue,' because he oversimplifies the complex nature of human desire, of authority, and of their interaction. Rieff's explanation for this is that 'Marcuse does not comprehend the sentimentality thrusting behind enlightened reason.'[53] Rieff asserts that in Marcuse's theory an important aspect of the philosophy of eros is lacking, because originally the god Eros was considered 'playful, cunning, cruel and unmanageable; Hesiod thought Eros damaged the mind. Long since, the acts of the original and dangerous god, disguised finally as harmless little Cupid, were used up; the god, abandoned, ceased functioning.'[54] In Marcuse's theory the capricious and therefore dangerous nature of Eros has disappeared too, based on the assumption, says Rieff, that in human eroticism there is no problem of sublimity at stake. Rieff points to the crucial issue that in eroticism the horrible is concealed, controlled with interdictory forms.[55] An aestheticizing of reality is tantamount to the release of 'the horrible,' as he suggests in his analysis of *The End of the Road.*

This failure to appreciate the problem of sublimity rests on a very ancient philosophical confusion: 'Marcuse's ancient mistake is to associate the good with desire – more precisely, with the incitement of desire.'[56] Rieff replies like this: 'Rather, to recognize desire is to recognize its relation to power. That double recognition leads to every true good, as a discovered limit of desire. The good is always true and beautiful by opposing the inseparable dynamics of desire and power.'[57] Based on this criticism Rieff describes the philosophical foundation of his theory of cultural dynamics succinctly: 'What is good can only emerge in interdictory form ... All true ethics are ethics of self-deprivation ... The moral life begins with renunciation; the therapeutic life begins with the renunciation of renunciation.'[58]

The Instability of Culture

Rieff comments on Marcuse's concept of desublimation like this; '[it is] a new-fangled term of mystification to cover its real meaning, i.e. temptation. I prefer the old name; it both conceals and reveals what is dismissed in the concept sublimation.'[59] The mystifying concept of desublimation blurs the operation of the interdict, as well as the fact that 'sublimation' is never stable. As for the latter point, we must recall what Rieff writes about mysticsm in *Triumph of the Therapeutic.* The utmost psychic stability and social integration is attained when the individual unites mystically with 'the god-term' of the culture he or she lives in. These moments are rare, however, and their results always unstable. Every mystical experience of stability is followed by new temptations.[60] These unstable complexities of psychic and social integration are blurred by the theorists of counterculture, says Rieff. These 'rhapsodes' seduce their (predominantly young) followers by presenting a mystifying theory to them that promises a 'total solution' for their problems and those of society.

Psychic integration is never stable, and neither is social integration. Every group develops a 'participation mystique' with rituals that have the same integrative functions for the group as mysticism has for the individual. In these rituals the community unites itself with the character-ideal that has penetrated the social order from the cultural order. This ideal assists in moulding the individual instinctual impulses into one 'common will' of the group. The result of this process does not lead to a stable situation either: 'Such a tremendous inversion of will does not often penetrate a social order nor for very long before it is displaced by more tolerable sublimations, remissive openings of possibility.'[61] Here Rieff resumes previously described theoretical notions, formulating his idea of the essence of 'sublimation.' In the line of thinking *from* the sublime, Rieff describes the founding of a culture as the installation of an interdictory modality. This is a dialectical process. The transcendent interdicts acquire a social form, but in that process they undergo a transformation which makes them 'tolerable.' Thus there is a dialectic of interdictory activity, which is essentially a curbing of human possibility and remissive activity ('sublimation'), which discloses new openings of possibility. This is how Rieff thinks of his double dialectic in culture in *Fellow Teachers.*[62]

All this sounds very abstract. What if we think of the biblical story of the revelation of the law to Moses as told in Exodus 20? Rieff seems to retell the story in cultural-sociological terms, including the repeated relapses during the hard journey of the Jews through the desert and in subsequent Jewish history.

Preconditions for a Return of the Interdicts

Concealed in irony and other elements of style we find in *Fellow Teachers* the beginnings of a new line in Rieff's thinking about culture. Apart from his cultural criticism and reflections on cultural discontinuity, Rieff starts thinking about the possibilities of cultural continuity. Most of modern social theory is not useful for this, because of the theoretical problems I described above. To conceptualize the cultural function of authority adequately a new approach must be developed. Rieff uses different terms for this approach, such as 'culturology'[63] and 'science of limits.'[64] The basic idea is that authority cannot be deconstructed or destroyed. The only thing that can happen is that we lose sight of how authority works. To restore that sight we have to develop new perspectives on this problematic.

A point of departure for Rieff is the recognition of the ethical importance of death as an ultimate boundary. This importance is undercut in modern culture because of the denial of the importance of guilt. 'Death had been judgment, the final trial of one's own life ... Death was the ultimate form of repayment. But without guilt and the resolution of guilt, death became meaningless. If death is meaningless because men are guiltless, then life, too, becomes meaningless because its end is no conclusive calling of quits.'[65] So Rieff locates the origin of meaning in life in the recognition of limits, with death as the supreme case. This ought to be the starting point for a theory of the cultural function of authority. 'To see the beginnings of a science of limits the scientists themselves will have to recognize the outside limit: that men must remain under the authority of death, the interdict of interdicts. It follows that the second interdict, in the historical order of our culture, is at once against the recreation of life in the laboratory and the taking of life in the abortion clinic. Under this double authority, a science of limits can then explore a life that is again made meaningful.'[66]

Here we see how Rieff indicates the beginning of a reply to the technical rationality of the therapeutic that tries to evade any substantial moral choice. As I suggested above, Rieff's concept 'interdict' seems closely related to the biblical concept of prohibition (which appears in its most essential form in the Ten Commandments). This concept seems to have been made inoperative by modern, critical approaches in science and art and the concomitant spread of therapeutic thinking. The interdictory form belonged to the cultures of religious man and political man. The culturology or science of limits that Rieff wants to develop must operate in a new social and cultural situation that requires new interdicts. Here Rieff sketches the most elementary forms of that approach, resting on the fundamental interdicts concerning life and death. Specifying those forms is to be done by constructing a codex: 'As the moral sciences and the arts must signify, so law codifies the interdicts and their remissions, which are the elementary forms within which god-terms articulate the forms themselves.'[67]

So, whether we recognize it or not, life sets our limits. Western culture had its modalities to reconcile man with this. In Rieff's thinking modern culture is a revolt against these forms. We have broken down the forms of reconciliation with life's limitations. According to Rieff's idea of cultural dynamism as developed in *Triumph of the Therapeutic*, Western culture always provided for new codifications of interdictory forms after a period of cultural crisis. The essence of modernity, however, lies in the breaking down of this cultural dynamism. So restoring the cultural operation of authority means creating a new form of this dynamism.

Here Rieff points again at the transcendent origin of authority. 'Who are to be our truth-tellers – better say, our guilt-provokers? I do not know. I am without authority; moreover I do not seek what cannot be sought. Authority is given or it is fraudulent; it cannot be taken by force or ambition. That was one of Weber's main errors in his theory of charisma.'[68] Here we need to recall that in Rieff's theory authority, as a dynamic of interdictory forms, belongs to the primary cultural process or 'the interior space' of culture. The origin of authority lies in this 'realm' of the cultural order and is dialectically linked to the social order. For Rieff it is crucial at this point that a new dynamic of interdictory forms cannot be generated in the social order and then penetrate into the interior space of culture. 'It is barely possible that interdictory forms, without which relations between reverence and justice, culture and social system, cannot be maintained, may be prepared from the outside in.'[69]

To let a new dynamic of interdictory forms come into existence the forces of modernity have to be countered. Contemporary judicial systems, for example, are not aimed at maintaining awe for interdictory forms. Because people are punished too little, the authority of interdictory forms deteriorates in the social order, says Rieff.[70] As an alternative he proposes to repay committed transgressions in kind, because 'once the transgressive sense is exercised, it will grow more acute. Then the transgressor will again subserve authority rather than subvert it.'[71] In

Fellow Teachers Rieff doubts whether in the near future 'a culture of militant, opposing truths can be reorganized to teach again fear of and in Law – and respect for presiding presences.'[72] We may hope, however, for a renascence of guilt, because 'the therapeutic movement has not yet penetrated deep down into the culture class order, but dominates only the strata at the transgressive top, the commercialized middle stratum and the false (bohemian) bottom. ... The inner truth of an authoritative symbolic has not been completely evaginated.'[73] This inner truth, which Rieff describes in *Fellow Teachers* as 'residual inwardness,' can only do its work when the therapeutic movement is counteracted. 'The therapeutic movement halted, a science and art of limits well begun, there would be some hope for a society in which art and science are clearly distinguished from, and related to, other actions.'[74]

Crucial in this process of reconstruction is the tragic sense. Rieff asserts that in premodern Western culture people knew that blaming persons was terribly dangerous, that the effects may be double, both good and evil. 'It is only upon this tragic sense, of the dangers to soul inherent in any judgmental action, and not upon the endless expressional quest for the identity of self, that the interdicts may be reconstructed.'[75] An aspect of the tragic sense is the way authority operates in a social order. Rieff thinks that punishment should always be an instrument of those in power, as if so to establish their authority. This power has its price because it is itself subjected to the power of an authority that is not in their service. Nobody, however, has as yet been able to separate power from authority. Distinguishing the two properly always remains a hermeneutical task, says Rieff. 'There is an unresolvable tension between power and authority that is only concealed by the modern concept of legitimation.'[76] Connecting the two in adequate ways is a delicate task, risking tragic failures, because the powerful are not obliged to be fearful enough for that authority which is not theirs. Therefore Rieff suggests this: 'Instill fear in the powerful; the powerless will follow and so revive the constitution of authority.'[77]

This reconstruction process also requires another vision of the cultural function of guilt than the modern one. In Rieff's theory guilt is the normal relation of the individual to authority. When guilt is tabooed, as it is in modern culture, we lose sight of how authority operates. Rieff pleads for a theory of punishment that aims at rediscovering our missing knowledge of guilt. 'No matter how great our technological capacity to produce comfort, the higher knowledge is of how to create a greater, constraining inner discomfort confident in its teaching of self-limit.'[78]

In a very ironic fantasy Rieff proposes a way of countering the contemporary judicial system and turning it into something that helps to generate guilt as a precondition for a new dynamic of interdictory forms. We could use the 'remissive tendency' in contemporary criminal law to encourage a scientific campaign to shut down all the prisons, except for those in which criminals are waiting for capital punishment. 'Then executions might be made public; this public offering to the interdicts could constitute a grand remissive occasion at which ordinary, less scientific numbers of the public would celebrate the terrible nearness of every interdict to its transgressions.'[79] Here Rieff alludes to the phenomenon of public anatomy as it was practised in the late Middle Ages and during the Renaissance. In Amsterdam, for example, these were annual events, in which a criminal was dissected, having been hanged the day before. In this public anatomy the archaic idea lived on that the criminal had violated the sacred order. This transgression had to be atoned for with a public sacrificial ritual.[80] To make the modern public execution therapeutically effective, in other words to have it generate a feeling of awe for the law, there should be no publicity, says Rieff. The victim ought to remain anonymous, I presume because Rieff wants to focus attention on the crime and its meaning. The exact nature of the crime is never to be reported, but is to be inferred by the public from the punishment. The reason for this is evident; when the public is able to infer the committed crime from the punishment, it can do that because an inner sensibility for transgressiveness is operative in the spectators. Then the interdicts are operative ín the event itself, without having to be made explicit. Here is presupposed Rieff's idea that morality only works unconsciously. In *Triumph of the Therapeutic* he formulates that idea like this: 'A culture survives principally, I think, by the power of its institutions to bind and loose men in the conduct of their affairs with reasons which sink so deep into the self that they become commonly and implicitly understood – with that understanding of which explicit belief and precise knowledge of externals would show outwardly like the tip of an iceberg.'[81]

This example of the public execution illustrates how the character of Rieff's irony has changed in *Fellow Teachers*, compared with his earlier works. Rieff is much more sarcastic now, probably because he thinks that the sensitivity for transgressiveness in Western culture has decreased to such extent that shocking his readers like this is necessary to make his point.

On History, Social Sciences, and Jewish Tradition

Three important themes for Rieff's metasociology have so far been put to the fore in this chapter in fragments only: the role of history in Rieff's thinking, the cultural task of the social sciences, and Rieff's relation to Jewish tradition. I will deal with them now more systematically, as a contribution to a description of this metasociology. (The section on the role of history is an elaboration of the discussion on the same topic from Chapter 3.)

The Role of History in Rieff's Thinking

Rieff launched the term 'the therapeutic' in *Triumph*. In *Fellow Teachers* he keeps on using it to refer to the cultural type that he thinks dominates late-modern Western culture: 'The therapeutic is the first free human, unrelated to any dominating presence or class; he is the universal Man who comes after neuroses succeed souls and ethics – after shows succeed sacraments.'[82] Here Rieff refers, again ironically, to the modern conception of freedom. Modern man considers himself free when he has shaken off the influence of interdictory forms. Were he ever to attain this goal, the therapeutic would be free and autonomous and inwardly empty, without deeply rooted resistances against the temptations of experience. According to Rieff, that is the unique characterisitic of modernity. 'To be radically contemporaneous, to be sprung loose from every particular symbolic, is to achieve a conclusive, unanswerable failure of historical memory ... Barbarians have never existed before. At the end of this tremendous cultural development, we moderns shall arrive at barbarism. Barbarians are people without historical memory. Barbarism is the real meaning of radical contemporaneity. Released from all authoritative pasts, we progress towards barbarism, not away from it.'[83]

The progressive modernization of Western culture shows that the hunger for liberation from authority is deeply rooted. Rieff develops a genetic explanation for this modern hunger, from a psychohistorical perspective.[84] His starting point is contemporary culture, which is dominated by the therapeutic. This first free man in history acquired his freedom with therapy in all its cultural forms. Then Rieff follows the track back into psychohistorical time. Therapy has this kind of psychohistorical pedigree: 'Therapy is that form which degrades all contents, for use by those who will succeed the late nineteenth- and early twentieth century psychologizers, themselves successors to moralizers, themselves regular successor types to all primitive spiritualizers.'[85] That is one movement back in psychohistorical time. In another passage Rieff mentions the 'Christian cultists,'[86] whom he calls 'remissive spiritualizers of Jewish law and order.'[87] In this passage Rieff seems to define the 'primitive spiritualizers' from the previous citation more precisely as 'Christian spiritualizers of Jewish law and order.' Whatever Rieff's ideas about the relation of Christianity to the Jewish law may be, for us it is more important at this point to see that Rieff traces back the origin of the interdictory form to the Jewish law. Along this diachronic track of Western psychohistory, as well as along the synchronic track of analysis of modern social sciences and art, Rieff discerns a central theme in Western psychohistory: the demolition of the, originally Jewish, interdictory form.

In a laudatory review of *Fellow Teachers,* Norman Brown cites the first of the two aforementioned psychohistorical sequences[88] and points out that Rieff's psychohistorical vision has a lot in common with the cyclical model of Giambattista Vico (1668–1744), the founding father of modern historical philosophy. Vico asserts that the history of Western culture can be described in terms of a cyclical succession of four eras. The first is the age of the gods, followed by the age of the heroes. The third age is that of men, which is succeeded by a period of barbarism, after which the cycle starts anew.

Based on a comparison between Rieff and Vico, Brown says that for both 'the great historical process in a long range view is a process of secularization, or profanation,'[89] culminating in modernity. Rieff's genetic analysis of therapy in *Fellow Teachers* links closely to his analysis of the fundamental changes in function and content of 'therapy' in the cultural ages of economic man and psychological man. Rieff indeed says that these changes involve a thorough erosion of the role of faith in Western societies. Brown thinks that *Fellow Teachers* is an important book because it anticipates 'the return of the gods.' Rieff rediscovers the necessity for the category of the sacred. He thinks, however, that Rieff is too pessimistic in his interpretation of modernity: 'We share a feeling of the barbarism of our present interlude, but Vico's cycle moves forward to a fresh beginning with a fresh age of the gods, which Rieff cannot see.'[90] This difference between Brown and Rieff rests on a difference over the transgressive character of modernity, conceived around the concept of orgy as the model of a transgressive social event. 'It is possible that we have to extend the notion of orgy as being an institution which individuals need to being also an institution which history needs. That is to say, great historical periods may end, or have to end, in that orgy out of which they can be reborn.'[91]

Here Rieff and Brown meet back to back. In *Fellow Teachers* Rieff calls the orgy the most original institution,[92] but says that in an orgy nothing can be liberated that can revitalize culture. The idea that the orgy can have such a function rests upon a false conceptualization of how expressive and limiting and/or controlling forces form institutions. Here Rieff's criticism is analogous to his criticism of Marcuse's ideas about sublimation. The erotic powers, which are said to determine the vitality of a culture, can only exist in a dialectical relation to the limiting forms from which these powers get their cultural form. Therefore a theory of cultural change or innovation can never be conceived of thinking about the erotic powers only, because they cannot exist separately from their limiting forms.

From this perspective I want to return to Rieff's thesis that the transgressivity of modern culture is not aimed at cultural innovation. This implies that there is transgressivity that does contribute to this innovation. Indeed we find in *Fellow Teachers* this passage: 'Instinct is only one new name for the original therapeutic dissolution of law and order.'[93] Rieff acknowledges the necessity of a regular dissolution of law and order and calls it therapeutic. This essential transgressive cultural function is in Rieff's theory reserved to a cultural elite. Within the order of the arts and sciences the elite are allowed to transgress existing limits to create new 'interior spaces.' This permission for transgressivity needs to be viewed in close connection with the limiting forces to which the transgressive forces are dialectically related, in two ways. First, Rieff thinks that absolute systems of limitation are operative in the order of the arts and sciences. The secret of artistic creation is that something new is created from within that system that transcends the existing limits or forms. The second dialectic is that between the social order and the order of the arts and sciences. The social order demands a restraint of the aesthetic capacity to invent new interior spaces because they can be a threat to the (symbolizations of) the interior spaces of the existing social order. On the other hand, the arts and sciences must be granted a certain freedom of that restraint because that is necessary for the secondary cultural process. Without this process, in which the cultural principles from the primary cultural process get their cultural shape and are being communicated in the social order, no social order can exist.

In Rieff's sociological theory this double dialectic is the motor of history, which keeps a culture alive because it provides it with new cultural forms. Rieff conceals this 'positive function' of transgressivity in his polemic against the theorists of counterculture. Probably he wants to be very careful in writing about the cultural necessity of transgressivity in a time that has turned transgression into a cultural principle.

It may be true that Rieff 'rediscovers the necessity for the category of the sacred,' but Rieff is also very critical of metaphysical theories of the role of history like Brown's. Rieff's reply to Brown's optimism is a criticism of modernity that is very often interpreted as cultural pessimism by Rieff's critics. To do this too easily, I think, risks the danger of missing the theoretical point at stake here. Beneath Rieff's criticism of Brown there is a debate with Hegel. 'The basic illusion Hegelian thought has projected upon the world is its optimism. Optimism ... has an eschatological dynamic, as theology and politics have always had.'[94] Rieff's criticism of Hegel applies to Brown's idea of history, too. As I showed in Chapter 3, Rieff holds to a more dialectical view of history. Inspired by Freud he tries to escape a Hegelian projection of a 'total scheme' on unruly reality and history, on the one hand. On the other, he defends the role of the transcendent in culture and its history. He conceives of cultural history as a history of great ideal-types that were formative for Western cultural history. History for Rieff is tradition, a chain of hermeneutical circles. More and more of these chains were broken or are bound to break.

Departing from this real threat of cultural discontinuity, Rieff tries to imagine how the process of restoring the links can be started. Here the teacher has a historical task or vocation. Implicitly referring to the ideal of *Bildung*, Rieff says that the teacher has to initiate the student in the interior spaces of the cultural artefacts from the cultural canon. Doing this initiation, the student gets integrated in the cultural order, after which he or she has the task of creating his or her own interiority, aided by these experiences. This process is the heart of the formation of individual identity, as well as of tradition. Whether a new cultural elite will come into existence that can fulfil its historical task is a question science is not able to answer. Rieff seems to follow Weber on this point: 'As Weber saw it, whether there will be new prophets or mechanized petrifaction is something that absolutely cannot be foreseen.'[95]

The Cultural Task of the Social Sciences

The task of the university is to contribute to the formation of a cultural elite. Rieff calls the university 'a sacred institution ... Because the university must be the temple of intellect, uniquely unchangeable in that respect, it is a sacred institution, the last in our culture.'[96] I suggest that this be read as an ironic statement because elsewhere in *Fellow Teachers* Rieff says that teachers are not preachers. In general, in *Fellow Teachers* Rieff criticizes a development that tends to transform the university into a bureaucratic 'factory of knowledge' in which far too many students are being educated to become 'problem-solvers.' The book is a cry from the heart to his fellow teachers to fight against the destruction of the ideal of *Bildung* in the academy. Implicit in this call is a vision of the cultural task of the social sciences.

Rieff calls himself a 'scholar-teacher of sociological theory.'[97] In a strict sense that is correct because his work shows that, despite his very interdisciplinary orientation, his vast knowledge of other discplines is used to reflect on the development of sociology as a discipline. Modern sociology 'has sadly neglected the whole notion of the autonomous realm of culture.'[98] According to Rieff, the causes for that are to be sought in the foundations of modern sociology: 'By Saint-Simon and Comte, and by their followers, faith was changed fundamentally into the final and most inclusive science, Sociology, with its endless projects of change, acutely personal and yet organized for our health, education and most general welfare.'[99] Modern sociology is 'therapeutic,' too, in Rieff's critical sense, and is, just like psychoanalysis, a 'crisis-science': 'According to Rieff, the quivering public instabilities of too many personality doctors and their patients are traceable to the instability of their culture. Psychiatry leads back to sociology.'[100]

The roots of modern sociology lie in the crisis caused by the emergence of modernity in Western culture and its effects on Christian culture: 'After August Comte, much of modern sociology has struggled for diagnostic ideas refined and yet wide enough to encompass the spectacle of a death so great in magnitude and subtlety.'[101] Rieff's criticism of modern sociology is the same as his criticism of psychoanalysis. Both disciplines are one-sided because they take as their point of departure the idea that modern man has to free himself from 'the old culture' with its cultus and morality.

To be able to fulfil its therapeutic task, sociology struggled to find a morally neutral position out of reach of the old culture and its sciences. It was found in the modern, positivist sciences. Rieff speaks of a 'positivist takeover,' in the first third of the nineteenth century.[102] Thus on a meta-theoretical level, sociology embraced the idea of transformative theory and fully rejected the idea of conformative theory. Every orientation on a 'transtemporal conception of reality'[103] was let go, or better, had to be banned. To attain this total release of the authority of the 'old culture' sociology became 'reflexive' or, in other words, 'critical of all inherited interdictory motifs.'[104]

It is precisely this transformative character of modern sociology that makes it unservicable for developing a sociological theory of culture, says Rieff. The heart of culture lies in the interdicts that originate in the transcendent realm of culture: 'A false generalization of the natural sciences has generated a fatal superiority of facts over culture itself. So long as we accept this fatal superiority, as if facts do really speak for themselves and that all important ones are other than matters of interpretation, there can be no science of limits.'[105] Therefore Rieff formulates the starting point for a sociology in which a theory of culture can be developed like this: 'The predicate of sociological analyses of the moral should be that "Man," the most capacious off all types, is capable of everything. That predicate, the possibility of action without limit, must lead sociological analyses to insights that are defensive.'[106] This is how Rieff raises attention in the realm of the social sciences for the problem of sublimity.

The most salient feature of Rieff's sociological theory of culture is that he tries to bring back into sociology the problem of transcendence that was banned from it by its founding fathers. With this Rieff stands in the tradition of Max Weber, Emile Durkheim, Marcel Mauss, and Johan Huizinga, according to the sociologist Benjamin Nelson. They were Rieff's predecessors 'in the massive amount of work [that] remains to be done if we are to get anywhere near a satisfactory understanding of the tumultuous sociocultural processes exploding across our 20th century world ... It is against these larger horizons that the work of Rieff needs to be appreciated.'[107]

Rieff, the 'Jew of Culture'

An adequate point of departure for a short reflection on Rieff's relation to Jewish tradition, which is closely linked to his relation to Christianity, is his description of the university as 'the temple of intellect.' That image invokes associations with a central theme of Jewish history and tradition; the destruction of the second temple in Jerusalem in 70 CE and its consequences for Jewish culture. That destruction was an important catalyst in a process in which the character of Jewish culture was changing fundamentally. The emergence of the synagogue, which diminished the cultural importance of the temple and the sacrificial service, refers to a new conception of cultus, in which the scriptural tradition gradually became the heart of Jewish culture. The Mishna and Talmud are the main scriptural products of a Jewish culture in which studying Torah as the central sacred text was considered of vital importance. This study was not conceived of as a purely cognitive or rational act, but was at the same time an act of devotion. Thus the temple on the Temple Mount (in Jerusalem) was transformed into the 'temple of feeling intellect.'

In the foreword of *Fellow Teachers* Rieff mentions the fact that the book was written in the Codrington Library of All Souls College in Oxford. How full of meaning this is when viewed from the perspective of the previous paragraph! According to Rieff, the traditional, respectable university is transformed into a 'factory of knowledge' and is in danger of losing its function as a breeding-place for a cultural elite. Oxford, as he sees it, is a bulwark of the struggle against this development. Rieff's proposals for a restoration of the university clearly reflect the idea of the university as a 'temple of feeling intellect.' That implies that in his work his relation to Jewish tradition appears primarily as a theoretical relationship. Rieff's interest is in *dynamics*, and Jewish tradition for him is a model of how culture works. On the level of content he says that he knows little about these traditions and that he is 'merely retelling motifs from Israel's family romance.'[108] In a footnote he says that he is 'not learned in the tradition.'[109]

In *Fellow Teachers* Rieff gives a cultural-theoretical definition of being Jewish, in passages dealing with a typological counterpart of psychological man, whom he calls 'the Jew of culture.' The most important passage is this: 'Our own culture has taken form in credal organizations.[110] Priesthoods and intelligentsias are but two of the forms credal organization, ancient and modern, may take. However, the defense of it, implicit in my theory of culture, does not make me an advocate of some earlier credal organization. In particular, I have not the slightest affection for the dead church civilization of the West. I am a Jew. No Jew in his right mind can long for some variant ... of that civilization. Its one enduring quality is its transgressive energy against the Jew of culture.'[111] Let us have a look at different aspects of this partly very cryptical statement.

What first catches the eye is that Rieff very strongly condemns Christianity here. This happens rarely in his work, but there is indeed a very important point at stake here, concerning the relation between Judaism and Christianity, the anti-Judaic character implicit in certain Christian ideas. This passage is clearly related to the one about the genesis of therapy as a cultural form. According to Rieff, a central theme in Western cultural history is the demolition of the, originally Jewish, interdictory form. 'The Christian mystery-cult evolved into the most terrible rationalizing of transgressiveness ever to curse our culture.'[112] This is a very ironic version of the idea that secularization proceeds from the very foundations of Christianity itself, usually put in terms of rationalization and disenchantment. Christian culture is demolished by 'the triumph of the therapeutic' and now the roots of that process are traced back into Christianity itself. Rieff has his own way of reacting to Christian anti-Judaism.

More important than Christian anti-Judaism for Rieff is the question of how his fellow Jews relate to their own cultural background. A recurring theme in his work is his criticism of Jews who fritter away their identity and thus undercut Jewish tradition from within. In *Fellow Teachers* he aims his arrows at Marx and Freud, and elsewhere at people like Martin Buber, Woody Allen, and the Jewish legal scholar Robert Burt.[113] The essential theme here is that these people approach Jewish tradition therapeutically, evading the central theme of the importance of the interdicts that endow Judaism with its moral and religious character. In Rieff's eyes Freud is the 'champion identity-basher,' because he tried in *Moses and Monotheism* to unravel 'the Mosaic presence' which is decisive for Jewish identity. The figure of Moses as lawgiver, in Rieff's words, as 'supreme interdictory figure,' plays a central role in the Jewish religion. Freud tried to explain away the influence of Moses, the *Urgestalt* of authority, as a neurotic psychological process and thus undercut the idea of the transcendent origin of (Jewish and Christian) religion.

In his analysis of *Moses and Monotheism* in *Fellow Teachers* Rieff ingeniously connects the fate of Christianity to Freud's ultimate attempt to settle accounts with religion. 'Freud has given us a superb hint of a non-responsible cadre, the therapists. In his theory of the inward historical genesis of morality, Freud mimed his own ancient, dying, interdictory fathergod carried like law inside the psyche of the guiding cadre, the followers of Moses. His story of culture, in its origins, both reveals and conceals the end of a moral order first settled upon us, as our inheritance, by the history of Israel.'[114] Between the lines Rieff here aims at Christianity, which declared itself the inheritor of Israel. Christianity is lethally ill in Western culture and seems to receive the death-blow from the therapeutization of culture, in other words, from Freud. Rieff does not think that Freud succeeded in carrying out his aim as far as Jewish identity is concerned. He demonstrates that Freud, after all, repeats the 'primal crime' (of the killing of the father). Freud 'killed' Moses, but in doing that *Moses and Monotheism* became the repetition of the primal crime itself. Freud, like Oedipus and Hamlet, attempted to break the repressive design of his life, but only 'succeeded in retracing it.'[115]

Who is, finally, this 'Jew of culture' who recurs throughout *Fellow Teachers*? A Jew of culture is somebody who resists the changes put forward by the 'technicians' and the 'revolutionairies.'[116] The technicians promote a type of academy in which managers rule the game and in which research must primarily have practical relevance for society. The same goes for the revolutionaries, whose main goal is to politicize the university. In short, the Jew of culture fights against developments that result in the teaching of merely transformative theory in the academy.

This ideal-type also fights a cultural struggle. 'We mere teachers, Jews of culture, influential and eternally powerless, have no choice except to think defensively: how to keep ourselves from being overwhelmed by that unique complex of orgy and routine which constitutes modernization and its totalitarian character type, using the language of trust against authority – without which trust cannot exist.'[117] We have already seen that the transgressivity of that character-type is connected to 'order-hopping'; it tries to transform ideal images concerning man and society which were invented in modern theory and art into social reality. According to Rieff, this can only lead to anti-culture, because in a real culture life is not confused with art and science. The mighty power of an aesthetic creation ought to remain aesthetic and should not be politicized. This power 'rightly belonged to Beethoven and Michelangelo, in their work, not to the condotierri,[118] or Hitler, in theirs. An extremely rare talent does not emerge in transgressions; rather in works of art, or science, that control their own spheres with full interdictory force, called "form." Within its culture, every art work constitutes a system of discrete limits, each a paradigm of how culture works; none are sovereign beyond themselves. A universal culture is a contradiction in terms. We Jews of culture are obliged to resist the very idea.'[119]

In sum, Rieff seems to consider Jewish tradition as a model for a high culture, which has a historical task in Western culture. In *Fellow Teachers*, he has described what that task is in late modernity, concealed in irony and ambiguity. I focused here on Rieff's theoretical relation to Jewish tradition. Rieff's Jew of culture is, of course, a theoretical construction. Rieff's relation to historical Jewish tradition is another story, which can only be written after biographical research has been done. During my visits in 1996, 1999, and 2001, Rieff repeatedly said that he wants to be considered a Jewish scholar and that his relationship to Jewish tradition is crucial for an adequate understanding of his work. The fact is, however, that in the written works that were the basis for my research, Rieff is much less explicit about this issue.

6

Late Modernity as Second Culture Camp

In the publications of his later period, Philip Rieff expands his theory of the cultural significance of authority into a theory of sacred order. In the earlier works, Rieff tended to focus on cultural discontinuity caused by cultural modernization. In a later article, 'By What Authority?' (1981), he suggests that we 'may be at the end of modernist inversions of sacred order.'[1] In the later works Rieff adds a second line of thought, in trying to envision cultural continuity. An ambivalent tension between thinking in terms of cultural discontinuity and continuity characterizes this later work. Rieff also tries to retrieve the academic style he gave up in *Fellow Teachers*. We will see that he strives to be more systematic, if that word can ever be applied to his work. To develop a thorough approach to the role of the sacred in culture Rieff devises a new psychohistorical model, which is based on the nineteenth-century idea of Kulturkampf. Rieff's basic idea of the 'second culture camp'[2] is that the transition of the twentieth to the twenty-first century is essentially a situation in which several philosophies of life – or Weltanschauungen – are struggling for cultural dominance. The result of that struggle is unpredictable. We live, in other words, still in a transitional time, as Freud realized sharply. Rieff's theory of sacred order can be read as an attempt to imagine a new cultural situation beyond modernity as 'anti-culture.'

Authority as Sacred Order

First I will deal with the texts from the 1980s in which much of the terminology that Rieff uses in his writings in the 1990s about sacred order is developed. The first text is the article 'By What Authority? Post-Freudian Reflections on the Repression of the Repressive as Modern

Culture' (1981). As the title indicates, the article is closely connected to the text about repression, 'One Step Further' (1979), which I dealt with in the previous chapter. According to Rieff, repression is the basis of culture. In *Fellow Teachers* this idea was formulated in terms of a theory of interdictory form. This thesis invites the question of the origin of this interdictory form, which Rieff adresses in 'By What Authority?'

In 'By What Authority' Rieff formulates the origin of authority in a manner that resembles his ideas about order and chaos that I described in Chapter 3: 'Authority is the achievement of rank order out of a primacy of possibilities so slow to change that primary possibility itself can only be inferred from secondary imaginings of it. Those secondary imaginings, generally named "Culture," direct humans in the manner and matter of what to deny to themselves.'[3] In those imaginings, in culture, the interdictory forms do their work. Those forms originate in the primary cultural process. From now on Rieff regularly uses the term 'sacred order' for this 'realm' of culture. In this form authority has a repressive function, but is not itself generated in the repressive process. This is how Rieff revises Freud's theory on the origin of repression. This form of authority cannot be changed with therapy, says Rieff.

From this starting point Rieff reinterprets Freud's idea of a 'crisis of authority' that underlies his theory of culture:

> 'Imagine an authority that will not fail and cannot disappear. What, then, of its crises? I imagine that we mortals can only enact, and re-enact the raising or lowering possibilities of action stipulated in the social organization of our received culture. Any reference to a 'crisis of authority' in contemporary American culture would refer to those strange pleasures that may be taken in lowering acts, or thoughts, within a vertical order of possibilities in their primacy. From that primacy culture delimits its operative acts.'[4]

This is a very abstract and condensed passage which requires 'unpacking.' Let us analyse the passage in parts.

'Imagine an authority that will not fail and cannot disappear. What, then, of its crises?' In his theory of culture Rieff inverts the perspective of the Freudian theory of sublimation and the inherent culture criticism. He diverts our attention from the instincts and directs it towards authority. He demonstrates that in such criticism of culture a manipulation of superego symbolism is at stake. Authority, or rather the attempt to break down authority, is the real theme, concealed in a theory of the libera-

tion of an 'authentic core' of human being that is supposed to reside in the instincts.

'I imagine that we mortals can only enact, and re-enact the raising or lowering possibilities of action stipulated in the social organization of our received culture.' In the first part of this sentence ('I imagine that') Rieff underscores the ideational character of his work. Here he thinks about 'the highest formalities,' in this case about a new image or vision of the operation of authority in culture. We should also recall Rieff's idea of formative principles that penetrate the social order from the cultural order and stipulate forms of morally accepted behaviour ('secondary cultural process'). What we can imagine, as 'mortals,' or in other words, on the level of the secondary cultural process, are 'the raising or lowering possibilities of action' (this is what he called the codification of law in *Fellow Teachers*). This amounts to the idea that the coming into existence of formative principles for moral behaviour is not an empirically accessible phenomenon for us because it belongs to the primary cultural process. The only thing we can do is try to determine to what extent our behaviour brings us closer to or distances us from a common character-ideal and its normative implications.

Here Rieff in fact steps 'beyond critical thinking.' He says that we can never observe from a distance how authority works. We always do that from within the existing social order, which stipulates forms of moral and immoral behaviour. This also brings us to the dialectical character of his theory. In this process the social order helps to create culture by making the cultural principles visible, audible, and tactile. In his later work Rieff stresses that it is unthinkable to have a social order at all without this interaction. In every culture there operates a specific version of this dynamic interaction between a sacred order and a social order. For Rieff Freud is the great analytic investigator of this dynamic, who tried to interfere in it: 'Freud made over into a negational faith the most illusory hope of all modernizing theories, including his own: that sacred order is finally abolished and only its affects linger. But sacred order is taking an eternity getting itself abolished. In theory, psychoanalytic therapy is interminable, but is only so because of the interminability of that which it addresses.'[5]

'Any reference to a "crisis of authority" in contemporary American culture would refer to those strange pleasures that may be taken in lowering acts, or thoughts, within a vertical order of possibilities in their primacy.' Rieff again inverts the modernist perspective on authority. He is not looking for the origin of repression (as locus of the origin of authority), but instead for

the origin of the pleasure that modern man takes in lowering acts that must lead to a liberation of the influence of traditional authority. Rieff asserts that the central motif in modern Western culture is to break down the 'primacy of the interdictory form' and to replace it by the 'primacy of possibility:' 'Anything goes' or 'why not?' are the modern creeds.

'From that primacy culture delimits its operative acts.' Rieff uses the term 'primacy' ironically. According to his cultural-sociological theory, the primacy of possibility can never be superior, for when that motif dominates in a culture it is in fact an anti-culture, in which the operation of interdictory forms is fundamentally impeded. Theoretically such a culture must end in total chaos or barbarism. Such a desublimating culture would be destroyed by the destructive instinctual forces it can no longer control. Really superior in Rieff's theory is the interdictory form.

Rieff's Neo-conformative Theory of Culture

The previous subsection is an example of how Rieff analyses modern culture in his later works. The notion of a dynamic interaction of a sacred and a social order is constitutive for his entire work, but it is only elaborated fully in the later phase. This dynamic can only be imagined with conformative theory. Rieff's later work can be called *neo-conformative* because he tries to imagine a culture beyond modernity, in which the social order / sacred order dialectic is restored. He develops aspects of this neo-conformative theory of culture by thoroughly analysing essential aspects of modern culture.

Rieff's central point of criticism of modern Western culture is the inversion of transcendence. This culture does not trace its source and vitality back to the mystery of a transcendent God, but to the idea of the crucible of human desires which Freud called the unconscious and which always remains mysterious, too. This sacrosanct belief in the instincts, as the true core of the self, makes modern man blind to the central role of authority in culture.

Sacred order is expressed in a social order in the form of a symbolic order. This expression of a symbolic order is a specific task that Rieff calls 'illuminative act': 'Works of art, acts of thought, all sensibility and expression, are even more illuminative than they are operative.'[6] The operative and illuminative aspects of human acts can be distinguished but not separated because both aspects tend to merge. Rieff mentions as an example that hands can be washed as an illuminative gesture and operatively as well. 'Both acts tend to merge; by that mergence, authority is carried in its culture. There can be no culture without authority as the mergence of illuminative and operative acts. From illuminative acts, which ordain the direction of operative acts, life takes its meanings and culture its energies.'[7] About this direction Rieff says this: 'An act, in culture, can only become operative in the vertical. Try as we may, we cannot live horizontally in the vertical world of culture; to prostrate oneself would be to live beyond the range of authority; such a life – such a culture without an authority that is either raising or lowering, and both, is impossible.'[8]

Here I must refer again to the point that Rieff made in *Mind of the Moralist* about Freud's conceptualization of the unconscious. Freud did not conceive of the unconscious as primarily a notion of *form* as in classical ontology, but as a *substrate* of unconscious desires. These instincts have their own logic (of the primary process). For Freud the agent that forms and/or controls the unconscious is always secondary. The forces that repress instinctual energies are generated in the repression itself, which Rieff rejected as tautological. Rieff arged that Freud repressed the idea that the interdict is the primary form of culture and origin of repression. Still, Freud was close to this point, says Rieff, in his theory of 'primal repression.'[9] What Freud called primal repression can more adequately be called 'the unrelievable pressure, in any and all cultures, against the primacy of possibility. That primacy cannot happen even in our wildest imaginings.'[10] Thus, against Freud, Rieff makes the notion of form primary in his theory of culture. The primacy of form implies the primacy of order in culture. 'Chaos is itself an order. Within a vertical of specifically operative acts become illuminative, the most disorderly acts take their positions in an order that is sacred. Those positions, in sacred order, must be, wherever they are, raising or lowering.'[11]

Modern thinking has alienated Western man from this dynamic. Rieff agrees that there is a 'crisis of authority,' but shifts the analytic perspective in the same way that Nietzsche does in the story of the death of God. Nietzsche makes the madman cry out that the people around him do not realize that they have killed God themselves. Rieff's assertion runs parallel – modern man does not realize that he kills authority with his faith in the idea of a crisis of authority: 'A crisis of authority derives not least from some more or less intellectually elaborate failure to understand that authority, higher and lower, is immortal and unalterable in its form.'[12] Man may or may not understand how authority works; nevertheless, its influence he will never escape. 'In that form, unchangeably vertical, every lowering act produces the pain or fear humans experience as true guilt; every raising act produces a saving sense, as of being redeemed from guilt or of a remission from pain or fear. A certain inversion now characterizes our common and received sense of what is lowering and what is raising in the form of authority.'[13] Rieff connects this theoretical idea of inversion to historical events like this: 'Our great Enlightenment, the slow work of the centuries since the Renaissance, has ended catastrophically, in our time, not in the failure of authority, as is widely believed among the late enlightened themselves; rather the catastrophe of our enlightenment lies in the success of its lowering movements. Gulag and Dachau, torture and terror, are the dry-eyed children of our enlightenments.'[14]

Thus Rieff's philosophy of trangressiveness is elaborated in his later works. The concept of 'primacy of possibility' is put next to the concept of the character-ideal from his earlier works. People can identify 'upward' with the character-ideal, leading to raising acts which Rieff calls 'interdictory acts.' People can also identify downwards with the primacy of possibility, leading to lowering acts which Rieff calls 'transgressive acts.' These identification processes are always in the vertical, says Rieff. In a visual image the concepts of the character-ideal and primacy of possibility are two coordinates of a vertical line which Rieff calls 'the vertical of authority.'

But living is making compromises as well and this is not always a matter of force majeure. A great deal of our behaviour is not motivated by an idealizing identification. Rieff assserts that there is always a certain indifference towards ideals. All cultures denote in their symbolic order, through stories, images, and music 'the vast body of experience within which a certain indifference ... to any right way prevails. I call this life space of human indifference the *remissive mode*, where what is otherwise not to be done may be done, pardonably ... Life is led mainly in a remissive muddle.'[15]

Rieff uses the term 'remission' in his earlier works, too. The way it was defined then was not sufficient for the theory he wants to develop in his later works. In his earlier works Rieff focuses on one coordinate of the vertical of authority: the identification with the character-ideal or the striving after goodness. That invites the question of how Rieff explains the existence of evil in his theory of culture.[16] To address that problem he develops his philosophy of transgressivity. Rieff formulates the relation between remission and transgression like this: 'Remissions subserve the interdicts above them; or, if they expand unpardonably, subvert the interdicts, and thus become transgressions, masked as rationalities or enlightenments.'[17] In late modern Western culture transgressivity, the structural and systematic indifference towards sacred order has become dominant, says Rieff.

Rieff asserts that this cultural dominance of transgressivity is unprecedented in the history of Western culture. At the same time he maintains that this attempt to break down authority is doomed to failure. However much we identify with transgressive ideals, we will always have to recognize that authority is inevitable. Our lives may be a remissive muddle or 'spent in a remissive flux,' as he says elsewhere, but 'the order of that flux is unchanging – I daresay, sacred.'[18] In this later statement Rieff implicitly takes a position in the philosophical debate on what I call 'the ontological status of the sacred.' This debate revolves around the question whether the sacred really exists or not. Rieff thinks that this question is the masked refusal to recognize that the origin of our thinking always evades us. The question refers more to human thought ('ideation') than to a 'really existing sacred order.' Rieff recognizes this problematic in Shakespeare's *Hamlet*: 'Hamlet was nothing like a therapeutic. Concealed as it is revealed behind his manifest question of parents, was Hamlet's latent parent question: whether or not he belonged to sacred order. Concealed as it is revealed behind that parent question is another even more ancient: whether sacred order is or not.'[19]

I want to summarize this section in a schema, which is a visual illustration of Rieff's 'aesthetics of authority' (Fig. 6.1).

A New Psychohistorical Model

The last important text that Rieff published is 'The Newer Noises of War in the Second Culture Camp: Notes on Professor Burt's Legal Fictions' (1991).[20] This the most encompassing formulation of his later theory of culture, in which Rieff summarizes his earlier texts. One characteristic of this piece strikes the eye immediately: Rieff hardly mentions Freud explicitly anymore. The text focuses on other 'inverters of sacred order' like Friedrich Nietzsche, Franz Kafka, James Joyce, Wallace Stevens, Marcel Duchamp, and Jacques Derrida.[21] Still, Freud is more prominent implicitly than it may seem, as is illustrated by a remark on Stevens's work that Rieff made in an interview: 'You find in Stevens remarkably poetic versions of Freudian theory.'[22]

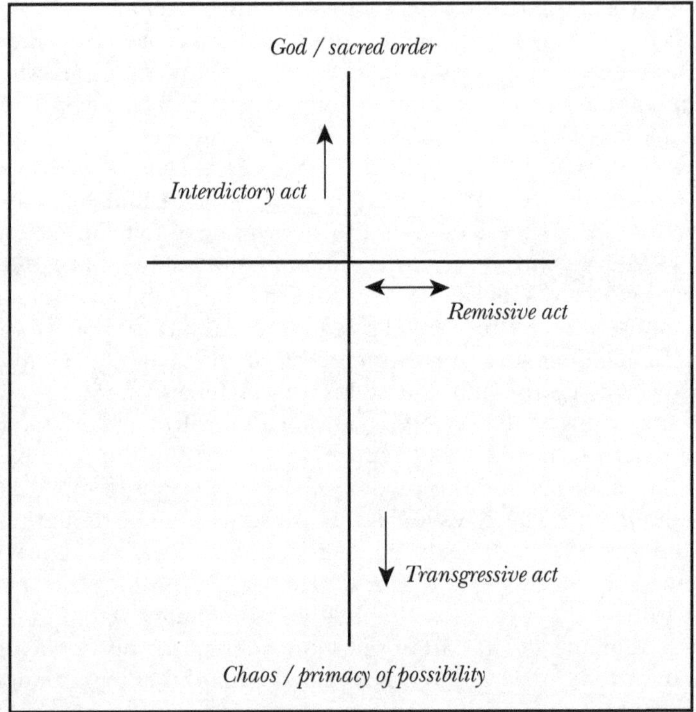

Figure 6.1 An image of Rieff's aesthetics of authority

Rieff's Last Definition of Culture

The idea that repression is the basis of culture returns in a new form: 'Culture is the form of fighting before the firing actually begins ... That cultural work is the matter and manner of disarming competing cultures, inside and outside its previously bounded self. In its disarming manner, a culture makes the political means of enforcement, armed force, unnecessary.'[23]

Rieff also reformulates the second central notion of his theory, the dialectic between sacred order and social order. For this he uses the concept 'creation.' Culture does not just drop from the skies, he says: 'There are no uncreated worlds.'[24] Chaos as the total lack of order can only exist in our imagination. Culture is created when the social order uses cultural principles (interdictory forms or 'primal forms,' as he calls them in his earlier works) to express itself. The formation of such principles and/or forms is not ours, but belongs to a transcendent sacred order. This is not a static situation, but a fundamentally unstable one. Its basic condition is the fight, and in this continuous struggle it is constantly renewed: 'Our church civilization is being, like all others, constantly re-created.'[25]

This creative process of culture formation can only be grasped when we have an eye for the importance of sacred order for culture: 'Unending, world creation comprises the task of culture: namely, to transliterate otherwise invisible sacred orders into their visible modalities – social orders.'[26] The literal meaning of the verb 'to transliterate' is 'to represent (a word, etc.) in the closest corresponding letters of a different alphabet or language.'[27] When we apply this definition to Rieff's usage of the verb, he seems to aim at the translation of the 'signs' of the sacred into the language of the social order. Translating is always interpreting because it is impossible to transfer the signs of one semantic field into another directly. The act of translating presupposes a whole translation technique, which includes a theory of signs and signification (semiology) and a theory of the interpretation of those signs (hermeneutics). The idea of finding the 'closest corresponding signs' refers to the very complex character of the transformation of the language of the sacred order into that of the social order. This requires a lot of attention, concentration, and dedication. The example of the study of the Torah, in Jewish tradition comes to mind, and likewise the, sometimes ardent, debates in the Mishna among rabbis about the meaning and implications of a passage of the Torah, sometimes even about a single letter or punctuation mark.

In his later work Rieff rejects the separation of the transcendent and the immanent, the sacred and the profane. The reality of the sacred is very concrete, a point which he illustrates with a paraphrase of a text from Deuteronomy: 'Meaning in the world is very near, the most personal body knowledge to be observed.'[28] This is a paraphrase of a passage from Deuteronomy 30:14: 'It is a thing very near to you, upon your lips and in your heart ready to be kept.' The 'thing' at stake here are the interdicts of the Torah. Those interdicts do not arrive in our hearts and upon our lips just like that. This is exactly the task of culture: to transliterate religious language from the religious traditions into forms of expression. Actually, Rieff's own texts can be considered part of this secondary cultural process. He 'transliterates' the religious language from the Torah into the sociological language of his theory of culture. Here we see that Rieff resumes the problematics of the three case studies from *The Triumph of the Therapeutic: Uses of Faith after Freud.* He presented the theories of Jung, Reich, and Lawrence as diagnostics for the modern disruption of the interaction between a sacred (symbolic) order, on the one hand, and the social and psychological order on the other.

With the concept 'transliteration' Rieff describes another aspect of culture. 'As transliterating institutions of sacred order into social, cultures are what they represent: "symbolics." '[29] Rieff calls this the '*is-ness*' of culture. As symbolic order culture *is* what it represents. Thus the sacred and the profane are inseparable. The symbolic order cannot exist apart from or outside the social order. Man makes the world as such habitable by describing it symbolically. Think of the story of creation, for example, in which Adam gives names to the animals. 'Cultures are the habitus of human beings, universal only in their particularities, symbolically inhabited.'[30] The symbolic activity is 'universal,' but at the same time Rieff rejects the idea of a 'universal culture,' as he did in *Fellow Teachers,* too.

For Rieff the term 'symbolics' apparently is not adequate, because he introduces another term: 'Cultures are what they represent: "symbolics" or, in a word that represents what it is, "worlds."'[31] He does not explain his preference for the term 'world' over the term 'symbolics' here explicitly, but I surmise that he is reacting against the contemporary usage of the term, especially the tendency to neglect the moral aspect of symbolics and the problem of authority. In the theory presented in this text, just as in *Triumph of the Therapeutic,* 'the religious problem is identical with the moral and the moral with the cultural.'[32] The term 'world' unites the symbolic, religious or transcendent, and moral aspects of culture.

Three Worlds

In the new psychohistorical model the central concept is not, as in the older model, the character-ideal as a typological person, but a typological culture. In 'Newer Noises' Rieff introduces the idea of 'typological worlds': 'In these notes, my typological observations divide into three symbolics or worlds that I shall number chronologically: *first, second and third.*'[33] In contemporary Western culture these three worlds are at war. Before I can describe in more detail how Rieff imagines this 'second culture camp' I must point out the distinctive feature that distinguishes these worlds from each other, what Rieff calls their 'symbolic particularity.' This has nothing to do with the kind of symbols extant in a culture.

There are many cultural differences on this point. In Christian cultures, for example, the cross is a central symbol, whereas in Buddhist cultures the wheel has this role. In Rieff's theory symbolic particularity is a dynamic concept, which pivots on the way a culture imagines authority and how it relates to authority.

In a section called 'a synchronic of three cultures,'[34] Rieff describes the concepts of the three worlds more elaborately. This section deals with late modern culture in which three typological worlds are at war with each other simultaneously. Of course, Rieff does not give neat definitions, but for the sake of clarity I will try to describe each world as separately as possible, starting with the first.

'Every world, until our third, has been a form of address to some ultimate authority.'[35] The term 'first worlds' is a typology for pagan cultures. About the way the relation to ultimate authority was imagined Rieff says this: 'Ultimate authorities in pagan worlds, various as Platonic Athens and aboriginal Australia, had something essential in common: mythic *primacies of possibility* from which derived all agencies of authority, including its godterms.'[36] The term 'primacy of possibility' is the central one in this description. Rieff also uses it in 'By What Authority?' with regard to Freud's concept 'the unconscious' and, more generally, to the way the origin of authority is imagined in modernity. In 'Newer Noises' Rieff uses the term primarily to typify pagan, first worlds, but there surely is a connection to modernity as well, as we shall see when he describes the typology of the third world.

In 'Newer Noises' we find the same ironic play with words as in *Fellow Teachers*. He uses the acronym 'pop' for 'primacies of possibility,' 'pop,' as a further description of the typology of the first world: 'Whether Platonic essences or aboriginal dreamtimes, an all-inclusive *pop* once characterized highest authority there, being above all and in all its agent authorities in all first worlds.'[37] According to Rieff, it is typical for pagan cultures that in the way authority is imagined 'human possibility' is the central idea, as not being subjected to a primal limiting (or forming) principle. So there is a reference to an ultimate authority in first worlds, but Rieff thinks that this is not a revealed authority, but one created by man himself: 'Of first worlds ... I ask my leading question: whether any remain in ultimate authority other than as a recycling of their aesthetic.'[38]

The typology of the second world refers to Rieff's ideas about the vertical of authority that I introduced earlier in this chapter. We saw that Rieff supposes that authority is inevitable and that we therefore always live in a vertical of authority. The central notion of the typological second world is the idea that 'what we are is constituted by where we are in sacred order.'[39] In first worlds the importance of this notion is recognized, too, but the crucial point at which the two worlds differ typologically is the way the origin of authority is imagined. Characteristic for the second world is the belief that the primacy of form is crucial for authority. 'Creation' is the cultural form with which the second world strives to imagine the origin and operation of authority. In pagan thinking it is the substrate (desires, in their different cultural forms of expression) that is primal, not form. Later on I shall go into Rieff's ideas on creation and their relation to revelation more elaborately. First I must describe the typology of the third world.

In 'Newer Noises' Rieff writes that our late modern worlds or symbolics should be called 'anti-cultures' because they do not translate sacred order into social.[40] This is the most distinctive difference between the typological second and third world. The third world differs essentially from the first on the point that in the third world there is no reference at all to one or the other ultimate authority. This did exist in the first world in the form of a mythic primacy of possibility or 'pop.' In the third world this pop is being recycled in fantasy versions. For Rieff pop music is the pre-eminent cultural artefact of the third world. From the perspective of this theory of sacred order he gives this criticism: '*Pop* inventions refer to readings of themselves alone, toward some supreme fiction at which not even virtuoso readers can arrive in this historical life.'[41]

Here Rieff cryptically comments on the modern inversion of direction in thinking about the sacred, as he did in *Fellow Teachers* with regard to Freud. 'The ultimate' is not something we can conceive of, in the form of a product of our imagination (a fiction), but comes from 'the other side.' But still that is what is done or tried in modern culture. To enable human imagination to produce fictions like this, it has to be freed from traditional forms of imagination that forbid this. Think, for example, of the prohibition in the Jewish tradition of pronouncing the name of God, which symbolizes the transcendent origin of God. Here Rieff elaborates on his ideas of transgressiveness as the foundation of modern culture. Modern cultural elites, which he calls 'radical remissive elites,' try to break down the traditional, religious forms of imagination through a radical criticism of culture. He criticizes their ideological intentions like this: '*pop* worlds are created more or less consciously to remain readings of a free future. Freedom now is as it never was and cannot be. ... Third worlds propose an unprecedented present age without moralities and religions.'[42] Rieff is convinced that this attempt is bound to fail: 'The symbolic of creation is no more eliminable from our second world than the doctrine of commanding truths.'[43]

In this description of the three typological worlds it catches the eye that when Rieff defines the first and third worlds he takes the distinctive feature of the second world as a starting point, that is, the transliteration of sacred order into social order. Rieff defends this 'thinking from within the second world' as his given hermeneutical position: 'There is no meta-culture, no neutral ground, from which the war of the worlds can be analyzed.'[44] He says that 'every sociologist, like every other human being, lives within his own incommunicable yet normative *habitus*. Mine is, uncertainly as any other's in our late second and emergent third worlds, in our second.'[45]

Creation and Revelation

In 'Newer Noises' Rieff returns once more to the question of the origin of authority, to which the third world does not have a consistent answer. The second world does have an 'answer': revelation. The second world has as its foundation the idea that culture is based on an ultimate authority that reveals itself in the formative principles of a culture. Revelation and creation are closely related in the second world, as is illustrated by the primal story about this in the second world: Genesis. Ontologically speaking, in the second world being is anchored in the authority which reveals (and conceals!) itself in His revelations to mankind. Genesis would be the Ur-story about the forms in which this takes place. In Exodus that is elaborated, because God reveals Himself in more specific ways, culminating in the revelation of the Ten Commandments. The truth of those commandments, 'true as they are commanding and only so, [lies] in the old word for that connection [between truth and commandment], "revelation."'[46]

Rieff demands attention for the role of the formative and limiting cultural principles which are shifted aside in modernity with its ideology of freedom and autonomy of the individual. He does that in 'Newer Noises' by interpreting theological concepts in his own, interdisciplinary way. Rieff reads the stories from Genesis and Exodus from the perspective of fight as the basic sociological form of culture. Thus he refines his concept of the dialectic between the social and the sacred orders: 'The fight for being there, as it emerges ever after Exodus 3:14, is within – in medieval culture, called the *psychomachia* – as it is without me. An habitable peace would be unprecedented. Peace would require perfect public abidances in one world or another, without a trace of fusion and its confusions: an impossible culture.'[47]

In this fight it is the task of culture to defend the primacy of the interdictory form. Rieff reads Genesis and Exodus, and other passages from the Torah, as symbolic accounts of this task. Rieff does not go into this explicitly, but I think he aims at the idea of how God conquers primal chaos ('tohu wabohu' in Hebrew) in Genesis. This primal chaos does not own itself beaten, but resurges again and again in the created world. Here the problem of sublimity is at stake again. Thus we come upon a fundamental meta-theoretical problem that needs to be dealt with before I can continue my description of the meaning of Genesis and Exodus from a Rieffian perspective.

Viewed meta-theoretically the difficult problem of the relations between theory and reality are here at stake again. It is useful to recall Rieff's ideas about the primary cultural process, about which he said: '[the term] primary process refers to an insurgent reality that is the predicate of all realities. Therefore, order is never primary.'[48] When we think of previous statements of Rieff about chaos and disorder we end up with a paradox, because he also thinks that chaos as such can only exist in our imagination, never in reality. Still, disorder, in the form of the primary process, is the foundation of reality. According to Rieff, this paradox was put into words very poignantly by Wallace Stevens, who said that 'every order is a disorder and every disorder an order.'[49] Rieff reformulated the paradox like this: 'The theory of order and analysis always fragments into a disorder which only thinking is able to relate.'[50] Here Rieff aims at the relation of theory and reality. The reality that theory tries to grasp is itself a phenomenon in which order and disorder are intertwined. The theory about order that tries to understand this fragments reality by analysing it. Only the thought process itself can bring unity into this fragmented knowledge. This is a unity which exists in theory. The order that man imposes on reality can never be identical with the order of reality, because the order of reality always has a transcendent origin. This tension between theory and reality, order and chaos, the sacred and the profane can never be resolved. The phenomenologist G. van der Leeuw, whom Rieff admires very much, formulates this problem very eloquently: 'Our time is full of yearning for the lost unity of life. Everywhere efforts are being made to replace the tangent planes with concentric circles. We have had our fill of limited "realms," and justly so. But this yearning must not tempt us to try to revive the primitive, nor even to erase the boundaries; least of all should we anticipate all that only exists in the eschatological sense, that is, through the grace of God.'[51]

Now, let us return to Genesis and Exodus. From a Rieffian perspective we read in Genesis and Exodus that God conquered the primal chaos, but this chaos resurges again and again. So, within the 'framework' created in the beginning of Genesis the process of creation continues in the first part of the book and in Exodus. This story of creation is at the same time the story of the coming into existence of God's people, Israel. After the death of the last patriarch, Joseph, the people of Israel find themselves under severe repression in Egypt. The pharaoh had become afraid of the growing power of Israel and had enslaved them. Then, in Exodus, we read how God calls Moses to liberate His people. Once freed, God gives His people the 'means' with which they need never live again as they did in Egypt. He reveals His law to live with in the land that He had promised to the patriarchs in Genesis. These stories from the Torah are, of course, at the same time symbolic or mythic stories in which the existential condition of the individual and the people it belongs to is at stake.

Modern, secularized man has developed a completely new way of envisioning this fight for existence, a totally new aesthetic. That product of modern imagination Rieff calls 'third world.' It is typical for the typological third world 'that '*pop* first worlds' have been recycled in a variety of disarming assaults by third worlds upon the exclusive and intolerant aesthetic of authority by which our seconds have continuously reconstituted their embattled identities.'[52]

This latter statement is programmatic for the part of 'Newer Noises' that follows on the introductory sections. From many different perspectives Rieff analyses a great number of modern pieces of art and a number of philosophical, theological, and social theoretical texts,[53] which are relevant for his theory for two reasons. First, every perspective makes visible an aspect of the typical modern phenomenon they all have in common, the attempt to break down authority in its sacred order. Second, Rieff interprets them in the same way as he interprets Freud's theory of culture in his later works: as attempts to decipher the dynamic of culture. His hermeneutical starting point is that in these pieces of artistic creation the operation of sacred order was repressed, but that this repression can be, to some extent, unmasked and deciphered using the right method. Thus it can be shown how in these works the authority of sacred order is operative, however hard their authors or creators deny that to themselves. Rieff considers them, just like Freud, 'negational theorists of sacred order.'

The Second Culture Camp

With this information about Rieff's new psychohistorical model we can take a closer look now at his idea of second culture camp. According to Rieff, there is no scientific neutrality. He criticizes the concept like this: 'To read our worlds at war is to participate unavoidably in the fighting. Value neutrality amounts to a taking of third world sides ... There is no neutral ground to be found in this or in any world.'[54] For that fight between the typological worlds the Germans had a compound word, says Rieff: 'Kulturkampf.' In this fight brute force was the last resort. The first resort has been to words: 'The historical task of culture is always and everywhere the same: the creation of a *world* in which its inhabitants may find themselves at home and yet accommodate the stranger without yielding their *habitus* to him.'[55]

This task of the creation of habitable worlds is the task of a cultural elite, says Rieff. The fight between different worlds is also a fight between cultural elites. Viewed like this there is a continuous line in Rieff's work, from his master's thesis on Coleridge, via *Fellow Teachers* – a passionate appeal to his fellow teachers to take up their cultural task – to 'Newer Noises.' In different forms Rieff repeats the theme of a defeat of a cultural elite, very often clerical, by a 'therapeutic elite' which betrays its cultural task. In the German nineteenth-century Kulturkampf we can find an analogous example. In the Germany of Bismarck there were fights, in the first instance with words, between the National Liberal Party and the triumphalist Roman Catholic hierarchy, which had been revitalized by the dogma of infallibility in matters of faith and morals adopted in 1870. 'The aim of the National Liberals was to shift the German Catholic imagination away from the church to the state.'[56] At a certain moment words alone no longer sufficed. 'Law is the ultimate weapon, before any turn to harder ware, in a *Kulturkampf* ... The pope responded to newly restrictrive laws by forbidding clerical conformity to them. In turn, the state dismissed clerical resisters from their duties and, moreover, suspended their salaries. Elites of the Kulturstaat, both Catholic and Protestant, then learned a fatally rational and enduring lesson: the high price of being other than indifferent to the temptation of opposing the *machtsstaat*.'[57]

This high price was paid only by a few, says Rieff. 'A consequent and prudent *adiaphora* [literally: indifference],[58] operating in a range from clerical indifference to conformity, endured from that Bismarckian Kulturkampf against the Church to Hitler's against the founding nation of that second world from which all church civilizations take their supersessive readings.'[59] With 'supersessive readings' Rieff refers to Christian interpretations of Christianity as the 'new Israel.' Here Rieff continues the polemic against Christian anti-Judaism from *Fellow Teachers.* In 'Newer Noises' Rieff draws a logical conclusion from his theory of the importance of the interdicts for the formation of culture. The 'prototypes' of the interdicts are the Ten Commandments from the Torah. Therefore the Jewish people must be considered 'the founding nation' of the typological second world.

Rieff draws a line from the Bismarckian Kulturkampf to the Holocaust and other totalitarian horrors of the twentieth century. He considers the destruction camps like Gulag and Dachau as the horrible results of the presuppositions of modernity. Rieff also suggests that totalitarianism has acquired a new face at the end of the twentieth century. The new totalitarian figures need not be as monstrous as, for example, Hitler's Nazis. Rieff's aforementioned analyses of cultural artefacts in 'Newer Noises' can also be read as attempts to make these new figures of totalitarianism visible. They are figures that embody the typological third world which is continuously at war with the second world.

A Casus on Identity

I want to give one illustrative example of Rieff's analyses of 'artefacts of the third world' that follows the introductory part of 'Newer Noises.' Rieff examines the book *Two Jewish Justices, Outcasts in the Promised Land.* It was written by a 'fellow teacher,' the American Jewish scholar of law Robert A. Burt, and published by the University of California Press in 1988. In his book Burt compares the philosophies of law of two important American Jewish Supreme Court justices: Louis Dembitz Brandeis and Felix Frankfurter. Brandeis (1856–1941) was a very socially engaged lawyer and became the most important adviser of President Woodrow Wilson for his policy of New Freedom. From 1916 to 1939 Brandeis was the first Jewish justice of the United States Supreme Court, where he belonged to a progessive minority, which turned into a majority under President Franklin D. Roosevelt. Brandeis played an important role in the Zionist movement. Felix Frankfurter (1882–1965) was a very close, younger friend of Brandeis. Unlike Brandeis he was not born in the United States, but together with his parents immigrated from Europe. A distinctive difference between these two justices, as Burt sees it, is their definition and use in jurisprudence of the status of insider and outsider in American society.

Burt distills their philosphies of law from the decisions they wrote or led in many cases and situates them in the contemporary social context. This was a time of radical social change, which involved great social turbulence, challenging the authority of existing social institutions. Briefly, Burt's thesis is that the main contrast between the philosophies of law of Frankfurter and Brandeis appears in their completely different reactions to these social changes. In his jurisprudence Brandeis always tried to induce the two opposing parties to discussion and thus achieve consensus. He thought that this was the way towards new social stability. Thus the boundaries between social insiders and outsiders were not strictly demarcated. Burt connects that approach to Brandeis's activities on behalf of the Zionist movement, in which he helped to fight for a new, legally recognized home for Jews, who had always been outcasts in so many societies. Brandeis was very sensitive to the needs of social outcasts and helped them in the struggle for a just place in American society. Frankfurter, on the contrary, tended more to counter social turbulence by upholding established authority. He appealed very strongly to established American values.

Burt draws historical parallels between the era in which the two justices worked and the end of the twentieth century. He understands Frankfurter's position, but eventually Burt sides with Brandeis. He calls Brandeis's perspective 'prophetic' because he thinks that Brandeis understood best the radical implications of the social changes at the end of the nineteenth century when the United States underwent rapid transition from a predominantly agricultural to a modern, industrial society. Traditional social structures were dissolving. According to Burt, at the end of the twentieth century that process had progressed to a stage where no ethnic group is so dominant in the United States that it can determine who is insider and who is 'stranger' or 'guest.' The American is permanently a guest in his or her own society. In other words, the 'outsider status, homelessness, is pervasively experienced in American society today – not simply among those groups customarily conceived in this way, such as blacks or Jews, but generally.'[60] Burt thinks that Americans can learn a lot from the wisdom of the Jewish Justice Brandeis and his vision of the social function of authority.

The parallel with Rieff's interpretation of Freud's work is evident. Like Brandeis, Freud reflected on the (psychological) implications of radical social changes which brought the modern individual into intrapsychic and social tension. Freud developed a therapy in which the individual unlearns to identifiy with traditional figures of authority. Thus, says Rieff, Freud catalyzed the demolition of authority in all its cultural and symbolic forms inaugurated by modernity. Typical for modernity is the absence of any common system of symbols. According to Rieff, that is what Burt calls 'homelessness,' for it is precisely the historical task of culture to create a 'habitable world.' Burt thinks that the Jews know this experience of homelessness very well, and therefore Americans can learn a lot from men like Brandeis who transformed such experience into a practice of law.

Rieff does not agree at all with the way Burt conceives of homelessness and the underlying reference to Jewish identity. Burt says that Brandeis identified with outcasts. According to Rieff however, 'identification with the outcast is a third world fantasy.'[61] He thinks that Burt mutilates the idea of Jewish identity. 'Only so does it become possible to describe the significance of Jewishness in American life without reference to Israel.'[62] With 'Israel' Rieff apparently means the Jewish tradition, because he formulates his theoretical criticism of Burt's book with texts from that tradition in which the problem of outcasts is at stake. He cites, for example, Leviticus 20:22–3, where God, in Rieff's interpretation, forbids Israel to identify with the outcast. Israel must abide in its own, sacred identity and is therefore not allowed to identify with 'the customs of the nations': 'Outcasts are criminals in sacred order.'[63]

Rieff asserts that we can find in Genesis 1:26 a description of this sacred identity of the Jews. The first part of this verse from the Torah is: 'Then God said, "Let us make man in our image and likeness."' In the typological second world it is believed that man is created in God's image after His likeness. This is a metaphorical description of the idea that man as a social being lives in sacred order. Or, more accurately, man is himself a nexus of social and sacred order or is so at least when he lives according to the idea that he was created in God's image and after His likeness, with all the normative implications. In third world thought this idea is inverted. It is believed that authority originates in the process of man identifying with the not-self or the Other. Authority cannot be imagined differently than as a 'function of identification.' The conception of authority developed in that manner is fundamentally *from* the human *to* the order of authority. That inverts the second world idea of an absolute authority that fundamentally transcends the human condition and that reveals itself to mankind. Modern man creates himself, from identifications with authority figures he chooses for himself. This belief leads to what I called 'cultural alienation' in previous chapters. Through this alienation modern man cuts himself off from sacred order. Rieff's formulates this idea in 'Newer Noises' thus: 'In third culture doctrines, specially in their Freudian versions, authority is a function of identification which is hermetically sealed away from the commanding truth of identity in the sacred self of Genesis 1:26.'[64]

So, Rieff disagrees with the way Burt defines Jewish identity. He considers Burt's 'legal fictions' as a piece of scholarly work based on third world thought: 'There is the mildest of menaces at work in Professor Burt's disarming text on the "significance of Jewishness in America life."'[65] Rieff calls the connection that Burt makes between being Jewish and the outsider status 'a third world fiction.' His book 'makes a text, but not a world.'[66] Burt's work is an 'attack from within' on the fundamentals of Jewish identity. Typologically spoken this is an example of an attack of the third world on the second world, or of second culture camp.

At stake here is Burt's suggestion that he is dealing with a central issue of late modern culture: the pathological social and psychological consequences of the lack of a common symbol system. Burt tries to imagine an adequate theoretical response to this problem. When evaluated from the perspective of the second world, Burt's pledge can only be considered an extreme form of modern thought. Modern texts such as Burt's are not 'registrations of a sacred order,' but products of the transgressive imagination of modern man. On the symbolic level there is a crucial difference between second world and third world texts: 'Sacred scripture, Jewish second world recorded, is not a text; not in the sense Burt's book is a text, nor Nietzsche's, nor Borges.' The true *Torah/teaching* way is not as literature, not as poetry. If there is a poetry of Law, then that poetry is in the obedient mind's eye open to see because it feels absolutely the commanding truths of sacred order in its own self: confident in its faith relation.'[67]

A typological difference between the second and the third world is described here as the difference in attitude towards sacred texts. Rieff demonstrates in 'Newer Noises' how Joyce in *Finnegans Wake* breaks down the sacred order of the second world by distorting important texts from the Torah with puns in such a way that the new meaning is the total opposite of the original meaning. (Rieff, by the way, is a master himself in this literary technique!) Burt does the same, mutatis mutandis, in the way he uses Jewish tradition to argue for the importance of Jewish identity for American society. He also destroys the core of the concept of Jewish identity. To penetrate into the truth of sacred texts another attitude is required, that of the 'obedient mind's eye,' than the attitude he distills from modern prose or scholarly fiction. Thus Rieff draws an unbridgeable dividing-line between the literature of the third world and the sacred text of the second, which calls to mind the distinction in the Jewish tradition between Torah and the rest of the religious scripture that is 'mere explication.' There may exist examples of profound modern literature, but it can never provide access to sacred order as the ontological foundation of culture and social order. Modern literature always remains 'fiction,' which is transgressive when it does not acknowledge the division between profane and sacred text, between profane and sacred order.

7

Rieff: Prophet of a Post-secular Culture

Philip Rieff was stigmatized as a very conservative thinker. Apart from the question whether he really is the conservative and cultural pessimist he is said to be,[1] I find it more relevant to investigate his theoretical message. Rieff contributes to the 'massive amount of work that remains to be done if we are to get anywhere near a satisfactory understanding of the tumultuous sociocultural processes'[2] that exploded in the twentieth century. In this concluding chapter I will first summarize the three major concepts that emerged in my reading of Rieff's work. After that I will evaluate Rieff's work from three perspectives. The first refers to his style. Rieff is a language artist, but the way he used this literary gift made his work very inaccessible. *Why did he choose to write in such an extremely difficult style?* Second, when we take into account that Rieff was a major theoretical figure in the social sciences in the 1960s, this question arises: *Why is it that nothing like a 'Rieff school' developed in the social sciences?* This issue is explored by comparing Rieff's work and career to those of Peter Berger, who is considered one of the most influential social theorists of the post–Second World War period.[3] The third issue comprises the major part of this chapter: *What is the relevance of Rieff's work for current debates on (de)secularization and 'new religion'?*

Rieff's Major Concepts

For Rieff, authority is the pre-eminent problem for the analysis of modern culture. However, Rieff is not just a classical defender of 'law-and-order.' I have already mentioned his critique of counterculture, which is explained by the focus on authority in his work. Rieff thinks that the primary task of culture is to curb human desire. Therefore he considers the interdict the primary form of culture. In late modern Western culture this curbing of desire is still a touchy subject, which is often repressed. The essence of Rieff's polemical response to this is that he moulds his theory of the sacred into a theory of authority. This theory is a critical instrument with which he breaks open modern theories of subjectivity. In the line of social constructionist thinking, Rieff criticizes theories that pit the self against society. Rieff proposes a non-dualistic anthropology, which enables us to clarify how 'inner' personality structures are intimately interwoven with 'outer' social structures.

In my reading of Rieff's work, three main conceptual categories emerged: (1) the two kinds of theory (conformative versus transformative) on the level of meta-theory; (2) the importance of transcendence for culture; and (3) the interrelation of nature (desire or eros) and culture (authority) or, analogically, of the sacred and the profane. (This third category includes the problem of sublimation.) I will summarize each category, in this order.

I presented Rieff's theory as a reflection on the cultural-historical meaning of the Enlightenment which, according to Rieff, was an important catalyst in the slow emergence of a new type of theory.[4] In his early works Rieff conceives of this development as a rupture in Western cultural history. In later works Rieff's opinion on this issue gradually changes. He thinks that this transformative type of thinking has acquired its place in late modern Western culture, but it cannot be more than a transgressive movement that theoretically must end up in an anti-culture. The 'second culture camp' is the logical consequence of modernity. A crucial difference between premodern conformative theory and modern transformative theory is that the former presupposes the existence of a transcendent order in reality. This order is conceived of as the origin of existence and is the realm in which man searches for answers on existential questions about himself and the world.

Rieff's theory can be called 'neo-conformative' because he brings in transcendence as a conceptual category in the social sciences. Examples of this are the notion of a transcendent cultural order from which formative principles penetrate into the social order, the notion of the transcendent origin of repression (based on a theory of the interdict as the origin of that repression), and the theory of sacred order from Rieff's later works. Transformative theory is based on the denial of the importance of the sacred for the social sciences. Rieff's neo-conformative theory criticizes transformative theory.

Starting from this main distinction at the meta-theoretical level and stressing the importance of transcendence, Rieff develops a very idiosyncratic view on three concepts that play a major role in a psychoanalytic theory of culture: desire or eros, authority, and sublimation. Rieff asserts that from a cultural-theoretical perspective it is an important point for Freud that man, on the one hand, must to a great extent renounce his instinctual nature. To revitalize the contemporary 'tired civilization' of the West, the rights of nature need to be partly restored. Freud closely connected sublimation to his libido theory and thus turned nature and culture into antagonists of each other. On the other hand, Freud had an eye for the importance of repression for culture. Therefore, says Rieff, it is crucial for an adequate interpretation of Freud's theory of culture to recognize that Freud was deeply ambivalent on this point. Freud struggled his entire life with the problem of authority as the necessary curbing of desire. Rieff digs up this 'forgotten problematic' and extrapolates it to the central issue of his own theory of culture. In Rieff's theory, culture is not conceived of as the expression of human desire, through the 'vicissitudes of sublimation,' but as the result of the 'categorical imperative of repression' which is so intimately woven into desire that it can never be exhaustively analysed how this repression works. Rieff inverts the directions in his 'science of limits': repression or limitation of human desire is the central theme, instead of the expression of it. Cultural innovation is only possible when modern man ceases to expect salvation from the instincts.

The idea of the intimate mergence of nature and culture, or of the sacred and the profane, can be found in various forms in Rieff's work. In his first book, Rieff develops an interpretation of Freud's theory in which this idea is an important issue. In his last published article he recognizes this 'intimicy of repression' in Deuteronomy 30:14. We have seen that this idea is the basis for a critical theory of culture which is an alternative for cultural theories that are based on sublimation.[5]

Rieff's Style

Rieff's first two books are written in a predominantly academic style. As he becomes older, his style becomes more cryptic, sometimes even aphoristic. His magnum opus texts consist mainly of short sections of one or several paragraphs, written in a Nietzschean style. About this magnum opus Rieff writes the following:

> The work will be published in three volumes – or, conceivably, four, with a

> few hundred illustrations. The text will weave around the illustrations, each of which will be fully examined in the theoretical context of the text ... Throughout each volume there are uses of poetry, philosophy, history, theology, music, psychology, art history and other disciplines .... My concluding work is synoptic ... The manuscript is broken, like the culture it examines, into a jumble of fragments that I have locked in, one to another, so to unify late 'second culture' thought in the humanities and social sciences. Call the style *bricolage.*[6]

Thus, Rieff's choice of style is closely related to the object of his research: fragmented late modern Western culture. However, one may wonder whether it is not possible to write about that in a more accessible way. Rieff seems to have three reasons for his peculiar style. The first is didactic. He assumes that the frames of reference of his readers are immersed in modern thought. That is no fertile ground for his culture criticism, which is a vehement attack on the modern ideal of self-realization. That criticism would be rejected if he would formulate it plainly. Therefore Rieff uses stylistic means such as irony.[7] One of the few theologians who pays serious attention to Rieff's work, Peter Homans, offers a sharp analysis of this aspect of it. He maintains that the powerful effect of Rieff's work lies in its capacity to drench the reader's awareness with metaphor, irony, parody, inversions, wit, sarcasm, and bitterness. 'Through his style,' says Homans, 'Rieff conveys to the reader what he thinks "it feels like," psychologically, to be cut off from the past, the "existential" condition which he insists Freud has forced upon the unsuspecting modern.'[8] I think that Rieff's aims coincide with that of a psychoanalyst, who strives for a therapeutic process in which the analysand becomes aware of and gains insight into the hidden motives that determine the analysand's desire for self-knowledge.[9] In parallel fashion, Rieff aims at making his readers aware of the critical motifs of de(con)struction of authority and transcendence that have pervaded modern thought.

Second, this awareness is more than cognition. Rieff wants to evoke a deeply felt awareness of an existential situation. He uses the aforementioned stylistic means to have his message enacted in the reading process itself. In this respect, Rieff's work may be compared to that of George Bataille, who also created a sociology of the sacred. Like Bataille, Rieff thinks that in late modern Western culture the tendency prevails to break down participation in the sacred. At this point Rieff's analysis of the work of D.H. Lawrence is important because, according to Rieff, Lawrence contrived to develop a 'second faith,' a successor to the sterile rationalism of science.[10] 'In Lawrence, the compassionate nineteenth-century science of religion was transformed into the characteristic religiously intimate poetry of the twentieth. Our lyric, with its tendency to evoke private worlds without end, has gone creedal at the same time that our prose has gone anti-creedal.'[11] Since scientific discourse has gone 'anti-creedal,' Rieff maintains, again like Bataille, that poetry is the only medium that is left in late modern culture to write about the sacred. This can be read as a methodological critique of empiricism which rejects this participation in the sacred. Rieff unmasks this empirical objectivity (including the idea of 'value neutrality') as part of the modern project to deconstruct the sacred. Rieff's alternative is to try to develop a style that allows critical analysis, but does not destroy its object – the sacred – in the analysis.

A third reason for Rieff's choice of style has to do with the tension between the theoretical and the personal in his work. We saw that Rieff called the typological second world, in which religion and the sacred are vital forces, his 'normative habitus.' That methodological position accords with Rieff's critical choice to develop his theory of culture not from the perspective of human desire (which is the central issue for the cultural third world), but from the problem of authority (which is the central issue for the cultural second world). Of course, Rieff is aware that this implies fundamental hermeneutical questions because nobody is able to separate himself from his own, historically determined, hermeneutical position. In *Triumph of the Therapeutic* and especially in *Fellow Teachers* he tackles this problem very ironically and calls himself as modern as the people or the ideas that he criticizes.[10] This complex and playful shifting between the personal and the theoretical cannot be put into a neat, linear argument.

The Reception of Rieff's Work: Rieff Compared with Berger

We have seen that the degree to which Rieff's work is forgotten should not be exaggerated. The term 'triumph of the therapeutic' and the one he coined before that, 'psychological man,' are still part of the contemporary sociological imagination.[13] The point is that most people lost track of his work since the publication of *Triumph of the Therapeutic*. It is therefore unknown that in the little work he published since then, Rieff developed an intriguing contribution to the field of cultural sociology that is applicable to research on 'new religion.' If we take into consideration that Rieff had a prestigious position in a major academic instution until 1993, many questions arise. How to explain this decline in his academic prestige? Why is his theory of sacred order so unknown? Why is there no 'Rieff school' in sociology? Of course, a few things are too obvious to not mention them. Rieff 'perished' because he did not publish. The 1970s and 1980s were not the most favourable climate for a conservative like Rieff. Also the inaccessibility of *Fellow Teachers* and later texts undoubtedly plays an important role. But are these sufficient explanations? We will explore this issue further by comparing Rieff's work and career with that of Peter Berger, who is considered one of the most influential theorists in the field of the sociology of religion of the past four decades[14] and has developed a 'faithful sociogy.'[15]

The basic reason for comparing these two writers is that for both of them 'transcendence' and 'social order' are key notions.[16] More specifically they share 'a Barthian impatience with the dilutions of transcendence'[17] that they perceive in modern forms of religion. There are other important similarities. They both consider themselves and are considered to be conservatives. Whereas Rieff adopted 'Old England' and its high culture as a 'cultural homeland,' Berger calls 'the vanished world of the Habsburg monarchy,' of which he absorbed the roots in his upbringing in Central Europe, 'a useful vantage point from which to observe the inanities of our own time.'[18] This cultural conservatism came to the fore most poignantly in their critical attitudes towards counterculture in the 1960s.

There are important differences, too, which may help to explain the poor reception of Rieff's work. I cannot give more than hints at these because a thorough answer requires more extensive research on Rieff's biography and sociological research in the field of American social science generally over the past four decades. First, both Rieff and Berger may be cultural conservatives, but that seems to imply different things in each case. Berger considers himself politically right of centre, but theologically liberal. But even in his political stance, Berger rejects what he calls the 'monomaniacal preoccupation with the issues of abortion and homosexuality' of the neo-conservative movement. On these issues Berger has been in the middle, as for abortion, or decisively liberal, as for homosexuality.[19] Rieff was always very reserved in writing explicitly about his political preferences, but these are precisely the two issues that he would fulminate against openly.[20] Next to things like his adopting an 'Oxfordish' accent and a very idiosyncratic way of dressing himself, this may have contributed to a disproportional attention to his conservatism. This may have blocked the way for an adequate interpretation of his irony and other stylistic idiosyncracies that he increasingly used to convey his theoretical message: A message that is not at all unambiguously conservative. Berger, on the other hand, managed to prevent this one-sided association of his conservatism with his theoretical work.

Two other important issues are the differences of style and of literary proliferation. As for the latter, I want to stress that we must not only think quantitatively. Although Rieff published just two books in the period 1959 to 1970, whereas Berger published nine, Rieff managed to build up an enormous prestige. Probably the predominance of psychoanalysis and Rieff's brilliant analysis of its cultural influence in well-written books were sufficient for that. In the 1970s, Berger published another eight books and Rieff only one. From then on the argument of proliferation does seem to play a major role, next to that of style. Apart from theoretical works, Berger keeps on producing very accessible books in which he applies the theoretical insights that he developed to societal, economic, and religious issues. Rieff never bothered with the latter. Maybe he counted on his pupils to do this for him. I am reminded of a passage in the preface of the first edition of *Mind of the Moralist*: 'Great masters need great disciples; it is a prerequisite of greatness among those who found movements. Calvin had his Beza, Luther his Melancthon, Marx his Engels. Each disciple was great, not in his own right, but in relation to his master, whom he interpreted to the world.'[21] Berger may have been his own Melanchthon to a large extent. (After all he has always been a convinced Lutheran.) He has also been director of the Institute for the Study of Economic Culture of Boston University since 1985. This is 'one of the most concrete ways in which Peter Berger has shaped the field.'[22] Rieff never 'interpreted himself to the world,' nor did he get 'disciples' who would do this for him. He also never held influential positions in major research institutes.

Another important difference between the careers of both writers is their reaction to counterculture. I have already mentioned that both severely criticized this cultural movement.[23] Whereas Berger was able to transform this criticism in widely read, academic books, Rieff reacted differently. Here I follow Kenneth Piver's assertion that 'a profoundly inner conversion has been at work and that *Fellow Teachers* is a snapshot of the transition.'[24] What precisely happened to Rieff is not clear yet, but it definitely had a detrimental effect. In *Fellow Teachers*, for example, Rieff chooses a stylistic means to criticize the way academic books are written and read: he chooses to develop many major theoretical ideas in very lengthy footnotes. Of course, Rieff was aware that the footnotes would be overlooked by most readers, except for the careful ones. In my opinion, this amounts to academic suicide. Rieff's vehement reaction to counterculture and its effect on academic life forced him to a retreat from public discourse – a retreat from which he would never recover. In an interview one of my interviews with Philip Rieff in 1999, he said that he regretted the style of *Fellow Teachers*. He wanted to experiment with another, more personal style. However, if he were to write the book again, he would choose another style, he said.

At present, 'a retour à Rieff' in social theory seems highly improbable. Rieff's work does not appeal to contemporary social science because the current concerns with poststructuralism and/or postmodernism no longer see psychoanalysis – an essentialist grand narrative – as relevant. There are few attempts to integrate psychoanalysis into social theory.[25] Furthermore, precisely because Rieff holds to the ideal of grand theory he does not fit in the pigeon-holes of the 'studies' approach that has overtaken academic research and teaching. Rieff's main contributions to his own discipline probably are his interdisciplinary investigations of a sociological theory of culture, a subject that has been one of sociology's stepchildren. In the sociological bestseller *Habits of the Heart*, Robert Bellah and his co-authors advocate the development of this field: 'It is that synoptic view, at once philosophical, historical, and sociological, that narrowly professional social science seems not so much capable of as uninterested in ... Such a social science does not need to be "reinvented," for the older tradition has survived side by side with narrowly professional social science and requires only to be encouraged and strenghened.'[26] This similarity with Rieff's work is not recognized in *Habits*, by the way. Bellah and colleagues only refer in footnotes to Rieff's ideas on the emergence of psychological man, citing his early works.

If any renewed interest in Rieff's work is to be expected, it should come from this kind of 'synoptic theorists.' Berger is one very important example of this. He evolved from a secularization theorist to a desecularization theorist. This brings him very close to theoretical questions that Rieff deals with in his later work on sacred order.

Rieff on Religion and (De)secularization

The issue of the fate of religion in modern Western culture must be addressed in an interdisciplinary way, combining theological, philosophical, and social-theoretical perspectives. But is it possible to do that with theories that exclude transcendence as a relevant category? In other words, what does Rieff's criticism of modern social theory mean for the interdisciplinary study of religion? This issue is dealt with in the first part of this chapter. In the second part I will show that Rieff developed from a 'classical theorist of secularization' to a theorist of 'post-secular culture.' The central question is: how does Rieff's work relate to the recent turn to 'desecularization' in social science, philosophy, and theology that we witness in the work of authors such as Peter Berger and Gianni Vattimo? To answer this question a preliminary task is to summarize Rieff's description of religion because the diagnosis by which we identify the place of religion in contemporary Western societies depends to a great extent on what definition of religion we use.

Interdisciplinary Theory: Rieff Compared with Milbank

It is striking that Rieff does not reflect explicitly on the problem of interdisciplinary theory in his published work. However, implicitly there are strong resonances of the problem aptly described by Clifford Geertz like this: 'The establishment of a common language in the social sciences is not a matter of mere coordination of terminologies or, worse yet, of coining artificial new ones; nor is it a matter of imposing a single set of categories upon the area as a whole. It is a matter of integrating different types of theories and concepts in such a way that one can formulate meaningful propositions embodying findings now sequestered in separate fields of study.'[27] Rieff wants to contribute to the development of this approach. The theories of the disciplines he draws from are as 'broken' as the 'late second culture' they examine, but Rieff's goal is to connect the theories of the humanities, social sciences, and theology. About his magnum opus he writes that 'if these books do their job, the humanities and the social sciences should be, in some signifying degree, reunited. I intend a unifying theory and praxis.'[28] The best example of that is how he gradually brings more and more theory and cultural phenomena under the common denominator of 'therapy,' which he develops into the even more encompassing concept of 'third world' in his magnum opus.

Rieff strives after unifying late 'second culture' thought in the humanities and social sciences. This implies a critique of all modern social theory that is meta-theoretically transformative, which means that it excludes transcendence as a relevant category in its theorizing. Only those strands of social scientific thought that are able to comprehend the proper place and role of transcendence in social and cultural processes can be unified with other theoretical perspectives into a theory of culture. At this point we may compare Rieff's position to that taken by the theologian John Milbank in his book *Theology and Social Theory*.[29] There Milbank asserts that modern social theory is inadequate for the study of religion because it is unable to comprehend transcendence as the essential characteristic of religion.

In *Theology and Social Theory*, Milbank uses a Foucauldian 'archeological' method and describes how the idea of the secular came into being as an invention of modern thought. First steps towards this were made in the thirteenth century. Later on they were elaborated into a 'new science of politics,' of which Machiavelli, Hobbes, and Spinoza are the great architects, according to Milbank. This modern political science opened up a new space for reflection, but could itself not comprehend the secular completely. This inherent and constitutive lack had to be supplemented in the eighteenth century by 'political economy' and 'speculative history,' and in the nineteenth century by the new disciplines of 'economics,' 'sociology,' and 'anthropology,' says Milbank.[30] He approaches the construct of 'the social' that is developed in these disciplines in a similar way. He also stresses the fact that theology played an important role in the development of the concepts of 'the secular' and 'the social.'

From a methodological point of view, Milbank makes the following important choice in developing his postmodern political theology: 'In retracing the genesis of sociology I have opened the way, not to denying "reduction to the social," but rather to casting doubt on the very idea of there being something "social" ... to which religious behaviour could be in any sense referred.'[31] Thus, Milbank deconstructs the modern constructs of the social and the secular. He denies that there is any social action definable or comprehensible apart from its peculiar linguistic manifestation, from the inexplicability of a particular symbolic system.[32] The construction of the objects of theology or the social sciences are inherently connected to the histories of these disciplines and their interaction. Milbank calls the modern social sciences 'new modern stories, which arose partially as an attempt to situate and confine faith itself.'[33] That has much in common with the way Rieff describes the emergence of modern social theory in his meta-theoretical terms, namely, as 'a response to the death of the gods and also as a weapon for killing off those surviving, somehow, in our moral unconscious and cultural conscience.'[34] As for the 'archeological' aspect of their theories, Rieff and Milbank seem to share their critical conclusions.

Milbank also rejects the idea that theology needs the mediation of the social sciences, in the sense that the social sciences present theology with a social object that is perfectly described and perfectly explained.[35] A major motif in Milbank's analyses of modern social theory is to demonstrate that this theory is based on an ontology ('meta-narrative') which is incompatible with Christian ontology (which is also the ontological basis of Christian theology). He therefore proposes to stop the dialogue between theology and the social sciences. At this point Rieff and Milbank seem to agree only partially. Rieff's meta-theoretical scheme also distinguishes sharply between the 'meta-narratives' of modern social theory and theology. In a later version of this scheme, namely, his theory of the second culture camp, he implies that the social sciences must be considered artefacts of the third world, based on transformative theory, whereas religion and theology are based on conformative theory and belong to the second world. These worlds are at war and thus incompatible. However, a fundamental difference occurs when we compare their ways of envisioning new approaches in developing theory. Milbank claims that theology has its own meta-narrative, including a vision on the social-historical dimensions of reality.[36] He thinks that (political) theology ought to be more self-conscious and develop this vision. This cannot be done in dialogue with the social sciences, which implies that Milbank rejects interdisciplinarity. Rieff chooses another option, namely, to try to reunify the humanities and social sciences. Working through the theoretical implications of this difference seems to me an important methodological contribution to an interdisciplinary theory of culture.[37]

Rieff on Religion

After our methodological inquiry, we now turn to one of the core issues of the debates on desecularization and new religion: the definition of religion. To describe the various meanings of the term 'religion' in Rieff's work, Peter Homans offers us a useful theoretical framework.[38] He argues that religious studies define religion in three ways: (1) as transcendence (theological orientation), (2) as order (sociological and social-anthropological orientation), and (3) as spontaneity (psychological orientation).[39] Each of these definitions of religion is, for the most part, in conflict with the other two, creating a pluralism at the level of religious thought which he considers the main problem in the scientific research concerning religion. I will give a short description of each of the three approaches.

Religion as transcendence: Studies of this type concentrate on the ontological and epistemological aspects of religion. Religion is interpreted as transcendence. The most typical gestalt of transcendence is that of a God whose existence is believed to lie beyond the realm of finite self-awareness. Homans refers to theological existentialism, which in the first instance gives an analysis of the human self in relation to dimensions of existence that are immanent, that is; accessible to human thought. This is followed up by an analysis of aspects of religion that relate to an order of existence that transcends the immanent. This order is called existential.[40]

Religion as order: In this type of studies religion is approached in terms of its capacity to confer order, primarily social order, upon life as a whole.[41] As in the theological orientation, the religious reality is conceived of as a reality beyond finite, human consciousness. However, such studies bracket the truth claims of this reality, by asserting that religion is a projection of immanent forces arising from the matrix of social and historical interaction. Furthermore, instead of a discussion of the transcendental character of religion, it seeks to analyse the structure of religion in terms of its capacities to confer order. Religion projects a system of images composing a cosmic order that unites ethos ('the mood and style of everyday life') and world-view by rendering the ideas of order socially convincing and thus creating certitude.

Religion as spontaneity: Here the focus is not upon epistemological or ontological aspects of a realm of existence which transcends human history, nor is it about roles, values, and norms which are mediated through the social order. Instead, religion is understood primarily in terms of affectivity and emotion expressing the spontaneous immediacy of personal consciousness. Religion is described as a highly experiential range of significant states of feeling encompassing many major moods of life, including joy, peace, and devotion, guilt, loyalty, obligation, mystery, wonder, and surrender. Insofar as elements of transcendence appear in this approach to religion, it is as objectified and organized forms of spontaneity in religious experience.[42]

In the next section I will sketch how Rieff approaches religion from each of the three perspectives. This is not the same as defining religion, which Rieff never does. He finds all efforts at doing that futile.[43] I will also deal with questions concerning the social scientific and theological study of religion that are implied in Rieff's approach of religion as transcendence and as order. (At that point I will leave out the category of religion as spontaneity, because it does not fit in Rieff's approach.)

Religion as Spontaneity

There is not much place for the idea of religion as 'organized spontaneity' in Rieff's theory because that is incompatible with his idea of the double dialectics of nature and culture or of expression and limitation. Religion does its work primarily in the controlling mode. As such it offers ways of expressing human desire. From a Rieffian point of view the idea of organized spontaneity is a contradictio in terminis. There is some room in Rieff's theory of religion for human spontaneity, but only as a secondary function of religion: as a remission of the controlling functions of religion that we can find in the ecstatic or orgiastic aspects of it. Probably for polemical reasons Rief stresses the importance of the controlling mode of religion. He undergirds this theoretically with a theory of transgressivity. He recognizes the cultural importance of transgressive behaviour, but the right to this kind of behaviour is in Rieff's view reserved to a cultural elite. This is closely connected to Rieff's definition of a cultural elite, which hinges on the idea that an elite consists of people who recognize the primacy of form as interdictory force and as the precondition for their transgressive activities.[44]

Religion as Transcendence

Rieff asserts that neither man nor the social order he lives in has an innate morality. The origin of morality is to be found in a transcendent cultural order ('the superior level of the cultural system') from which higher, organizing principles penetrate into the myriad of human activitities. The operation of these principles can be discerned in repression. Rieff revises Freud's theory of repression in such a way that repression refers to the operation of interdicts, which are the most elementary cultural forms. These interdicts are not 'human fictions,' but originate in the transcendent cultural or sacred order and are revealed to us. In his 'neo-conformative' theory, revelation is the concept with which Rieff describes the dynamic interaction between the sacred and the social order.

As for the social scientific study of religion, Rieff's introduction of the category of the sacred or transcendent touches the heart of sociology. In the introduction I referred to Bryan Wilson's analysis of the early sociological enterprise, that, on the one hand, accorded religion a central place in its interpretation of social development. On the other hand, however, it assumed that modernization of culture inevitably would lead to a decline of religion. This idea was elaborated as the secularization thesis. So 'the question of religion is historically inseparable from the subject matter of the social sciences,'[45] but gradually 'secularization' became the dominant paradigm to conceive of the relation between culture and religion. Religion was conceptualized as a withering 'function,' banished to the realm of the private. An exemplary case, according to Rieff, is the theory of Max Weber who in his approach to religion, as did Freud, took the passions as a starting point, rather than authority. What Weber calls different types of faiths, Rieff refers to as 'a functionalized psychology of motive.'[46] Weber's concept of faith reduces faith to therapy (in Rieff's cultural-theoretical sense).

Thus the secularization thesis was the main instrument with which modern social science tried to 'situate and confine faith.' Secularization primarily consists in the emergence of new ways of coming to grips with reality and changing it.[47] What has occurred during the past century can be viewed as follows: Independently, new conceptual models and specific methods have developed which, each in its particular way, attempted to amass knowledge and to alter reality. These models and practices were no longer concerned with the coherence of overall 'knowledge' nor with the general results of their independent interventions. 'The process of secularization deployed itself without having to justify itself. Religion was left at the side. Its language was not disputed. Rather, one merely placed another language next to it.'[48] The way Rieff introduces the category of the sacred in social science is his polemical response to this confining and neglecting of religion in contemporary social science.

Rieff asserts that the only way of escaping this inadequate approach to religion is by introducing transcendence as a category sui generis in social theory. It seems that Rieff wants to steer a middle course between two positions. One is that of theological existentialism. This confirms the autonomous status of the transcendent, but it does this through a strong apologetic reaction to the social sciences' criticism of religion.[49] This reaction implies a big problem for the interdisciplinary research of religion because it poses an unbridgeable gap between theology and the social sciences. Rieff wants to avoid this methodological dead end by asserting that religion can only be studied in its social and psychic forms of expression. But Rieff also rejects the reductionist approaches that reduce religion to these expressions and are blind to its sui generis character. One example of Rieff's approach is the theory of culture as the merging of illuminative and operative acts. Sacred order is revealed in illuminative acts that merge with operative acts.

In this sense, Rieff really is a 'prophet of a post-secular society.' Long before the present 'desecularization of the world' urged social theorists like Peter Berger to openly denounce the secularization thesis, Rieff rejected the thesis on theoretical grounds. The new models of thought and practice mentioned in the previous paragraph can be compared with Rieff's 'third worlds.' He does not leave religion at the side, but uses premodern religious thought as a critical perspective from which he analyses the 'third worlds' of modern culture. The crucial difference between faith and therapy in Rieff's theory of culture hinges precisely on the way the transcendent is conceived of. Thus he calls secularization theory to account.

Rieff's sacred sociology can be considered truly theological, according to Patrick Vandermeersch's description of the task of the theologian: 'For him, God's transcendence as well as the distinction between true faith and superstition are central themes.'[50] The traditional insistence that God abides in His own sphere, that His name is unspeakable, that His presence can be conceived only as absence, and the interdict against any depiction of God, all point to the unique character of the 'reality experience' which constitutes the core of religious faith, according to Vandermeersch. He specifies the task of the theologian as keeping this experience as pure as possible or, rather, in purifying it time and time again despite the distortions that arise when the experience is transmitted. The issue of the 'reality experience,' which constitutes the core of religious faith that Vandermeersch raises here, involves the problem of transcendence. For it is typical for this type of reality experience that it involves us in a participation in the sacred. This participation has become highly problematic in modern culture. At this point, too, there is an important connection to the work of John Milbank. To explain this, I need to refer back to the section on Rieff's style. We saw that a salient feature of Rieff's style was the capacity to evoke the feeling of being cut off from the past, of discontinuity, that comes with modernity. Rieff, like Milbank, would trace this disrupting effect of modernity to the core problem that man is cut off from the experience of participation in the sacred. Rieff responds to this problem by writing about the sacred only in a poetic scientific prose. Reading it invokes an experience in which one feels the object of it – the sacred, at work, although always at a proper distance.

With the form and substance of his theory of sacred order, Rieff calls into question what Milbank termed 'the entire post-Scotist legacy of modern thought.' 'It was Duns Scotus who for the first time established a radical separation of philosophy from theology,' says Milbank. 'Eventually this generated the notion of an ontology and epistemology unconstrained by, and transcendentally prior to, theology itself ... By contrast, in the Church Fathers or the early scholastics, both faith and reason are included within the more generic framework of participation in the mind of God.'[51] The comparitive research that I proposed earlier of Rieff's work with Milbank's, from a methodological perspective, may take this issue of participation in the mind of God as its starting point. Finally, both Rieff and Milbank contribute to a new theory of religion, in which its social and transcendent aspects are conceived of in a non-reductionistic manner.

Religion as Order

We saw that in Rieff's theory of culture the religious problem is identical with the moral and the moral with the cultural. Rieff says that our inner lives cannot be expressed as such, but need modes of communication between what is inside ourselves and what is outside. In these processes the individual externalizes his or her inner life and thus becomes a social being. Every culture produces its communication modes, its aesthetic. I have shown that this theoretical position must not be viewed as a reduction of religion to morality, or of religion to culture, but instead as a theoretical enterprise aimed at developing interdisciplinary theory that escapes the functionalization of religion (and authority). What we usually call 'culture' is the result of an interaction between higher formative and organizing principles and human possibility. Religion plays an important role in this, without being totally absorbed by it.

I clarified Rieff's view on this point by referring to the concept of interior space. This can be considered a counterpart of the concept of symbolic order. Before going into that I must make a preliminary terminological remark. Whereas symbol theory is very important in Rieff's work, he never uses the term 'symbolic order.' My explanation would be that Rieff wants to do justice to the fragmented nature of late modern culture. In that culture there are symbolics, but there is not a symbolic *order*.[52] Equally significant is the fact that he starts using the term 'sacred order' in his later works. Apparently it is necessary to introduce the element of order to develop his neo-conformative idea of postmodern culture in which the dialectic between sacred order and social order is restored.

So, we may understand Rieff's concept of interior space more accurately as a counterpart to the symbolic in culture. In this interior space religion does its work, together with morality. I described Rieff's ideas about this under the heading of the primary cultural process. In that process human desire receives its form, which is at the same time a limitation of possibilities. Rieff distinguishes two religious modes, an erotic and a doctrinal or controlling one, which are merged. In the doctrinal mode of faith a doctrine is internalized, thus becoming functionally anti-instinctual. In the other mode faith is ecstatic or erotic; then the instincts can express themselves more directly in orgiastic behaviour or in mystic states of mind that release the subject from traditional authority. In *Triumph of the Therapeutic* these modes are relatively equal to each other. In his later works Rieff develops his theory of the interdicts and calls the controlling mode primary.

Rieff says that religion does not influence all aspects of life, but only those that give a certain assurance of salvation, whatever that may mean concretely in a specific cultural situation. In his theory of culture this salvation refers to a state of being released from a multitude of conflicting desires. This assurance is the basis for adequate moral behaviour because it stems from an identification with the ruling character-ideal which is so strong that the tuning of the individual's instinctive impulses to this ideal succeeds.

According to Rieff, these processes take place in the cultus of a culture. In the cultus the individual communicates with the interior space of culture, with instruments provided for by culture, like liturgy, academic teaching, or the arts. In *Fellow Teachers*, for example, Rieff defines the tasks of academic teaching as performing the 'scores' of our dead masters. When performed adequately, God enlivens their minds in us, so that we can see what lives in them. Then we can communicate with the interior space shaped by them and thus inherit our share in the living authority of our great predecessors. This is an example of the idea of 'penetration of higher, organizing principles from the superior level of culture (or cultural order) into the myriad of human activitities.' It also illustrates how the liturgical, pedagogic, aesthetic, and ethical merge in Rieff's theory.[53] The idea of transliteration of sacred order into social order from Rieff's later works sets forth this line of thinking. I take it to be a cultural-theoretical version of the theological concept of the incarnation of the creative word (*logos*). This theoretical paradigm of how culture works can be applied to specific cultural realms, like liturgy, the arts, and the sciences, in order to decipher the working of culture of which they are reflections. Thus Rieff's work presents a provocative view of the role of religion in a culture, which must be sought inside the walls of the church as well as outside. Religion is operative in all cultural realms. The modes of operation change because of cultural changes. I will elaborate on that in the next section.

To conclude this section I will highlight one very important criticism of Rieff's views on the relationship between religion and culture. In Rieff's thought religion and the arts are closely connected, yet he rejects what he calls 'a religion of art,' referring to the modern idea that the arts can take over the role of religion as a mediation of the sacred. This reflects Rieff's idea that the arts and sciences are the secondary cultural process, in which the cultural principles that stem from the primary cultural process get their cultural forms. Interdicts are the primary form of culture, says Rieff. Is Rieff's theory of culture thus safeguarded against reductionism? Christopher Lasch does not think so. Lasch accuses Rieff of developing a 'religion of culture.'[54] He asserts that since *Fellow Teachers* Rieff has increasingly developed a religious definition of culture, in which he considers culture the essential source of social order. This implies that Rieff's conceptualization of religion is functionalist, says Lasch, however much Rieff himself maintains that he rejects the ideas of Kant, Freud, and Weber on this point: 'Culture may well depend on religion ... but religion has no meaning if it is seen merely as a prop of culture.'[55] Rieff, contends Lasch, fell prey to the same confusion of faith and institution when (in *Fellow Teachers*) he called the university 'a sacred institution' and described academic teaching as an initiation into the cultus of culture. Rieff then identifies the sacred too unambiguously with the institutions and the interdicts they enforce. About this confusion of faith with institution Luther and Calvin were very clear a long time ago, says Lasch.

Unfortunately, Lasch does not mention explicitly the later works of Rieff that he refers to in his criticism; therefore it remains unclear to what texts Lasch is referring exactly. Reading Rieff's articles from the 1990s I would say that he is more ambiguous than Lasch asserts. An essential point in Rieff's theory of the relationship between sacred and social order is that, as I assume intentionally, he leaves profound ambiguities intact. On the one hand, Rieff says that there are intimate connections between the sacred and the social. But on the other hand, the sacred always retains its transcendent character and can never be reduced to its social forms. Sacred order can be studied in no other forms than those it acquires in the secondary cultural processes, but the most elementary forms of culture belong to the primary cultural process and are therefore always transcendent. Rieff does not assert that religion is totally absorbed in its cultural functions and institutions or that the sacred is totally absorbed in the secondary cultural processes.

Rieff on 'True Religion'

The present 'desecularization of the world' urges us to redefine the secularization thesis. Instead of a decline of religion this upsurge of religion in various forms may testify to a cultural process in which religion acquires new forms that are gradually replacing traditional forms. This thesis, however, implies an important critical question: how do we justify calling this 'new religion' a 'true religion'? Is it not merely a 'pseudo-religion,' as Bryan Wilson asserts?[56] This invites the question of how we can study the relationship between traditional and new religion critically. The theoretical issue at stake is how to develop criteria to compare old and new forms of religion consistently. Wilson develops two criteria for 'true religion,' namely, 'reference to the supernatural' and 'effective social utopianism' (i.e., the ability to create and legitimate projects and action with the aim of transforming society). Wilson eliminates most of the so-called human potential movements, and in particular those influenced by New Age, because the former criterion is frequently present, but the latter is generally absent.

How does this relate to Rieff's theory? Rieff also criticizes the form of religion that was assessed so brilliantly by Bellah and colleagues in *Habits of the Heart.* They show that in America new religion may have different forms, and they all have one feature in common: they hold freedom and individuality as central values.[57] In this religion the self is deified, which makes it 'therapeutic' in Rieff's critical sense. In Rieff's theory, deifying the self cuts us off from the supernatural. That is how he distinguishes 'faith' from 'therapy.' So, the appeal to the supernatural may be present in self-seeking new religion, but Rieff would not consider this as real openness to the transcendent. As for the other criterion, I think it is more complicated to compare Rieff's theory with Wilson's assessment of these forms of 'new religion.' Rieff has been very critical in making transforming reality a central notion in the study of religion. He tends to identify religion with conformity. However, we must be careful to view this as straightforward conservatism. Rieff's stressing of conformity versus transformation of reality clearly is polemical. I also showed that Rieff is aware of the necessity of the category of change because no culture or religion is immutable.

Another aspect of the rise of new religion is the resurgence of religious fundamentalism throughout the world. Rieff's work contributes to the study of this phenomenon, too, as Lauren Langman has pointed out recently. I will summarize his valuation of this phenomenon from a Rieffian perspective. Fundamentalism, says Langman, is a response to the stress and moral challenges caused by rapid social change. It is a rapidly spreading return to more 'traditional' religious beliefs and practices. Fundamentalism can be understood as the 'triumph of repression over desire.' The decadence of secular modernity, which includes sexual equality and erotic freedom, the sterility of rationality, and, most of all, challenges to traditional authority structures, identities, and morals, has evoked a compensatory regression that demands subjugation to its stern moral dictates. But this subjugation destroys the artistic and aesthetic freedom that a cultural elite requires. 'While they may well reconstitute communities of faith, between their anti–intellectualism and censoring moralism, they are the enemies of culture.'[58] Langman's assessment from a Rieffian perspective makes clear that religious fundamentalism, like New Age–type religions, also lacks features that would justify calling this phenomenon truly religion. Each religion ought to provide for the artistic and aesthetic freedom that a cultural elite requires. Without this freedom the danger of petrification of religious tradition is lurking.

In sum, Rieff's theory is a valuable contribution to the development of social theoretic concepts that enable us to assess the present upsurge of religion in its many varieties. Langman beautifully describes the essence of Rieff's work like this: 'Where can we find myths, beliefs and communities that would preserve our culture? Philip Rieff made us examine such questions; that was his mission.'[59]

Rieff and Desecularization Theory

In his early works, Rieff seems to be a classical theorist of secularization. Based on his psychohistorical model of the four ideal character types of Western culture, Rieff develops his thesis of the 'triumph of the therapeutic.' The inheritance of our cultural tradition becomes inaccessible because in modernity 'faith' is completely replaced by 'therapeutic thinking.' The latter is based on a wholly new Weltanschauung. Rieff's position becomes more complex in his later work. Thinking in terms of cultural discontinuity remains present in his works as one pole, but he juxtaposes another pole, thinking in terms of continuity between religion and late modern culture. At the beginning of the 1980s Rieff suggests very carefully that 'we may be at the end of modernist inversions of sacred order.'[60] Yet at the end of that decade he states explicitly that the sacred can never be deconstructed and that we always live in sacred order. Thus in Rieff's works an ambivalent tension develops between thinking in terms of continuity and thinking in terms of discontinuity, which gets shape in his theory of 'second culture camp' (second Kulturkampf). This method is otherwise not a fundamental change in Rieff's theory, but a shift of focus. Elements that were already present in earlier work are elaborated in later work. For example, Rieff's methodology of reading authors as '*negational theorists of sacred order*' from his magnum opus of the 1990s, could already be found in *Triumph of the Therapeutic* in 1966.

The concept of 'negational theory of sacred order' is based on an intriguing idea. Interpreting the works of atheist modern artists or scientists as intimations of this negational theory presupposes that the sacred was never absent from modern Western culture. It was merely repressed and, according to psychoanalytic logic, returned in distorted forms. Rieff's theory of sacred order is based on the shift in focus of his research that I indicated in Chapter 6. Rieff inverts the modernist perspective on authority. Rieff is not looking for the origin of repression – as locus of the origin of authority – but instead for the origin of the pleasure that modern man takes in lowering acts that must lead to a liberation of the influence of traditional authority. Rieff asserts that the central motif in modern Western culture is to break down the 'primacy of the interdictory form' and to replace it by the 'primacy of possibility.' In the following two sections I will argue that this shift in Rieff's work is well in line with the current shift to desecularization theory in the sociological and philosophical study of religion.

Religion as 'Hidden Ground' of Modernity

A preliminary point to be made is that it is not obviously appropriate to relate Rieff's work to the debates on the secularization hypothesis because he has always refused to use the term 'secularization.' This refusal is based on 'doubts that penetrative thrust inheres in the concept 'secularization.'[61] Rieff criticizes secularization theory because he thinks that it prevents research from getting to the real point at stake, which is the shifting role of authority in culture and of the religion that is based on this traditional authority. Secularization theory too easily postulates that (traditional) religion is in decline and that its role has been taken over by substitutes like art and science.[62] Based on this criticism, Rieff chooses to elaborate his theory of culture as a theory of 'authority in sacred order.' Rieff's thinking in terms of cultural discontinuity in his early work may in many ways resemble secularization theory as far as the fate of religion in modern Western culture is concerned. But on theoretical grounds, which he developed in his texts from 1973 to 1992, Rieff concludes that 'secularization' is impossible. The heart of culture is the interdict. This can only be denied, but never changed. The arts and sciences are not religion's successors. On the contrary, modern art and science have been fascinated by religion but have never succeeded in laying bare its essence. This problem is brilliantly assessed in Rieff's magnum opus texts with the method of interpretation of these arts and sciences as a negational theory of sacred order. In this way, Rieff laid bare that religion, as embodiment of the sacred, has always been the 'hidden ground' of modernity.

From this perspective, Rieff was a forerunner of the current debates on the secularization thesis. In 1975 Norman Brown wrote that 'the first thing to be said about "Fellow Teachers" is that it anticipated the return of the gods: Rieff rediscovers the necessity for the category of the sacred.'[63] At present the classical secularization thesis is being questioned in the sociology of religion because religion remains a substantial political and cultural factor worldwide. Cultural modernization has some secularizing effect, mainly because it ingrained plurality in our cultures. Plurality relativizes everything, including religion.[64] But modernization also provoked powerful movements of 'desecularization.' Second, religious institutions may have lost power and influence in Western culture, but old and new religious practices and beliefs have nevertheless continued in the lives of individuals.[65] Thus Rieff's elaboration of a theory of sacred order accords well with the 'turn to desecularization' in the contemporary sociologal and philosophical study of religion.

I will further illustrate my point with an example of the work of an important social theorist on desecularization, Danièle Hervieu-Léger, concerning the issue of the differences between American civil religion and 'Eurosecularity.' At stake is the complex problem of the relationship between culture and religion. I will show that Hervieu-Léger's theoretical position comes close to Rieff's. Hervieu-Léger is responding to Peter Berger, who brought up the issue of 'Eurosecularity.' Berger's argument goes like this: Compared with other parts of the world, Europe (and Canada) remain highly secularized. This matches with the secularization thesis, because this theory explains the decline of religion as a consequence of modernization. But how then to explain the huge and increasing influence of religion in the United States, undoubtedly the most modern nation of the world? 'One of the most interesting puzzles in the sociology of religion is why Americans are so much more religious as well as more churchly than Europeans,' says Berger.[66]

Hervieu-Léger replies to this by asking whether Europe is really as secularized as Berger maintains. She concedes that 'objective secularization' (in which the political sphere became autonomous from religion) and 'subjective secularization' (the emancipation of individual consciousness from ecclestical doctrine) are pervasive in Europe.[67] But that does not mean the end of religion. Europe does not have a civil religion like the United States does, but religion is merged with culture in different ways. To assess this issue, Hervieu-Léger agrees with Berger that secularization theory must be rejected as a general theory of explanation. How religion and culture are related can only be examined by contextualizing research. To proceed in this direction, Hervieu-Léger proposes two research perspectives: (1) a *genealogical* perspective, from which the different historical trajectories are studied in which modernity was constructed and the specific way religion inscribed itself in this, and (2) a *geographical* perspective, from which the institutions and collective actions, as well as the conscience and imagination of individuals ('mentalities') are studied that were embedded in the long run in a given society.[68] She mentions France as a particularly illuminating case because nowhere in Europe has institutional religion been further excluded from any social role than in that country. But in France, as in many other European countries, the nature and style of politics, the substance of political debates, the definition of public and private responsibility, etc., take shape in contexts in which religion remains a potent influencing factor.[69] Hervieu-Léger summarizes this with the following 'formula' of Jean-Paul Willaime: 'France is a secular (*laïque*) country whose culture is Catholic.'[70]

Hervieu-Léger's point is that this persisting influence of religion functions in a different way than it used to. It does not work primarily through churches that exercise their normative authority, but in more elusive ways, through the symbolic structures that the churches devised and that have permeated the culture. I think that this revision of secularization theory brings us near to basic issues of Rieff's work. Like Bellah, Hervieu-Léger pleads for a 'synoptic view,' at once philosophical, historical, and sociological. It takes this synoptic view to grasp the complex ways culture(s) and religion(s) are interrelated. I think that Rieff's theory of the dialectic between sacred order and social order is a powerful contribution to this theoretical development in the sociology of religion, which enables us to study more adequately the complex relations between culture and religion. More precisely, I think that Rieff's work is an important contribution to an elaboration of cultural-sociological theories of religion that deal with 'the anxieties of Tocqueville or Durkheim as to the future of democratic societies faced with the implications of renouncing ... the notion that there is a transcendent basis for social order.'[71] As for research on European societies, Rieff's work may be more useful than that of Berger, who is far more popular. Berger's perspective is clearly more American than Rieff's. This is another issue to be explored further.

Neo-conformative Theory and Postmodern Philosophy

The 'turn to desecularization' is an important theme in contemporary philosophy, as well. According to Jürgen Habermas, for example, we live in a 'postsecular society' since 11 September 2001.[72] Habermas seems to hold that this turn to religion implies a crisis of secularization. However, it seems more adequate to speak of a crisis of the *discourse* of secularization, as is illustrated by the discussions of the sociology of religion covered above. The underlying philosophical issue is the following: Postmodern philosophy denies the possibility of grounding reality in a metaphysical order of existence. This way of thinking presupposed the classic ontology that is rejected by postmodern philosophy. However, the upsurge of religion worldwide forced postmodern philosophy to put the theme of metaphysics high on the agenda again. How to take up the theme of metaphysics without regressing into old philosophical schemes that were previously rejected? In this section I want to indicate briefly that this topic pertains directly to the main theoretical thrust of Rieff's work, which is to develop what I call a 'neo-conformative theory.'

First I will summarize what the rejection of classical ontology by postmodern philosophy amounts to. In premodern Western culture metaphysics was based on the belief in an ideal world order, in a kingdom of essences that transcend empirical reality. This belief was thought to be the precondition for knowledge of reality and a criticism of the limits of this knowledge. In modernity, this metaphysical way of thinking was criticized and then replaced by other schemes for thinking about reality. The trajectories used to develop this criticism and devising alternatives vary. This is not the place to deal with that issue and the discussions they imply.[73] With an eye to Rieff's work the main issue of relevance is that it is broadly accepted that it is not necessary to believe anymore in an 'ideal order of existence' in order to construct a view on reality. The existence of God need not necessarily be denied anymore, but with the death of the classic ontology, the old ways of thinking about God were abandoned, too. Thus God is no longer the almighty architect of existence, ruling His creation from a realm outside. He has become a 'weak God' whose relation to His creation must be thought of in totally new ways that break through old dualistic schemes in which the transcendent is pitted against the immanent.

How does this 'weak ontology' relate to Rieff's idea of the transcendent? The first step is to relate it to Rieff's meta-theoretical scheme, more precisely to the term 'conformative.' As I made clear in Chapter 2, Rieff's description of conformative theory is precisely a circumscription of classical ontology. In a later chapter I labelled Rieff's theory of sacred order 'neo-conformative' because Rieff's theory of the interdict seems to presuppose this premodern ontology. The interdict is the form that helps us express our inner lives. It is through the fact that we are confronted with interdicts that we become aware of these otherwise inexpressible lives. I think Rieff's theory of the dialectic between desire and interdict is neo-conformative because the interdict seems to play the same role as faith did in classical ontology, where it was the precondition for knowledge of reality and a criticism of the limits of this knowledge. Rieff sees the function of the interdict as the way of 'bringing mankind to conform to the eternal and stable order of things as they really are.'

Rieff's choice of terms is provocative. The idea of conforming oneself to a pre-established cultural and moral order was and remains scandalizing, in a culture where individual autonomy is a core value. Rieff is clearly polemical here. He is very well aware that the premodern cultural order he refers to in his meta-theoretical scheme has receded into history. Late modern culture is fragmented. By using the prefix 'neo' I want to indicate that Rieff brings to the fore the problem of order in this new situation of cultural fragmentation. Maybe Rieff's theory of the interdict and the intimacy of repression can be interpreted as an attempt to envision a new localization of sacred authority, in a culture where traditional, institutionalized forms of authority and the sacred are waning. But then new questions arise, such as: How does Rieff's theory of the intimicy of repression relate to the concept of 'weak ontology'? What does Rieff's theory of the sacred, based on a theory of the aesthetics of authority, contribute to theological reflection on new gestalts of religion in a post-secular era?

I hope that by now I have made clear that Philip Rieff's work is far from obsolete and that it pertains to crucial theoretical questions of contemporary sociological, theological, and philosopical theories of culture, religion, and morality. I hope my book is a contribution to an adequate understanding of Rieff's work and its relevance. Research on this issue may get a new impulse when Rieff's trilogy is published. The present situation (September 2004) is that the faculty board of the University of Virginia Press has approved publication of the trilogy. Three scholars are preparing an introduction, each for one volume, and Kenneth Piver is general editor. The projected titles of the volumes and dates of publication are: *My Life among the Deathworks* (volume 1, 2005), *The Ultimate Murderer of Moses* (volume 2, 2006), and *Crises of the Officer Class* (volume 3, 2007).[74]

Notes

Introduction

1 Friedrich Nietzsche, *The Gay Science: With a Prelude in German Rhymes and an Appendix of Songs*, ed. B. Williams, trans. J. Nauckhoff (Cambridge: Cambridge University Press, 2001), pp. 119–20.

2 See Peter L. Berger, 'The Desecularization of the World: A Global Overview,' in Peter L. Berger (ed.), *The Desecularization of the World: Resurgent Religion and World Politics* (Grand Rapids, MI: Eerdmans, 1999), pp. 1–18.

3 According to Alexander, the term 'modernity' stems from the fifth century CE and has since become fashionable again twice, with different meanings, in the late Middle Ages and in the era of the Enlightenment. See Jeffrey C. Alexander, 'Modern, Anti, Post and Neo: How Social Theorists Have Tried to Understand the "New World" of "Our Time,"' *Zeitschrift für Soziologie* 23(3) (1994), p. 167. For Rieff 'modernity' is a term invented in the Enlightenment which we still use, with connotations like (scientific) rationality, progress, and individualization.

4 Bryan Wilson, 'The Return of the Sacred,' *Journal for the Scientific Study of Religion* 18(3) (1979), p. 269.

5 See 'Worlds at War: Illustrations of an Aesthetics in Authority; or Numbered Notes towards a Trilogy, of which the General Title is 'Sacred Order / Social Order,' in Eileen Barker, James A. Beckford, and Karel Dobbelaere (eds.), *Secularization, Rationalism and Sectarianism: Essays in Honour of Bryan R. Wilson* (Oxford: Clarendon Press, 1993), pp. 214–65.

6 Philip Rieff, *The Triumph of the Therapeutic: Uses of Faith after Freud* (Chicago: University of Chicago Press, 1987 [1966]), p. 4.

7 Rieff explicitly mentions these two terms only in *Triumph*. In my interpretation of Rieff's work I gave them a central function because they are very use-

ful for my present purpose. I will show that in later works Rieff uses other terms that refer to the same phenomena.

8 See Philip Rieff, *Freud: The Mind of the Moralist* (Chicago: University of Chicago Press, 1979 [1959]), p. 19.

1 A Bird's-Eye View of Rieff's Life and Work

1 As yet there is no biography of Rieff available. Most of the biographical data in this chapter I took from three interviews I had with Rieff in June 1999. Other sources are mentioned in the notes. A very useful text which describes Rieff's academic career and his main publications is Kenneth S. Piver, 'Philip Rieff: The Critic of Psychoanalysis as Cultural Theorist,' in Mark S. Micale and Roy Porter (eds.), *Discovering the History of Psychiatry* (New York/Oxford: Oxford University Press, 1994). A shorter, more popularizing article is Stephan Goode, 'In Praise of Things Past,' *Insight*, 8 March 1992, pp. 12–14, pp. 28–9.

2 I distinguish three main periods in Rieff's academic career: the early period from 1949 to 1966, the middle period from 1967 to 1972, and the later period from 1973 onward. This distinction is based on the date of appearance and the contents of Rieff's main publications.

3 See Richard H. King, 'From Creeds to Therapies: Philip Rieff's Work in Perspective,' *Reviews in American History*, June 1976, p. 291.

4 Ibid., 292.

5 Eugene Goodheart, 'A Postscript to the Higher Criticism: The Case of Philip Rieff,' *The Failure of Criticism* (Cambridge: Harvard University Press, 1978), p. 186 n4.

6 For reviews of *Freud: The Mind of the Moralist*, see Perry Lefevre, 'A Penultimate Ethic of Honesty,' *Christian Scholar* 43 (1959), pp. 329–34; John Dollard, 'Society, Too, Is on the Couch,' *New York Times Book Review*, 22 March 1959, pp. 7 and 26; Gordon Wright and Arthur Mejia Jr, *An Age of Controversy, Discussion Problems in Twentieth Century European History* (New York: Dodd, Mead & Co., 1964), pp. 416–21; and Philip Toynbee, 'Critique of Freud,' *Encounter*, April 1960, pp. 73–6. A later, also very positive, review if that in Richard H. King, 'From Creeds to Therapies: Philip Rieff's Work in Perspective,' *Reviews in American History*, June 1976, pp. 291–6. A very negative review by Frank Auld appears in *Religious Education* 55 (March-April 1960), pp. 153–5.

7 Sheldon D. Pollack, 'The Elusive Freud,' *Psychoanalytic Review* 71(4) (1984), p. 519.

8 Rieff published his first article in 1949. In the 1950s, 1960s, and early 1970s

Rieff's articles and book reviews were published in mainstream magazines such as *Commentary*, *Encounter*, *Partisan Review*, and *American Sociological Review*. A 'Bibliographia Rieffiana' can be found in Philip Rieff, *The Feeling Intellect: Selected Writings*, ed. Jonathan B. Imber (Chicago: University of Chicago Press, 1990), pp. 375–85. This bibliography is no longer complete because in the 1990s Rieff published two more, and important, articles (see the References in the present volume).

9 For a complete listing of Rieff's academic appointments, see Kenneth S. Piver, Philip Rieff: The Critic of Psychoanalysis as Cultural Theorist' in Mark Micale and Roy Porter (eds.), *Discovering the History of Psychiatry* (New York/ Oxford: Oxford University Press, 1994), pp. 191–215.

10 David Rieff, *Slaughterhouse* (London Vintage Books, 1996).

11 Philip Rieff (ed.), *The Collected Papers of Sigmund Freud* (New York: Collier-Macmillan, 1963), 10 vols.

12 Rieff reviewed this first American edition. Philip Rieff, 'He Discovered a New Image of Man,' *New York Times Book Review*, 19 July 1959, p. 1, 16.

13 Pollack, 'Elusive Freud,' p. 519. Marcuse was one of the leading theorists of the counterculture of the 1960s and 1970s. See Theodore Roszak, *The Making of a Counter Culture: Reflections on the Technocratic Society and Its Youthful Opposition* (London: Faber and Faber, 1970 [1968]).

14 See Jerry Z. Muller, 'A Neglected Conservative Thinker,' *Commentary* 91(2) (1991), p. 50.

15 'New Left' is a collective noun for those intellectuals who sympathized with Marxism as a theory and world-view, but not or to a much lesser extent with its institutional forms. The latter was a reaction to developments in the American Communist Party. (See Charles Kadushin, *The American Intellectual Elite* (Boston: Little, Brown, 1974), p. 13.

16 See Pollack, 'Elusive Freud,' p. 520.

17 Kadushin, *American Intellectual Elite*, p. 228.

18 Ibid.

19 Philip Rieff, *Fellow Teachers/of Culture and Its Second Death* (Chicago: University of Chicago Press, 1985 [1972]). Rieff had early premonitions of the changes in the academy induced by counterculture, as can be found in the article by Philip Rieff entitled 'The Mirage of College Politics,' *Harper's Magazine* 223, no. 1337 (1961), pp. 156–63.

20 Piver, 'Rieff,' p. 192.

21 However, Rieff is never straightforward. He muffles his own voice by writing mainly in the form of exposition. Whether this should be called a 'guise of exposition,' as Fine and Manning have suggested, is open to discussion. See Gary A. Fine and Philip Manning, 'Preserving Philip Rieff: The Reputation

of a Fellow Teacher,' *Journal of Classical Sociology* 3(3) (2003), p. 232. It may well be that Rieff has, e.g., pedagogical reasons for this mode of writing.

22 George Steiner, 'Sermon for Prophets' (review of *Fellow Teachers*), *Sunday Times*, 29 March 1975, page number unknown. Other reviews of *Fellow Teachers* are by Robert Boyers, V. Shiva Naipaul, Frank Kermode, and C.P. Snow.

23 Imber now teaches sociology at Wellesley College near Boston, Massachusetts. He edited a collection of Rieff's selected writings (*The Feeling Intellect*) and was appointed by Rieff as his literary executor.

24 Rieff, *The Feeling Intellect*, p. ix.

25 See: Frank Kermode, 'That Uncertain Feeling' (review of *Fellow Teachers*), *Times Literary Supplement*, 13 June 1975, pp. 638–9.

26 See Robert Boyers (ed.), *Psychological Man* (New York: Harper and Row, 1975), pp. 1–2.

27 *Salmagundi*, no. 20 (summer-fall 1972).

28 Rieff, *Fellow Teachers*, p. 1.

29 See Boyers, *Psychological Man*, pp. 1–2.

30 Ibid.

31 Rieff, *Triumph*, p. 2.

32 Christopher Lasch, 'The Saving Remnant' (review of *The Feeling Intellect*), *New Republic*, 19 Nov. 1990, p. 34. The twelfth chapter of Lasch's *The Revolt of the Elites and the Betrayal of Democracy* (New York: Norton, 1995), pp. 213–29), entitled 'Philip Rieff and the Religion of Culture,' is a short and good introduction to Rieff's work from the early and middle period.

33 Kadushin, *American Intellectual Elite.* The only reference to Rieff in this book is the publication about intellectuals that Rieff edited entitled *On Intellectuals, Theoretical Studies / Case Studies* (New York: Doubleday, 1969).

34 Personal communication with Piver, June 1999.

35 Piver, 'Rieff,' p. 193 and personal communication, June 1999.

36 C.P. Snow, 'Parochial Spies' (review of *Fellow Teachers*), *Financial Times*, Feb. 1975, page number unknown.

37 See note 26.

2 Rieff's Reading of Freudian Metapsychology

1 Philip Rieff (ed.), *The History of the Psychoanalytic Movement*, vol. 1, *The Collected Papers of Sigmund Freud* (New York: Collier-Macmillan, 1963), p. 10.

2 Rieff presupposes a lot of historical data about Freud and psychoanalysis in his writings, which make them hard to follow for less informed readers. Where necessary I refer to historical data taken from Peter Gay's biography of Freud entitled *Freud: A Life for Our Time* (London: J.M. Dent, 1988).

3 Rieff, *History*, p. 10.
4 See: Rieff, ibid., p. 45.
5 Philip Rieff, *Freud: The Mind of the Moralist* (Chicago: University of Chicago Press, 1979) p. 29. For the typification 'physiological versus psychological' see ibid., pp. 13–17.
6 Rieff follows Freud's description of basic concepts in his *History*, spread through several passages of this book. In a later article, called 'Psychoanalysis' (1922), Freud summarizes this succinctly: '*The Corner-stones of Psychoanalytic Theory.* – The assumption that there are unconscious mental processes, the recognition of the theory of resistance and repression, the appreciation of the importance of sexuality and of the Oedipus complex ... No one who cannot accept them all should count himself a psychoanalyst.' Rieff, *Character and Culture*, vol. 9, *Collected Papers*, p. 244.
7 Rieff, *History*, p. 14.
8 Ibid., p. 22.
9 Ibid., p. 17.
10 Ibid.
11 Ibid., p. 21. In this passage Rieff plays with the terms 'to choose' and 'to be chosen.' He also writes: 'Gods choose; men are chosen' (ibid., p. 21), which is a notion that has become inconceivable to modern man.
12 Patrick G.M. Vandermeersch, *Ethiek tussen wetenschap en ideologie* (*Ethics between Science and Ideology*) (Leuven: Peeters, 1987), p. 23.
13 Rieff, *History*, p. 15. Rieff's description of the role of religion in premodern culture is very similar to that of Marcel Gauchet. Gauchet described the essence of the relationship between religion and society in premodern societies like this: 'The key to the inter-relationship between religion and society ... lies in its radical conservatism which structurally combines co-presence to the origin with disjunction from the originary moment, combining unstinting conformity to what has been definitively founded with a separated foundation.' *The Disenchantment of the World: A Political History of Religion*, trans. Oscar Burge (Princeton: Princeton University Press, 1997 [1985], p. 25.
14 Rieff, *History*, p. 15.
15 Ibid.
16 Philip Rieff, 'History, Psychoanalysis, and the Social Sciences,' *Ethics* 63(2) (1953), pp. 109–10.
17 Ibid., p. 110 and n22.
18 'Therapy' thus means more than 'psychotherapy' in Rieff's thinking. In chapters 4 and 5 I will return to this subject.
19 Philip Rieff, without title, review of W.M. Simon, *European Positivism in the*

Nineteenth Century: An Essay in Intellectual History, *American Sociological Review* 30(5) (1965), p. 790.

20 Philip Rieff, review of *Communication and Social Order*, by H.D. Duncan, *American Sociological Review* 29(4) (1964), p. 603.

21 Philip Rieff, review of *Education and Sociology*, by E. Durkheim, *American Sociological Review* 22(2), (1957), p. 233.

22 See Rieff, *Mind*, p. 18.

23 Ibid., p. 14.

24 Ibid., p. 15.

25 Ibid., p. 339.

26 Rieff has always polemicized against the tendency to model social science after the positivist and empiricist scientific ideal. A good example can be found in Rieff's appreciative review of Franz Rosenzweig's *Understanding the Sick and the Healthy: A View of the World, Man and God* (1954): entitled 'On Frans Rosenzweig,' in *The Feeling Intellect: Selected Writings*, ed. by Jonathan B. Imber (Chicago: University of Chicago Press, 1990), pp. 97–8.

27 Rieff, *Mind*, p. 20.

28 Ibid., p. 29.

29 Ibid., p. 31.

30 Ibid., p. 34.

31 Ibid.

32 Ibid., pp. 35–6.

33 Ibid., p. 36.

34 Ibid., p. 37.

35 See ibid.

36 Ibid., p. 48.

37 Ibid., p. 46.

38 Ibid., p. 47.

39 Sigmund Freud, *Totem and Taboo*, vol. 13, *The Complete Psychological Works of Sigmund Freud*, Standard Edition (London: Hogarth Press, 1953 [1913]), p. 90, cited by Rieff in *Mind*, p. 47.

40 Rieff, *Mind*, p. 56.

41 Ibid., p. 64.

42 Ibid., pp. 290–1.

43 Rieff, *The Triumph of the Therapeutic: Uses of Faith after Freud* (Chicago: University of Chicago Press, 1958 [1966], p. 7n.

44 Gerry Watson, 'The Impossible Culture of the Therapeutic: An Essay on the Sociology of Philip Rieff,' *Compass: A Provincial Review* 5 (1979), pp. 39–62.

3 The Emergence of Psychological Man in Western Culture

1 Philip Rieff, *Freud: The Mind of the Moralist* (Chicago: University of Chicago Press, 1979 [1959]), pp. 4–5.
2 Philip Rieff, *The Triumph of the Therapeutic: Uses of Faith after Freud* (Chicago: University of Chicago Press, 1987 [1966]), p. xv.
3 Philip Rieff, 'Reflections on Psychological Man in America,' in *The Feeling Intellect: Selected Writings*, ed. by Jonathan B. Imber (Chicago: University of Chicago Press, 1990), pp. 3–4.
4 Rieff, *Triumph*, p. 40.
5 Yannis Gabriel, 'Freud, Rieff and the Critique of American Culture,' *Psychoanalytic Review* 69(3) (1982), p. 355.
6 See Don Browning, 'Philip Rieff: Psychological Man and the Penultimate Ethic of the Abundant Life,' in *Generative Man: Psychoanalytic Perspectives* (Philadelphia: The Westminster Press, 1973), p. 47. Browning quotes from the 1961 edition of *Mind*, p. 158. Gabriel suggests that 'Ricoeur's (1970) reading of Freud can be seen as an attempt to bridge the differences in emphasis between Rieff's interpretations of instinct and those of Marcuse and Brown.' 'Freud, Rieff and the Critique,' pp. 364–5 n1. Later on in this chapter I will summarize these differences. A short critical evaluation of Rieff's use of Freudian instinct theory is in Jeffrey Abramson, *Liberation and its Limits: The Moral and Political Thought of Freud* (Boston: Beacon Press, 1984), pp. 21–4.
7 Paul Ricoeur, *Freud and Philosophy: An Essay on Interpretation*, trans. D. Savage, (New Haven and London: Yale University Press, 1977 [1970]), p. 6.
8 Kerrigan suggests that Rieff's extrapolation of Freud's *Weltanschauung* into the character-ideal of psychological man is severely biased by his 'concerns about Western culture.' Other interpretations of the Freudian text are justified, which lead to totally different conclusions about Western culture, such as those of Richard Rorty. Kerrigan suggests that Rorty's position might be a friendly answer to Rieff's concerns. Unfortunately Kerrigan's criticism is based on a very limited reading of Rieff's work, i.e., only the seventh chapter of *Mind*. See William Kerrigan, 'Psychoanalysis and the Vicissitudes of Enlightenment,' *American Imago* 48(2) (1991), pp. 265–78. For a recent evaluation of Rieff's cultural-theoretical interpretation of Freud's works, see Howard Kaye, 'Rieff's *Freud* and the Tyranny of Psychology,' *Journal of Classical Sociology* 3(3) (2003), pp. 263–77.
9 See Philip Rieff, 'The Function of the Social Sciences and Humanities in a Science Curriculum,' in *The Feeling Intellect*, p. 241.

10 Rieff, *Mind*, p. 359n.

11 See Norbert Elias, *Über den Prozess der Zivilisation. Soziogenetische und Psychogenetische Untersuchungen*, vol. 1, *Wandlungen des Verhalten in den Weltlichen Oberschichten des Abendlandes*, 2nd ed. (Bern and Munich: Francke, 1969 [1939]), p. viii.

12 See Ricoeur, *Freud and Philosophy*, pp. 38–9.

13 Ibid., p. 39.

14 Rieff, *Mind*, p. 204.

15 Ibid.

16 Rieff does not clearly define the concept 'primal form.' In several passages of *Mind* he connects it to Freud's concept of 'prototype.' In one of those passages he connects Freud's prototype to the morphology that Goethe used in his botanical research. *Mind*, pp. 204–7. Goethe developed a theory of the *Urpflanze* as a prototype for later species of plants. A second example of primal forms is to be found in religion: liturgy or *cultus* can be considered an expression of the primal forms of culture. In *Triumph* Rieff develops the idea of the *cultus* as the prototype of a culture. (I will elaborate on this in chapter 4.)

17 Rieff, *Mind*, pp. 329–30.

18 Ibid., p. 168.

19 Ibid., p. 224.

20 Ibid., p. 160.

21 Implicit here is a polemical aspect of Rieff's interpretation of the Freudian text. According to Rieff, the importance of authority for Freud's thinking was neglected in the contemporary Anglo-American reception of the Freudian text.

22 I used the article by Bernard J. Bergen and Stanley D. Rosenberg, 'The New Neo-Freudians: Psychoanalytic Dimensions of Social Change,' *Psychiatry* 34 (February 1971), pp. 19–37. At some points I add information from Theodore Roszak, *The Making of a Counter Culture: Reflections on the Technocratic Society and Its Youthful Opposition* (London: Faber and Faber, 1970 [1968]).

23 Bergen and Rosenberg, 'New Neo-Freudians,' p. 25.

24 'Freud's error, Marcuse argues, lay in believing that scarcity and the Reality Principle were synonymous.' Roszak, *Making of a Counter Culture*, p. 105.

25 Bergen and Rosenberg, 'New Neo-Freudians,' p. 33. For a more detailed discussion of this problem, see this article, pp. 27–33.

26 'Mind is not necessarily a reformed whore. I see no reason to call every risen possibility by its Freudian name, "sublimation."' Philip Rieff, 'By What Authority? Post-Freudian Reflections on the Repression of the Repressive as Modern Culture,' in *The Feeling Intellect*, p. 333.

27 Rieff, *Mind*, p. 305.
28 Ibid., p. 210.
29 Peter Gay, *Freud: A Life for Our Time* (London and Melbourne: J.M. Dent, 1988), pp. 604–8.
30 Sigmund Freud, *Moses and Monotheism*, p. 145, cited in Philip Rieff, 'Kairos in Freud's Thought,' in *The Feeling Intellect*, p. 56. Rieff cites from the American edition (Hogarth Press, 1949) of the English translation by Katherine Jones of *Der Mann Moses und die monotheistische Religion*.
31 See Rieff, *Mind*, pp. 199–200.
32 Ibid., p. 212.
33 For a more detailed description of Rieff's analysis of the relation between 'historical truth' and 'psychological truth,' see Rieff, 'Kairos in Freud's Thought,' pp. 53–61, and Philip Rieff, 'Intimations of Therapeutic Truth: Decoding Appendix G in *Moses and Monotheism*,' in *The Feeling Intellect*, pp. 61–5.
34 An important debate between Freud and Jung about the nature of the unconscious is at stake here. Freud forcibly argued against Jung's adaptation of the theory of the unconscious, as we saw in Chapter 2. Rieff asserts that in Jung's theory the nature of unconscious processes is oversimplified because Jung turns the concept of the unconscious into the notion of an eternal and ideal (symbolic) order. Consequently, the unconscious was not a critical principle of explanation as in Freud's theory, but a 'total religious system.' See Philip Rieff (ed.), *The History of the Psychoanalytic Movement*, vol. 1, *Collected Papers of Sigmund Freud* (New York: Collier-Macmillan, 1963), pp. 9–26, and Rieff, *Mind*, p. 200 and p. 200n. For us the importance of this complex discussion is that correlated to the difference between the Freudian and Jungian definition of the unconscious is an important difference in the definition of the relationship between individual and collective processes. Freud, with his advocacy of the individual who suffers from the influence of metaphysical systems, accused Jung of blurring critical distinctions between these two processes.
35 Rieff, *Mind*, p. 252.
36 Ibid., p. 254.
37 Ibid., p. 294.
38 Ibid., p. 297.
39 Sigmund Freud, *The Interpretation of Dreams*, vol. 5, *The Complete Psychological Works of Sigmund Freud, Standard Edition* (London: Hogarth Press, 1968 [1900], p. 601 (editorial note).
40 In this seventh chapter Freud writes: 'It is true that, so far as we know, no psychical apparatus exists which possesses a primary process only and that such

an apparatus is to that extent a theoretical fiction. But this much is a fact: the primary processes are present in the mental apparatus from the first, while it is only during the course of life that the secondary processes unfold, and come to inhibit and overlay the primary ones; it may even be that their complete domination is not attained until the prime of life.' Freud, *Interpretation of Dreams*, p. 603.

41 Ricoeur, *Freud and Philosophy*, p. 112.

42 Personal communication with Rieff, June 1999. According to Rieff, chaos theory was very important for Romantic philosophy and science; see Rieff, *Mind*, p. 33.

43 Rieff's formulation is not complete. It is evident, however, that Rieff hints at the relation between consciousness and the unconscious.

44 Personal communication with Rieff, June 1999.

45 Ibid.

46 Rieff, *Fellow Teachers*, p. 2.

47 'Modality' is a way of knowing or being.

48 Rieff, *Triumph*, p. 6n.

49 Ibid., p. 16.

50 Megill (1985) distinguishes two modalities in the contemporary Freud interpretation, a modernist and a postmodernist one. See Allan Megill, *Prophets of Extremity: Nietzsche, Heidegger, Foucault, Derrida* (Berkeley: University of California Press, 1985), pp. 320–9. Both are based on the assumption of a crisis in Western culture that causes fragmentation and disorder, but their reactions to this crisis are different. In the modernist modality Freud is considered a thinker who strived to develop a strategy for ethical survival of the individual in the crisis of modernity. Rieff is the great exponent of this modality. The postmodernist modality is averse to this interpretation of Freud as a moralist. It considers the crisis of modernity not as a crisis, but as a possibility. Freud does not teach us how to *live*, but how to *read*. Freud is not just the interpreter of dreams, of the mind, of social life and culture, but he is the interpreter *tout court*. Next to Rorty, Megill mentions Derrida, who does not read Freud's texts as attempts to uncover hidden truths, but as a 'self-justifying play.' Whether Megill's evaluation of Rieff's work is still adequate may be questioned. It does apply to *Mind* and *Triumph*, but in texts of the early 1990s Rieff's opinion on Freud becomes far more critical. Further treatment of this specific topic is beyond the scope of my book, but a very valuable point of Megill's way of positioning Rieff is that it draws our attention to a significant point of Rieff's theory. Unlike the postmodern philosophers, Rieff does problematize the cultural fragmentation and disorder. In his later works 'sacred order' becomes a central concept.

4 Blueprint for a Theory of Culture

1 Rieff, *The Triumph of the Therapeutic: Uses of Faith after Freud* (Chicago: University of Chicago Press, 1987 [1966]), p. 12.
2 Ibid., p. 2.
3 Ibid., p. 14.
4 Ibid.
5 Ibid., p. 15.
6 Ibid., p. 14.
7 Ibid. An important weak point of *Triumph* is that Rieff hardly ever mentions those historical cases explicitly. Therefore the connection between Western cultural history and Rieff's 'psychohistory' must be reconstructed by his readers themselves.
8 Rieff, *Triumph*, p. 246.
9 Ibid., p. 247.
10 Ibid., p. 15.
11 Ibid.
12 Ibid.
13 Ibid., p. 16.
14 Ibid.
15 Ibid., p. 17.
16 In *Triumph* Rieff does not account for the differences between the concepts of 'faith' and 'religion' systematically. Theologically this implies many questions, but I think that they are not very relevant here because both terms apply to the same central theme of Rieff's thinking, the introduction of transcendence as a conceptual category into the sociology of culture.
17 Rieff, *Triumph*, pp. 34–5
18 Ibid., p. 35.
19 Ibid., p. 36.
20 This formulation is inspired by the term 'deconversion' that Rieff uses to typify modernity. Peter Homans has formulated the relation between deconversion and psychoanalysis like this: 'Psychoanalysis ... in Kierkegaard's words, plays the music backwards ... For psychoanalysis is a "deconversion," a spiritual perception calculated to unravel in the fashion of parody the formation of those very illusions that bind men together and give them the assurance that control, delay, and renunciation are all really worth the effort.' Peter Homans, *Theology after Freud: An Interpretive Inquiry* (Indianapolis and New York: Bobbs-Merrill, 1970), p. 151. The psychoanalytic concept of transference can be interpreted in the same way: 'Transference is a retrograde pro-

cess of going back in the dynamics of repression and the formation of the harsh superego' (ibid., p. 92).

21 Rieff, *Triumph*, p. 36.

22 Ibid.

23 Rieff, *Freud: The Mind of the Moralist* (Chicago: University of Chicago Press, 1979 [1959]), pp. 275–6. Rieff cites Sigmund Freud, *Totem and Taboo*, vol. 13, *The Complete Works of Sigmund Freud*, Standard Edition (London: Hogarth Press, 1953 [1913]).

24 Rieff, *Triumph*, p. 49.

25 Ibid., p. 51.

26 Ibid., p. 53.

27 Ibid., pp. 54–5.

28 Ibid., p. 54.

29 Ibid., p. 62.

30 Ibid., p. 65.

31 Ibid.

32 Ibid., p. 51.

33 Ibid.

34 Ibid., p. 52.

35 Ibid., p. 68.

36 Ibid.

37 Ibid., p. 69.

38 Ibid., p. 71.

39 Ibid.

40 Two pairs of concepts should not be mixed up. In his theory of theory Rieff distinguishes conformative theory from transformative theory. In the text above Rieff uses a distinction from another order, i.e., that of therapeutical experience. The two pairs of concepts are related, as I will show in the next section of this chapter.

41 Rieff, *Triumph*, pp. 73–4.

42 Ibid., p. 72.

43 Ibid.

44 Ibid. I assume that Rieff alludes to the pop-cultus of counterculture here, which was explosively growing in the period when he wrote *Triumph*. In that time pop music was the pre-eminent means of protest against traditional patterns of behaviour and thinking and of conveying that protest to others. In later works Rieff writes about Lou Reed and Madonna. See Philip Rieff, 'Worlds at War: Illustrations of an Aesthetics in Authority; or Numbered Notes towards a Trilogy, of which the General Title is "Sacred Order / Social Order,"' in Eileen Barker, James A. Beckford, and Karel Dobbelaere (eds.),

Secularization, Rationalism and Sectarianism: Essays in Honour of Bryan Wilson (Oxford: Clarendon Press, 1993), pp. 257–9).

45 Rieff, *Triumph*, p. 72.

46 This passage implies a fundamental revision of Freud's theory of religion. For Freud's geneticism in the explanation of the origin of religion Rieff substitutes a dialectic explanation. Thus Rieff does away with the reductionism in Freud's theory of religion.

47 Rieff, *Triumph*, p. 49.

48 Ibid., p. 75.

49 Rieff gives a similar aesthetic analysis of the essence of psychoanalysis: 'Rationalism came to abolish any particular content by which a commitment was justified. All that remained was the form of internalization, which likewise had to be seriously modified, according to psychoanalytic theory.' Rieff, *Triumph*, p. 201.

50 Ibid., p. 212.

51 Ibid., p. 123.

52 Ibid., p. 126.

53 Ibid.

54 See Rieff *History*, p. 17.

55 Rieff, *Triumph*, pp. 113–14.

56 Ibid., p. 134.

57 'Below the Unconscious of repressions, with its "cruel, sadistic, lascivious, predatory and envious impulses," Reich ... had discovered the pure Unconscious of "primary biological impulses." Instinct is pure, good and beautiful – until it becomes adultered by the repressions through which it must pass on the way to action.' Rieff, *Triumph*, p. 147.

58 Ibid.

59 Ibid., p. 188.

60 Ibid., p. 184.

61 Ibid., p. 206.

62 See ibid., p. 225.

63 Ibid., p. 213.

64 Ibid., p. 206.

65 Rieff asserts that Lawrence's work contains an important criticism of modern sociology which tends to conceptualize man's inner life as 'society individualized.' Lawrence points at the irreducible nucleus of human personality, the self. Rieff discusses this problematic more elaborately in three articles about the work of Charles H. Cooley, who also rejected conceptions of the relationship between human nature and social order that were too one-sidedly dualistic. See Philip Rieff, *The Feeling Intellect: Selected Writ-*

ings, ed. by Jonathan B. Imber (Chicago: University of Chicago Press, 1990), pp. 294–321.

66 Rieff, *Triumph*, p. 207.

67 Ibid., p. 77.

68 Ibid., pp. 226–7.

69 Ibid., p. 193.

70 Ibid., p. 194.

71 Philip Rieff, 'Eros Cross-Examined,' review of Anders Nygren, *Agape and Eros* (1953), in *The Feeling Intellect*, p. 141.

5 The Limits of Modernity

1 Michel Foucault, *The Use of Pleasure: The History of Sexuality*, vol. 2, trans. by R. Hurley (London: Penguin, 1992), p. 8.

2 Philip Rieff, 'The Function of the Social Sciences,' in *The Feeling Intellect: Selected Writings*, ed. by Jonathan B. Imber (Chicago: University of Chicago Press, 1990), p. 241.

3 Philip Rieff, *Fellow Teachers/Of Culture and Its Second Death* (Chicago: University of Chicago Press, 1985 [1972]), pp. 10–11.

4 Ibid., p. 11.

5 Ibid., p. 2.

6 Ibid.

7 An example is this: 'As the Marxist demonstrates, even the highest criticism, armed, will defend its own establishment soon enough and prevent mind from entering those interior spaces opened and shaped by our continuous interpretative sciences, in institutions reserved to that end.' Rieff, *Fellow Teachers*, p. 18.

8 Ibid., p. 76n.

9 Ibid., p. 24.

10 See ibid., p. 88.

11 Ibid., p. 115.

12 In the foreword of the third edition of *Fellow Teachers* Rieff mentions a slogan which he saw in a train somewhere and to his view refers to the essence of counterculture: 'E VIETATO VIETARE (It is forbidden to forbid)' (p. xiii).

13 Ibid., p. 21.

14 This is the epilogue of the third edition of *Freud: The Mind of the Moralist* (Chicago: University of Chicago Press, 1979 [1959]), pp. 358–97.

15 Ibid., p. 362n.

16 Ibid., p. 362.

17 See ibid., pp. 367–8. Rieff quotes from Sigmund Freud, *The Ego and the Id*, vol. 19, *The Complete Works of Sigmund Freud, Standard Edition* (London: Hogarth Press, 1953 [1923]), p. 18.

18 Rieff, *Mind*, p. 270.

19 Ibid., p. 368. Another text in which Rieff discusses this problem is entitled 'By What Authority? Post-Freudian Reflections on the Repression of the Repressive as Modern Culture,' in *The Feeling Intellect*, pp. 330–51, esp. pp. 335–7.

20 Rieff, *Mind*, p. 368.

21 Ibid.

22 Rieff, *Mind*, p. 362.

23 Rieff illustrates this idea with an analysis of Joseph Conrad's novel *Heart of Darkness* (1902). See Rieff, *Fellow Teachers*, pp. 187–90.

24 Rieff, *Fellow Teachers*, p. 69. Rieff cites from Sigmund Freud, 'Repression,' General Psychological Theory, Vol. 6, *The Collected Papers of Sigmund Freud* ed. and introduced by Philip Rieff (New York: Macmillan, 1963), p. 109.

25 Rieff, *Fellow Teachers*, p. 69.

26 Ibid. In *Triumph* Rieff uses the term 'control' for the limiting modality of culture, which is called 'the interdict' in *Fellow Teachers*. Rieff does not explain how these terms relate to each other.

27 Rieff, *Fellow Teachers*, p. 41.

28 Ibid., p. 69.

29 Spread throughout *Fellow Teachers* Rieff mentions Comte, Sohm, Durkheim, Weber, Sorel, and Geertz.

30 Rieff, *Fellow Teachers*, p. 69.

31 Ibid., p. 21.

32 Ibid., p. 182.

33 Ibid., p. 183.

34 Ibid., p. 39.

35 Ibid., p. 63.

36 Ibid., p. 64.

37 Ibid., p. 63.

38 Rieff, *Mind*, p. 332. According to Rieff, this therapeutic ideal is otherwise unattainable. In *One Step Further*, Rieff puts it like this: 'Both Oedipus and Hamlet attempted to break the repressive design of their lives; so did Freud. All succeeded only in retracing it.' *Rieff, Mind*, p. 379. In a later text he reformulates Freud's discovery, alluding to Kafka's story about the guard in the novel entitled *The Process*: 'Before this gatekeeping *Not* Freud sat all the main part of his intellectual life, without being able to know how cleverly he had

recognized sacred order.' Rieff 'By What Authority?' in *The Feeling Intellect,* p. 336.

39 Rieff, *Fellow Teachers,* p. 186.

40 Ibid., p. 185. Rieff does not mention where he found this in the Freudian text.

41 This thesis has far-reaching implications for a theory of the origin of authority: 'Would you like to know how to recreate authority? You would have to begin again outside yourself. A true interdictory authority can only be taught to us; it cannot be thought up by us.' Ibid., p. 137.

42 See Rieff, *Mind,* p. 32.

43 Rieff, *Fellow Teachers,* p. 186.

44 Rieff, 'By What Authority?' p. 333.

45 Rieff, *Fellow Teachers,* p. 186.

46 Ibid., p. 144.

47 Ibid., p. 206.

48 See Herbert Marcuse, *Eros and Civilization: A Philosophical Inquiry into Freud* (New York: Vintage Books, 1961 [1955]), e.g., p. 160.

49 Rieff, *Fellow Teachers,* p. 108n.

50 Ibid.

51 Ibid., p. 144n.

52 In *One Step Further,* Rieff formulates it like this: 'Sublimation' is to repression as Unitarianism is to Christianity: too high minded to be true.' Rieff, *Mind,* p. 387. The Freudian and Marcusian concepts of sublimation shut out the divine origin of the sublime, which in Rieff's theory is the interdict that stems from a transcendent cultural order. Freud's and Marcuse's points of view are tantamount to the denial of the divine origin of Christ by the Unitarians.

53 Rieff, *Fellow Teachers,* p. 206.

54 See ibid.

55 See Rieff, *Fellow Teachers,* p. 63, and the very long footnote on Edmund Burke's *A Philosophical Inquiry into the Origin of Our Ideas of the Sublime; With an Introductory Discourse Concerning Taste* (ibid., pp. 63n–66n). Rieff's criticism reminds me of Pier Paulo Pasolini's movie *Salo* in which this 'problem of sublimity' is at stake as well and in which 'the horrible' that is concealed in human eroticism is put under a cinematographic magnifying glass

56 Rieff, *Fellow Teachers,* p. 207.

57 Ibid.

58 Ibid., pp. 207–8.

59 Ibid., p. 185. Rieff's usage of the 'psychology of temptation' in order to criticize Freud's theory of eros and authority and Marcuse's revision of it, may

well be an attempt to fill the gap in Freud's theory that Paul Ricoeur describes like this: 'The psychology of temptation ... makes us acutely aware of the lack of a more original dialectic of desire and law. Paul Ricoeur, *Freud and Philosophy: An Essay on Interpretation,* trans. by D. Savage (New Haven and London: Yale University Press, 1977 [1970]), p. 204.

60 Rieff alludes to Martin Luther's '*Anfechtungen.*' See Rieff, *Fellow Teachers,* p. 181n.

61 Rieff, *Fellow Teachers,* p. 215.

62 In 'By What Authority?' Rieff resumes this criticism on the concept of sublimation. He connects it to critical comments on great modern art like that of Picasso and Joyce, whose works he considers attempts to bolt out of the interdictory form of modern culture. See *The Feeling Intellect,* pp. 333–4 and pp. 338–9.

63 Rieff, *Fellow Teachers,* p. 35.

64 Ibid., pp. 41–2.

65 Philip Rieff, 'Doctor to the body of the doctor of the mind,' review of *Freud: Living and Dying,* by M. Schur, *New York Times Book Review,* 18 June 1972, p. 24.

66 Rieff, *Fellow Teachers,* p. 42.

67 Ibid., p. 70.

68 Ibid., pp. 160–1.

69 Ibid., p. 162.

70 Ibid., p. 167.

71 Ibid., p. 162.

72 Ibid., p. 163.

73 Ibid., p. 164.

74 Ibid., p. 165.

75 Ibid., p. 165.

76 Ibid., pp. 165–6.

77 Ibid., p. 166.

78 Ibid., p. 167.

79 Ibid., p. 168.

80 Both William S. Heckscher (*Rembrandt's Anatomy of Dr Nicolaas Tulp: An iconological study* [New York: New York University Press, 1958]) and Mieke Bal (*Reading 'Rembrandt': Beyond the Word-Image Opposition* [Cambridge: Cambridge University Press, 1991]) mention this sacrificial aspect of the public anatomy.

81 Rieff, *Triumph,* pp. 2–3.

82 Rieff, *Fellow Teachers,* p. 120.

83 Ibid., p. 39.

84 A more conventional term in this respect would be 'mental history,' but that

concept is not adequate for Rieff's project because it does not conceptualize the problem of authority adequately.

85 Rieff, *Fellow Teachers*, p. 120.

86 The cultist is the psychohistorical predeccesor of the therapist. Just like the modern therapist assists the modern individual in analytic therapy, the cultist assisted the premodern individual in commitment therapy.

87 Rieff, *Fellow Teachers*, p. 120.

88 Norman O. Brown, 'Rieff's "Fellow Teachers,"' in Robert Boyers (ed.), *Psychological Man* (New York: Harper and Row, 1975), pp. 132–3.

89 Ibid., p. 132.

90 Ibid., p. 137.

91 Ibid., p. 141.

92 'Our psychological men aim to recreate the most contemporary of all institutions, the most fleeting and first: orgy.' Rieff, *Fellow Teachers*, p. 144n. 'The original cultic experience, that critical theory tries to imagine, and against which all interdicts must aim, is of orgy.' Ibid., p. 196, 'Instinct is only one new name for the original therapeutic dissolution of law and order. That dissolution had an institutional name: orgy.' Ibid., p. 98. 'That orgy is the one, only and original, totally democratic institution – the common Utopia of all our guru's, "fascist" and "liberationist" – is the key to a revival of interdictive knowledge.' Ibid., p. 162n.

93 Ibid., p. 98.

94 Rieff, 'A Jesuit Looks at Proudhon: Competition in Damnation,' review of Henri de Lubac, *The Un-Marxian Socialist*, in *Modern Review* 3(2) (1950), pp. 166–7; reprinted in and cited from *The Feeling Intellect*, p. 166.

95 Robert Boyers (ed.), 'Perspectives on the Therapeutic in the Context of Contemporary Sociology: A Dialogue between Benjamin Nelson and Dennis Wrong,' in Robert Boyers (ed.), *Psychological Man* (New York: Harper and Row, 1975), p. 174. In this text Rieff's work is compared with the works of important contemporary American sociologists such as Talcott Parsons, Erving Goffman, Thomas Luckmann, and Peter Berger.

96 Rieff, *Fellow Teachers*, p. 6.

97 Ibid., p. 1.

98 Boyers, 'Perspectives on the Therapeutic,' p. 144.

99 Rieff, *Fellow Teachers*, p. 32.

100 Ibid., p. 36.

101 Rieff, *Triumph*, pp. 1–2.

102 Rieff, *Fellow Teachers*, p. 48.

103 The term is Geertz's, to which Rieff refers in *Fellow Teachers*, p. 25.

104 Ibid., p. 116.

105 Ibid., p. 159.
106 Ibid., p. 21.
107 Boyers, 'Perspectives on the Therapeutic,' p. 178.
108 Rieff, *Fellow Teachers*, p. 203.
109 Ibid., p. 203n.
110 The creed is an important phenomenon for Rieff's theory. Rieff is interested in central or leading ideas that direct acting and thinking. The creed is an expression of the leading ideas of an organization.
111 Rieff, *Fellow Teachers*, p. 51.
112 Ibid., p. 170.
113 One of Burt's publications is the theme of a short case study in the next chapter.
114 Rieff, *Fellow Teachers*, p. 99.
115 Rieff, *Mind*, p. 379.
116 Rieff, *Fellow Teachers*, pp. 82n–83n.
117 Ibid., pp. 112–13.
118 *Condotierri* were leaders or members of gangs of soldiers, mainly in fourteenth- and fifteenth-century Italy, who hired themselves for warfare to parties (e.g., cities) that paid best.
119 Rieff, *Fellow Teachers*, p. 46.

6 Late Modernity as Second Culture Camp

1 Rieff, 'By What Authority? Post-Freudian Reflections on the Repression of the Repressive as Modern Culture,' in *The Feeling Intellect: Selected Writings*, ed. by Jonathan B. Imber (Chicago: University of Chicago Press, 1990), p. 335.
2 Rieff translates 'Kulturkampf' with the peculiar term 'culture camp.' As we shall see in this chapter, the more common term 'culture war' may seem more appropriate, because Rieff really thinks that a 'culture war' is going on. Rieff does not explain why he chose the term 'camp.' I think he had at least two reasons for that. First, the term 'culture war' refers to existing cultures that collide, as in Samuel Huntington's 'clash of civilizations.' Rieff's theory refers to an internal struggle in Western culture itself. Second, he wanted to stay close to the German term from which it is derived.
3 Rieff, 'By What Authority?' pp. 333–4.
4 Ibid., p. 332.
5 Rieff, *Freud: The Mind of the Moralist* (Chicago: University of Chicago Press, 1979 [1959]), p. 382.
6 Rieff, 'By What Authority?' p. 332.
7 Ibid.

8 Ibid.

9 In 'By What Authority?' Rieff does not go deeper into the problem of definition of this primal repression. He does so in another text ('Intimations of Therapeutic Truth,' in *The Feeling Intellect*, pp. 61–5), where Freud localizes the origin of repression in a false and neurotic sense of guilt. According to Rieff, this strategy ends in the same aporia concerning the origin of repression as I described in chapter 5.

10 Rieff, 'By What Authority?' p. 332.

11 Ibid.

12 Ibid., p. 331.

13 Ibid.

14 Ibid.

15 Philip Rieff, 'Worlds at War: Illustrations of an Aesthetics in Authority; or Numbered Notes towards a Trilogy, of which the General Title Is "Sacred Order / Social Order,"' in Eileen Barker, James A. Beckford, and Karel Dobbelaere (eds.), *Secularization, Rationalism and Sectarianism*: Essays in Honour of Bryan R. Wilson (Oxford: Clarendon Press, 1993), p. 244. This text summarizes 'The Newer Noises of War in the Second Culture Camp: Notes on Professor Burt's Legal Fictions,' *Yale Journal of Law and the Humanities* 3(2), 1991, pp. 315–88.

16 This part of his theory must in some way be related to Rieff's biography. When I visited Rieff he urged me to read a recent biography of Hitler. So when I use the word 'evil' here, the Holocaust resonates in the term.

17 Rieff, 'Worlds at War,' p. 244.

18 Rieff, 'By What Authority?' p. 332.

19 Rieff, 'For the Last Time Psychology,' *Salmagundi* nos. 74–75, 1987, pp. 101–17; reprinted in and cited from *The Feeling Intellect*, p. 363.

20 Rieff refers to 'Newer Noises' as a summary of the magnum opus of which the working title is 'Sacred Order / Social Order: Image Entries to the Aesthetics of Authority' and which should be published by the University of Chicago Press. See 'Newer Noises,' p. 315n and personal communication with Rieff, June 1999.

21 For a comparison of the styles of Rieff and Derrida, see Philip Manning, 'Philip Rieff's Moral Vision of Sociology: From Positive to Negative Communities – and Back?' *Journal of Classical Sociology* 3(3) (2003), p. 238 and 244–5.

22 Personal communication with Rieff, June 1999.

23 Rieff, 'Newer Noises,' p. 316.

24 Ibid.

25 Ibid.

26 Ibid.
27 *Concise Oxford Dictionary*, 9th ed. (Oxford: Clarendon Press, 1998), p. 1482.
28 Rieff, 'Newer Noises,' p. 346.
29 Ibid. pp. 316–17.
30 Ibid., p. 317.
31 Ibid.
32 Rieff, *Triumph*, p. 212.
33 Rieff, 'Newer Noises,' p. 317.
34 Ibid., p. 319.
35 Ibid.
36 Ibid.
37 Ibid.
38 Ibid.
39 Ibid., p. 318.
40 Ibid., p. 319.
41 Ibid., pp. 319–20. Rieff refers to Wallace Stevens, 'Notes toward a Supreme Fiction,' *The Collected Poems* (New York: Knopf, 1976), pp. 380–408.
42 Rieff, 'Newer Noises,' p. 320.
43 Ibid., p. 318.
44 Ibid., p. 319.
45 Ibid., p. 317.
46 Ibid., p. 318.
47 Ibid., p. 317. Exodus 3:14 is where God reveals himself as 'I am who I am.'
48 Personal communication with Rieff, June 1999.
49 Rieff refers to Wallace Stevens's poem 'The Idea of Order at Key West' (1936), published in the collection *Ideas of Order*: *The Collected Poems of Wallace Stevens* (New York: Knopf, 1961), pp. 128–30.
50 Personal communication with Rieff, June 1999.
51 Gerardus van der Leeuw, *Sacred and Profane Beauty: The Holy in Art* (New York: Holt, Rinehart and Winston, 1963 [1932], p. 332.
52 Rieff, 'Newer Noises,' p. 319.
53 Some examples are the following: A tableau of Marcel Duchamp, *Étant donnés: 1. La chute d'eau. 2. Le gaz d'éclairage*, on which the artist worked secretly from 1946 to 1966 and which according to Rieff is a key work for the understanding of transgressivity. The same goes for the main works of James Joyce, *Ulysses* (1922) and *Finnegans Wake* (1939) and for the work of Franz Kafka. Rieff refers frequently to Joseph Conrad's *Heart of Darkness* (1902), to J.L. Borges's *Ficciones* (1960), and to Wallace Stevens's *Notes towards a Supreme Fiction* (1942). Rieff also analyses works of Abelard, Nietzsche, and Derrida. And of course *good old Freud* appears on stage now and then. In many cases

Rieff analyses what he calls 'deathworks': the last work of an artist or author that summarizes all his or her previous work. This term is ambiguous because he also interprets these works as symptoms of the death of second world culture. Rieff also calls his own magnum opus his deathwork.

54 Rieff, 'Newer Noises,' p. 326.

55 Ibid. In this statement there is an historic allusion to the problem of being Jewish in the German state as it came into existence under Bismarck. There the basis for the German identity was a very nationalistic ideology that resulted in the anti-Judaism of the Third Reich and its horror. The Jewish identity presupposes a totally different way of thinking than the nationalist ideology, which made it a *Fremdkörper* in the German state. Rieff presents this problem of identity in 'Newer Noises' as a crucial problem for a theory of modernity. In the formulations he uses, there are allusions to the late modern problem of cultural pluralism. I will return to this problem in the next section.

56 Rieff, 'Newer Noises,' p. 327.

57 Ibid., pp. 326–7.

58 Here Rieff refers to an ecclesiastical theory: 'The doctrine of considering certain matters of small difference between churches in Christian praxis as most prudently treated with indifference ... Perhaps the greatest Christian theorist of adiaphora was Desiderius Erasmus.' 'Newer Noises,' p. 327, n29. He elaborates also in a more general and philosophical way on the theme of *adiaphora* in relation to the task of a cultural elite in several passages of 'Newer Noises.'

59 Ibid., p. 327.

60 Robert A. Burt, *Two Jewish Justices Outcasts in the Promised Land* (Berkeley: University of California Press, 1988), p. 3.

61 Rieff, 'Newer Noises,' p. 330.

62 Ibid., p. 333.

63 Ibid.

64 Ibid. This what the 'second death' from the subtitle of *Fellow Teachers* alludes to. Rieff takes over this term from the second chapter of Augustine's *The State of God*, which is about death. This second death is 'the death we die before our bodies die[,] when we are separated from God.' Jan Aarts and Marianne Broeder, 'Psychoanalyse en sociologie: Het debat Rieff-Vandermeersch' (Psychoanalysis and sociology: The Debate Rieff-Vandermeersch), *Sociologisch Tijdschrift* 11(3) (1984), pp. 503–29. Rieff speaks analogously about 'the second death of Western culture,' caused by modernization, which aims at banishing every reference to sacred order from culture and thus gets separated from God.

65 Rieff, 'Newer Noises,' p. 328.

66 Ibid., p. 332.

67 Philip Rieff, 'The Newer Noises of War in the Second Culture Camp: Notes on Professor Burt's Legal Fictions,' *Yale Journal of Law and the Humanities* 3(2), 1991, pp. 315–88.

7 Rieff: Prophet of a Post-secular Culture

1 See Kenneth S. Piver, 'Philip Rieff: The Critic of Psychoanalysis as Cultural Theorist,' in Mark Micale and Roy Porter (eds.), *Discovering the History of Psychiatry* (New York and Oxford: Oxford University Press, 1994), p. 191.

2 Robert Boyer (ed.), 'Perspectives on the Therapeutic in the Context of Contemporary Sociology: A Dialogue between Benjamin Nelson and Dennis Wrong,' in *Psychological Man* (New York: Harper and Row, 1975) p. 178.

3 Linda Woodhead, 'Introduction,' in Linda Woodhead, Paul Heelas, and David Martin (eds.), *Peter Berger and the Study of Religion* (New York: Routledge 2001), p. 1.

4 It is true that Rieff himself contributed to his being labelled as a reactionary culture pessimist. For example, in the introduction of *Fellow Teachers/Of Culture and Its Second Death* (Chicago: University of Chicago Press, 1985 [1972]) he does indeed write that he 'meditates a counterenlightenmnent' (p. x.), but it is clear that Rieff's intention is polemical there. I suggest to interpret this statement as a critical, programmatic one. It is better to read his work as an attempt to restore the scholarly ideal of the Enlightenment. Rieff thinks that modernization degenerated from a critical project into a dogmatic movement that is culturally destructive. In *Fellow Teachers* he writes this: 'The textbooks have miseducated us enlightened ones miserably, for generations, on the meaning of the Enlightenment. From Hume and Rousseau to Sorel, Freud and Fanon, the finest intellectuals in the tradition of the Enlightenment kept up their confident lack of confidence in the rational abilities of man. In contrast, by their "Enlightenment," received through cliché and textbook, the social servicing ex-religious elites who dominated Western culture increasingly since their origins in the eighteenth century insist to this day on exercising, unawares, a rationalistically-dressed sentimentalism derived from their betters, the Enlightenment theorists' (p. 146). Rieff wants to develop anew a critical scholarly approach that criticizes the existing culture and sciences systemically, as did the Enlightenment mutatis mutandis in its own era.

5 Other authors, too, point to the problems that the theory of sublimation delivers for an interdisciplinary theory of culture. For example, Howard

Kaye, a former student of Rieff's, has shown that neither Parsons nor the theorists of the Frankfurter School have succeeded in bringing together the sublimation theories of Freud and Weber into one common denominator without destroying the cultural-theoretical sophistication of both theories. See Howard Kaye, 'Rationalization as Sublimation: On the Cultural Analyses of Weber and Freud,' *Theory, Culture and Society* 9 (1992), pp. 45–74.

6 This citation is taken from an application form for a one-year fellowship of the National Endowment of the Humanities (April 1995) that Rieff enrolled for to finish his magnum opus.

7 Personal communication with Rieff, June 1999.

8 Peter Homans, *The Ability to Mourn: Disillusionment and the Social Origins of Psychoanalysis* (Chicago and London: University of Chicago Press, 1989), p. 299.

9 Patrick Vandermeersch, *La chair de la passion – Une histoire de foi: la flagellation* (Paris: Cerf, 2002), p. 240.

10 Philip Rieff, *The Triumph of the Therapeutic: Uses of Faith after Freud* (Chicago: University of Chicago Press, 1987 [1966], p. 189.

11 Rieff, *Triumph*, p. 199.

12 One example is this: 'Fellow teachers of resistance: do not wait in suspense for the neurotic facts to reverse themselves. I do not doubt they can be reversed – and I would prefer them so, because I prefer a more humane, less dynamic world, deeply graven interdicts etched in superior and trustworthy characters. Do not count on me ... I am at one with all you heterodoxologists.' Rieff, *Fellow Teachers*, p. 87.

13 Philip Manning, 'Philip Rieff's Moral Vision of Sociology: From Positive to Negative Communities – and Back?' *Journal of Classical Sociology* 3(3) (2003), p. 236. We may even find these terms used without reference to Rieff, e.g., Gary Dorrien, 'Berger: Theology and sociology,' in Linda Woodhead, Paul Heelas, and David Martin (eds.), *Peter Berger and the Study of Religion* (New York: Routledge, 2001), p. 28.

14 See Woodhead et al., *Berger*, pp. 1–7.

15 Paul J. Fitzgerald, 'Faithful Sociology: Peter Berger's Religious Project,' *Religious Studies Review* 27(1) (2001), pp. 10–17.

16 As for Berger's work, Woodhead summarizes the point like this: 'It is "in, with and under" human experience that he discerns "signals of transcendence" These he finds in the fundamental experiences of love, play, laughter, outrage at evil, hope in adversity. All in Berger's view, reveal an awareness of a deep order in the structure of things.' Woodhead et al., *Berger*, p. 7. In *A Far Glory* Berger himself writes this: 'I am ... inclined to think that the idea of a self over and beyond all socializations can be only determined in a view of reality that includes transcendence.' Peter L. Berger, *A Far Glory: The Quest*

for Faith in an Age of Credulity (New York: Anchor Books/Doubleday, 1992), p. 98.

17 Woodhead et al., *Berger*, p. 3.

18 Peter Berger, 'Postscript,' in Woodhead et al., *Berger*, p. 190.

19 Ibid., p. 191.

20 See Piver, 'Rieff,' p. 209.

21 Philip Rieff, *Freud: The Mind of the Moralist* (Chicago: University of Chicago Press, 1979 [1959]), p. xiv.

22 Woodhead et al., *Berger*, p. 5.

23 Although Berger protested against the Vietnam War in the 1960s, he was repulsed by most of the antiwar movement and virtually all of counterculture. See Gary Dorrien, 'Berger: Theology and sociology,' in Woodhead et al., *Berger*, p. 32.

24 Piver, 'Rieff,' p. 202.

25 See Lauren Langman, 'Philip Rieff's Mission: Character, Culture and Morality,' *Journal of Classical Sociology* 3(3) (2003), p. 292.

26 Robert N. Bellah, Richard Madsen, William M. Sullivan. Ann Swidler, and Steven M. Tipton. *Habits of the Heart: Individualism and Commitment in American Life* (Berkeley and Los Angeles: University of California Press, 1996 [1985]), p. 298.

27 Clifford Geertz, *The Interpretation of Cultures: Selected Essays* (New York: Basic Books, 1973), p. 44.

28 Application National Endowment for the Humanities, p. 2.

29 John Milbank, *Theology and Social Theory: Beyond Secular Reason* (Oxford: Blackwell, 1993 [1990]).

30 Ibid., p. 27.

31 Ibid., p. 102.

32 Ibid., p. 103.

33 Ibid., p. 245.

34 Philip Rieff (ed.), *The History of the Psychoanalytic Movement*, Vol. 1, *The Collected Papers of Sigmund Freud* (New York: Collier-Macmillan, 1963), p. 15.

35 Milbank, *Theology and Social Theory*, pp. 245–9.

36 Ibid., p. 247.

37 A useful bibliography can be found on: www.radicalorthodoxy.org.

38 I will not go into the difficult terminological issue of how to define or circumscribe 'religion,' 'the sacred,' and 'the transcendent,' and how they interrelate. I have indicated how the terms function in Rieff's discourse. That is enough for my introductory purpose. For further research I want to mention two texts. For the term 'the sacred,' a useful starting point may be found in Matthew Evans, 'The Sacred: Differentiating, Clarifying and

Extending Concepts,' *Review of Religious Research* 45 (2003), pp. 32–47. For religion (and its relations to the sacred and tradition), Danièle Hervieu-Léger's approach in *Religion as a Chain of Memory* (Cambridge: Polity Press, 2000 [1993]) is an important contribution.

39 Peter Homans, 'The Significance of Erikson's Psychology for Modern Understanding of Religion,' in Peter Homans (ed.), *Childhood and Selfhood: Essays on Tradition, Religion, and Modernity in the Psychology of Erik H. Erikson* (New Jersey: Associated University Press, 1978), p. 234.

40 See Homans, 'Significance of Erikson's Psychology,' pp. 249–50. Homans mentions Rudolf Bultmann, Martin Buber, Reinhold Niebuhr, and Paul Tillich as the most representative figures.

41 See ibid., pp. 251–3. Homans mentions Clifford Geertz, Victor Turner, and Peter Berger as the most representative figures.

42 See ibid., pp. 254–5. Homans mentions William James, Carl Gustav Jung, and Abraham Maslov as the most representative figures.

43 Rieff, *Fellow Teachers*, p. 25.

44 For a more detailed analysis of the contemporary cultural elite in Western culture from a Rieffian perspective, see Alan Woolfolk, 'The Therapeutic Ideology of Moral Freedom,' *Journal of Classical Sociology* 3(3), (2003), pp. 247–62, esp. pp. 252–5.

45 Hervieu-Léger, *Religion*, p. 14.

46 The three following passages from *Fellow Teachers* summarize Rieff's main criticism of Weber's theory of religion and of authority: 'Weber identified authority, as distinct from power, with service to ends, and ends with faith. But his faiths – "rational, humanitarian, social, ethical, cultural, wordly, or religious" – are a functionalized psychology of motive ... Not Weber, not any theorist of my acquintance, knows how to escape the modern functionalization of faith into therapy' (pp. 22–3.) According to Rieff, 'modern social theory too easily translated id into political criminality and that into new "authority" configurations. In their different ways, each with considerable ambivalence, Durkheim and Weber both sanctioned this wildly one-sided translation' (p. 116). Rieff's answer is this: 'Authority is given or it is fraudulent; it cannot be taken by force or ambition. That was one of Weber's main errors in his theory of charisma' (p. 161).

47 Here I follow the Belgian theologian and psychologist of religion Vandermeersch. See Patrick Vandermeersch, *Unresolved Questions in the Freud–Jung Debate: On Psychosis, Sexual Identiy and Religion*, Louvain Philosophical Studies (Leuven: Leuven University Press, 1991), pp. 23–4.

48 Ibid., pp. 23–4.

49 This was examined by Peter Homans in his *Theology after Freud: An Interpretive Inquiry* (Indianapolis and New York: Bobbs-Merrill, 1970).

50 Vandermeersch, *Unresolved Questions*, p. 277.

51 John Milbank, 'Knowledge: The Theological Critique of Philosophy in Hamann and Jacobi,' in John Milbank, Catherine Pickstock, and Graham Ward (eds.), *Radical Orthodoxy* (London and New York: Routledge, 2001 [1999]) pp. 23–4.

52 In previous chapters I did use the term 'cultural order.' As for the use of the term 'order' this is, strictly speaking, anachronistic because Rieff uses the term 'sacred order' only in his later works. My intention was to make clear how in Rieff's earlier works the later theory of sacred order is prepared. Rieff himself does not use the term 'cultural order' in those earlier works, but speaks of 'culture,' 'the cultural,' and 'cultural system.'

53 For the third time in this chapter, we stumble upon the issue of participation. Rieff's definition of the essence of academic teaching can be read as a cultural-theoretical transposition of Paul's definition of the working of the spirit in faith: 'Faith in Christ means responsive participation in the same divine pneuma that was active in Jesus who appeared in the vision as the Resurrected ... Justified through faith, we are at peace with God through our Lord Jesus Christ' (Romans 5:1). Eric Voegelin, *Order and History*, vol. 4, *The Ecumenic Age* (Baton Rouge and London: Louisiana State University Press, 1974), p. 242.

54 Christopher Lasch, *The Revolt of the Elites and the Betrayal of Democracy* (New York: Norton, 1995), p. 227.

55 Ibid., p. 228.

56 See Chapter 2 of Hervieu-Léger, *Religion*, pp. 23–41. My exposition of Wilson's position is taken from that text.

57 See Bellah et al., *Habits of the Heart*, pp. 235–7.

58 See Lauren Langman, 'Philip Rieff's Mission. Character, Culture and Morality,' *Journal of Classical Sociology* 3(3) (2003), p. 291.

59 Langman, 'Rieff's Mission,' p. 293.

60 Rieff, 'By What Authority?' in *The Feeling Intellect*, p. 335.

61 Rieff, *Fellow Teachers*, p. 51n.

62 Rieff formulates it cryptically like this: 'I doubt that penetrative thrust inheres in the concept "secularization." We can do better without "secularization." The concept obscures interdictory-remissive shifts of indirective content. Secularization especially encourages false homotonalities, an ease of transitions that may falsify true oppositions: as between pastors and professors, for example – as if becoming a Professor really does express in another form ... earlier religious aspirations.' *Fellow Teachers*, p. 51n.

63 Brown, 'Rieff's Fellow Teachers,' p. 132.

64 For a more elaborate description of the secularizing effect of cultural pluralisation, see Berger, *A Far Glory*, pp. 25–46.

65 In the sociology of religion Peter Berger is a leading theorist on this subject. In *The Desecularization of the World: Resurgent Religion and World Politics* (Grand Rapids: Eerdmans, 1999) Berger summarizes his thesis on desecularization, a subject about which he started writing in 1977. He maintains that the classical secularization hypothesis, to which he contributed a lot himself, must be considered bankrupt. See Peter L. Berger, 'The Desecularization of the World: A Global Overview,' in *Desecularization of the World*, pp. 1–18.

66 Berger, 'Desecularization of the World,' p. 10.

67 Danièle Hervieu-Léger, 'The Twofold Limit of the Notion of secularization,' in Woodhead et al., *Berger*, pp. 119–21.

68 Danièle Hervieu-Léger, 'Pour une sociologie des "modernités religieuses multiples": une autre approche de la "religion invisible" des sociétés européennes,' *Social Compass* 50(3) (xxxx), pp. 290–1.

69 Hervieu-Léger, 'The Twofold Limit of the Notion of Secularization,' pp. 124–5.

70 Ibid., p. 124. The British sociologist Grace Davie also downplays the thesis of 'Eurosecularity.' She develops the concept of 'vicarious religion' in order to explain the different, but persistent, role of religion in Europe. The idea of vicarious religion is that the main religious tasks are delegated to a small group of people who are supposed to represent 'the religious voice' at different places and times. See Grace Davie, 'The Persistence of Institutional Religion in Modern Europe,' in Woodhead et al., *Berger*, pp. 101–11.

71 Hervieu-Léger, 'Twofold limit, p. 114.

72 See Jürgen Habermas, *Glauben und Wissen* (Frankfurt am Main: Suhrkamp, 2001).

73 For example, in his *After Christianity* (New York: Columbia University Press, 2003) the Italian philosopher Gianni Vattimo argues that Nietzsche's idea of the death of God can be interpreted as an equivalent of Heidegger's idea of the end of metaphysics. He even argues that their deconstruction of old metaphysical schemes is a necessary step in a process of 'purification of the transcendent' which is well in line with the inner vocation of the christian religion. He thinks this purification as a 'kenosis,' in which 'a weak God' pours himself out completely in immanent reality. Don Cupitt also considers secularization in terms of purification; see Cupitt's *Religion's Own Philosophy* (London: SCM, 2000).

74 Personal communication with Philip Rieff and Penelope Kaiserlian, director University of Virginia Press, March 2004.

References

Aarts, Jan, and Marianne Broeder. 'Psychoanalyse en sociologie: Het debat Rieff–Vandermeersch' (Psychoanalysis and sociology. The Rieff-Vandermeersch debate). *Sociologisch Tijdschrift* 11(3) (1984), pp. 503–29.

Abramson, Jeffrey. *Liberation and Its Limits: The Moral and Political Thought of Freud.* Boston: Beacon Press, 1984.

Alexander, Jeffrey C. 'Modern, Anti, Post and Neo: How Social Theorists Have Tried to Understand the "New World" of "Our Time."' *Zeitschrift für Soziologie* 23(3) (1994), pp. 165–97.

Auld, Frank. Review of *Freud: The Mind of the Moralist,* by Philip Rieff. *Religious Education* 55 (March-April 1960), pp. 153–5.

Bal, Mieke. *Reading 'Rembrandt': Beyond the Word-Image Opposition.* Cambridge: Cambridge University Press, 1991.

Barth, John. *The End of the Road.* New York: Bantam Books, 1969 [1958].

Bellah, Robert N., Richard Madsen, William M. Sullivan, Ann Swidler, and Steven M. Tipton. *Habits of the Heart. Individualism and Commitment in American Life.* Berkeley and Los Angeles: University of California Press, 1996 [1985].

Bergen, Bernard J., and Stanley D. Rosenberg. 'The New Neo-Freudians: Psychoanalytic Dimensions of Social Change.' *Psychiatry* 34 (February 1971), pp. 19–37.

Berger, Peter L. *A Far Glory: The Quest for Faith in an Age of Credulity.* New York: Anchor Books/Doubleday, 1992.

– 'The Desecularization of the World: A Global Overview.' In Peter L. Berger (ed.), *The Desecularization of the World: Resurgent Religion and World Politics.* Grand Rapids, MI: Eerdmans, 1999, pp. 1–18.

– 'Postscript.' In Linda Woodhead, Paul Heelas, and David Martin (eds.), *Peter Berger and the Study of Religion.* New York: Routledge, 2001, pp. 189–98.

Boyers, Robert (ed.). 'The Therapeutic and the End of Culture.' Review of *Fellow Teachers/Of Culture and Its Second Death*, by Philip Rieff. *Review of Existential Psychology and Psychiatry* 12(3) (1973), pp. 258–64.

– 'Perspectives on the Therapeutic in the Context of Contemporary Sociology: A Dialogue between Benjamin Nelson and Dennis Wrong.' In Robert Boyers (ed.), *Psychological Man*. New York: Harper and Row, 1975, pp. 143–78.

– *Psychological Man*. New York: Harper and Row, 1975.

Brown, Norman O. 'Rieff's "Fellow Teachers,"' In Robert Boyers (ed.), *Psychological Man*. New York: Harper and Row, 1975, pp. 131–42.

Browning, Don S. 'Philip Rieff: Psychological Man and the Penultimate Ethic of the Abundant Life.' In Don S. Browning, *Generative Man: Psychoanalytic Perspectives*. Philadelphia: Westminster Press, 1973, pp. 32–59.

Burt, Robert A. *Two Jewish Justices: Outcasts in the Promised Land*. Berkeley: University of California Press, 1988.

Cherry, Conrad. 'Boundaries and Frontiers for the Study of Religion: The Heritage of the Age of the University.' *Journal of the American Academy of Religion* 57(4) (1989), pp. 807–27.

Cochran, Clarke E. 'The Thin Theory of Community: The Communitarians and Their Critics.' *Political Studies* 32 (1989), pp. 422–35.

Conrad, Joseph. *Heart of Darkness*. London: Penguin, 1995 [1902].

Davie, Grace. 'The Persistence of Institutional Religion in Modern Europe.' In Linda Woodhead, Paul Heelas, and David Martin (eds.), *Peter Berger and the Study of Religion*. New York: Routledge, 2001, pp. 101–11.

Dollard, John. 'Society, Too, Is on the Couch.' Review of *Freud: The Mind of the Moralist*, by Philip Rieff. *New York Times Book Review*, 22 March 1959, pp. 7 and 26.

Dorrien, Gary. 'Berger: Theology and Sociology.' In Linda Woodhead, Paul Heelas, and David Martin (eds.), *Peter Berger and the Study of Religion*. New York: Routledge, 2001, pp. 26–39.

Elias, Nobert. *Über den Prozess der Zivilisation: Soziogenetische und Psychogenetische Untersuchungen*, vol. 1, *Wandlungen des Verhalten in den Weltlichen Oberschichten des Abendlandes*. Bern and Munich: Francke, 1969 [1939].

Evans, Matthew. 'The Sacred: Differentiating, Clarifying and Extending Concepts.' *Review of Religious Research* 45 (2003), pp. 32–47.

Fine, Gary A., and Philip Manning. 'Preserving Philip Rieff: The Reputation of a Fellow Teacher.' *Journal of Classical Sociology* 3(3) (2003), pp. 227–33.

Fitzgerald, Paul J. 'Faithful Sociology: Peter Berger's Religious Project.' *Religious Studies Review* 27(1) (2001), pp. 10–17.

Foucault, Michel. *The Use of Pleasure: The History of Sexuality*, vol. 2. trans. R. Hurley. London: Penguin, 1992.

Freud, Sigmund. *The Interpretation of Dreams*, vol. 5, *The Complete Psychological Works of Sigmund Freud, Standard Edition*. London: Hogarth Press, 1968 [1900].

– *The Ego and the Id*, vol. 19, *The Complete Psychological Works of Sigmund Freud, Standard Edition*. London: Hogarth Press, 1953 [1923].

– *Moses and Monotheism*. Transl. by K. Jones. London: Hogarth Press, 1949 [1939].

Gabriel, Yannis. 'Freud, Rieff and the Critique of American Culture.' *Psychoanalytic Review* 69(3) (1982), pp. 341–66.

Gauchet, Marcel. *The Disenchantment of the World: A Political History of Religion*. Trans. Oscar Burge. Princeton: Princeton University Press, 1997 [1985].

Gay, Peter. *Sigmund Freud: A Life for Our Time*. London and Melbourne: J.M. Dent. 1988.

Geertz, Clifford. *The Interpretation of Cultures: Selected Essays*. New York: Basic Books, 1973.

Goode, Stephen. 'In Praise of Things Past.' *Insight*, 8 March 1992, pp. 12–14 and pp. 28–9.

Goodheart, Eugene. 'A Postscript to the Higher Criticism: The Case of Philip Rieff.' In *The Failure of Criticism*. Cambridge: Harvard University Press, 1978, pp. 84–104.

Green, Martin. 'A New Sensibility?' Review of *Against Interpretation*, by Susan Sontag, and *The Triumph of the Therapeutic*, by Philip Rieff. *Cambridge Quarterly* 2(1) (1966–7), pp. 55–65.

Habermas, Jürgen. *Glauben und Wissen*. Frankfurt am Main: Suhrkamp, 2001.

Hammond, Philip E. (ed.). *The Sacred in a Secular Age: Toward Revision in the Scientific Study of Religion*. Berkeley: University of California Press, 1985.

Heckscher, William S. *Rembrandt's Anatomy of Dr Nicolaas Tulp: An Iconological Study*. New York: New York University Press, 1958.

Hervieu-Léger, Danièle. *Religion as a Chain of Memory*. Cambridge: Polity Press, 2000 [1993].

– 'The Twofold Limit of the Notion of Secularization.' In Linda Woodhead, Paul Heelas, and David Martin (eds.), *Peter Berger and the Study of Religion*. New York: Routledge 2001, pp. 112–25.

– 'Pour une sociologie des "modernités religieuses multiples": une autre approche de la "religion invisible" des sociétés européennes.' *Social Compass* 50(3) (2003), pp. 287–95.

Homans, Peter. *Theology after Freud: An Interpretive Inquiry*. Indianapolis and New York: Bobbs-Merrill, 1970.

– (ed.) *Childhood and Selfhood: Essays on Tradition, Religion, and Modernity in the Psychology of Erik H. Erikson*. Lewisburg, Penn.: Bucknell University Press, 1978, pp. 231–63.

– *The Ability to Mourn: Disillusionment and the Social Origins of Psychoanalysis.* Chicago and London: University of Chicago Press, 1989.

Kadushin, Charles. *The American Intellectual Elite.* Boston: Little, Brown, 1974.

Kafka, Franz. *Metamorphosis and Other Stories.* Trans. W. and E. Muir. London: Minerva, 1990.

Kaye, Howard. 'Rationalization as Sublimation: On the Cultural Analyses of Weber and Freud.' *Theory, Culture and Society,* 9 (1992), pp. 45–74.

– 'Rieff's *Freud* and the Tyranny of Psychology.' *Journal of Classical Sociology* 3(3) (2003), pp. 263–77.

Kermode, Frank. 'That Uncertain Feeling.' Review of *Fellow Teachers/Of Culture and Its Second Death,* by Philip Rieff. *Times Literary Supplement,* 13 June 1975, pp. 638–9.

Kerrigan, William. 'Psychoanalysis and the Vicissitudes of the Enlightenment.' *American Imago* 48(2) (1991), pp. 265–78.

King, Richard H. 'From Creeds to Therapies: Philip Rieff's Work in Perspective.' *Reviews in American History,* June 1976, pp. 291–9.

Lang, Berel. 'About the Dead Speak []Only, [] Mainly, [] Some, [] No Good.' Review of *Fellow Teachers/Of Culture and Its Second Death,* by Philip Rieff. *Salmagundi* 71, 1986, pp. 227–5.

Langman, Lauren. 'Philip Rieff's Mission: Character, Culture and Morality.' *Journal of Classical Sociology* 3(3) (2003), pp. 279–95.

Lasch, Christopher. 'The Saving Remnant.' Review of *The Feeling Intellect: Selected Writings,* by Philip Rieff. *New Republic,* 19 Nov. 1990, pp. 32–6.

– 'Philip Rieff and the Religion of Culture.' In *The Revolt of the Elites and the Betrayal of Democracy.* New York: Norton, 1995, pp. 213–29.

Leeuw, van der, Gerardus. *Sacred and Profane Beauty: The Holy in Art.* New York: Holt, Rinehart and Winston, 1963 [1932].

Lefevre, Perry. 'A Penultimate Ethic of Honesty.' Review of *Freud: The Mind of the Moralist,* by Philip Rieff. *Christian Scholar* 43, 1959, pp. 329–34.

Lichtermann, Paul. 'Beyond the Seesaw Model: Public Commitment in a Culture of Self-Fulfillment.' *Sociological Theory* 13(3) (1995), pp. 275–300.

Lynch, William F. 'Psychological Man.' *America,* 25 Nov. 1967, pp. 635–7.

Manning, Philip. 'Philip Rieff's Moral Vision of Sociology: From Positive to Negative Communities – and Back?' *Journal of Classical Sociology* 3(3) (2003), pp. 234–46.

Marcuse, Herbert. *Eros and Civilization: A Philosophical Inquiry into Freud.* New York: Vintage Books, 1961 [1955].

Megill, Allan. *Prophets of Extremity: Nietzsche, Heidegger, Foucault, Derrida.* Berkeley: University of California Press, 1985.

Milbank, John. *Theology and Social Theory: Beyond Secular Reason*. Oxford: Blackwell, 1993 [1990].

– 'Knowledge: The Theological Critique of Philosophy in Hamann and Jacobi.' In John Milbank, Catherine Pickstock, and Graham Ward (eds.), *Radical Orthodoxy*. London and New York: Routledge, 2001 [1999], pp. 21–37.

Muller, Jerry Z. 'A Neglected Conservative Thinker.' *Commentary* 91(2) (1991), pp. 49–52.

Naipaul, V. Shiva. 'Hang-Ups, Crises, Rebirth.' Review of *Fellow Teachers/Of Culture and Its Second Death* by Philip Rieff. *Washington Post*, 12 January 1974, page number unknown.

Nietzsche, Friedrich. *The Gay Science: With a Prelude in German Rhymes and an Appendix of Songs*. Ed. B. Williams. Trans. J. Nauckhoff. Cambridge: Cambridge University Press, 2001.

Piver, Kenneth S. 'Philip Rieff: The Critic of Psychoanalysis as Cultural Theorist.' In Mark Micale and Roy Porter (eds.), *Discovering the History of Psychiatry*, New York and Oxford: Oxford University Press, 1994, pp. 191–215.

Pollack, Sheldon D. 'The Elusive Freud.' *Psychoanalytic Review* 71(4) (1984), pp. 515–27.

Ricoeur, Paul. *Freud and Philosophy: An Essay on Interpretation*. Trans. by D. Savage. New Haven and London: Yale University Press, 1977; 1st ed., in French, 1965.

Rieff, Philip. 'A Jesuit Looks at Proudhon. Competition in Damnation.' Review of *The Un-Marxian Socialist*, by Henri de Lubac. *Modern Review* 3(2) (1950), pp. 166–71. Also in *The Feeling Intellect*, pp. 163–7.

– 'History, Psychoanalysis, and the Social Sciences.' *Ethics* 63(2) (1953), pp. 107–20.

– 'Freud's Contribution to Political Psychology. Doctoral disseration, University of Chicago, 1954. (Unpublished, available on microfilm in the library of the University of Chicago).

– Review of *Understanding the Sick and the Healthy: A View of World, Man and God* by Fransz Rosenzweig. *Journal of Religion* 35(4) (1955), pp. 262–3. Also in *The Feeling Intellect*, with the title 'On Frans Rosenzweig,' pp. 97–8.

– 'Freudian Ethics and the Idea of Reason.' *Ethics* 67(3), part 1 (1957), pp. 169–83.

– Review, of *Education and Sociology*, by Emile Durkheim. *American Sociological Review* 22(2), (1957), pp. 233–4. Also in *The Feeling Intellect* with the title 'Emile Durkheim's *Education and Sociology*,' pp. 233–5.

– *Freud: The Mind of the Moralist*. Chicago: University of Chicago Press, 1979 [1959].

– 'The Function of the Social Sciences and Humanities in a Science Curriculum.' *Religious Education* 54(2) (1959), pp. 156–63. Also in *The Feeling Intellect*, pp. 237–47.

– 'He Discovered a New Image of Man.' Review of *Collected Papers* (5 vols.), by Sigmund Freud. *New York Times Book Review*, 19 July 1959, p. 1 and p. 16.

– 'Reflections on Psychological Man in America.' *What's New*, no. 220 (1960). Abbott Laboratories What's New Anniversary Issue. *Contemporary Comment* no. 13, pp. 17–23. Also in *The Feeling Intellect*, pp. 3–10.

– 'The Mirage of College Politics.' *Harper's Magazine* 223, no. 1337 (1961), pp. 156–63.

– *The Collected Papers of Sigmund Freud*, 10 vols. Edited and introduced by Philip Rieff. New York: Macmillan, 1963, vol. 1, *The History of the Psychoanalytic Movement*; vol. 2, *Early Psychoanalytic Writings*; vol. 3, *Therapy and Technique*; vol. 4, *Dora: An Analysis of a Case of Hysteria*; vol. 5, *The Sexual Enlightenment of Children*; vol. 6, *General Psychological Theory*; vol. 7, *Three Case Histories*; vol. 8, *Sexuality and the Psychology of Love*; vol. 9, *Character and Culture*; vol. 10, *Studies in Parapsychology*.

– Review, of *Communication and Social Order*, by H.D. Duncan. *American Sociological Review* 29(4) (1964), pp. 602–3.

– Review, of *European Positivism in the Nineteenth Century, An Essay in Intellectual History*, by W.M. Simon. *American Sociological Review* 30(5) (1965), pp. 790–1.

– *The Triumph of the Therapeutic: Uses of Faith after Freud*. Chicago: University of Chicago Press, 1987 [1966].

– *On Intellectuals: Theoretical Studies / Case Studies*. Ed. Philip Rieff. New York: Doubleday, 1969.

– 'Doctor to the Body of the Doctor of the Mind.' Review of *Freud: Living and Dying*, by M. Schur. *New York Times Book Review*, 18 June 1972, pp. 23–4.

– *Fellow Teachers/of Culture and Its Second Death*. Chicago: University of Chicago Press, 1985 [1972].

– 'Intimations of Therapeutic Truth: Decoding Appendix G in Moses and Monotheism.' *Humanities in Society* 4(2–3) (1981), pp. 197–201. Also in *The Feeling Intellect*, pp. 61–5.

– 'By What Authority? Post-Freudian Reflections on the Repression of the Repressive as Modern Culture.' *The Feeling Intellect*, pp. 330–51. This is a shortened and revised version of a text with the same title published in J. P. Diggins and M. E. Kann (eds.), *The Problem of Authority in America*. Philadelphia: Temple University Press, 1981, pp. 225–55.

– 'For the Last Time Psychology.' *Salmagundi* nos. 74–5 (1987), pp. 101–17. Also in *The Feeling Intellect*, pp. 351–65.

– *The Feeling Intellect: Selected Writings*. Ed. Jonathan B. Imber. Chicago: University of Chicago Press, 1990.

– 'The Newer Noises of War in the Second Culture Camp: Notes on Professor Burt's Legal Fictions.' *Yale Journal of Law and the Humanities* 3(2) (1991), pp. 315–88.

–, 'Worlds at War: Illustrations of an Aesthetics in Authority; or Numbered Notes towards a Trilogy, of which the General Title is "Sacred Order / Social Order."' In Eileen Barker, James A. Beckford, and Karel Dobbelaere (eds.), *Secularization, Rationalism and Sectarianism: Essays in Honour of Bryan R. Wilson.* Oxford: Clarendon Press, 1993, pp. 214–65.

Robinson, Paul A. *The Freudian Left: Wilhelm Reich, Geza Roheim, Herbert Marcuse.* New York: Harper and Row, 1969.

Roszak, Theodore. *The Making of a Counter Culture: Reflections on the Technocratic Society and Its Youthful Opposition.* London: Faber and Faber, 1970 [1968].

Snow, C.P. 'Parochial Spies.' Review of *Fellow Teachers/Of Culture and Its Second Death,* by Philip Rieff. *Financial Times,* 27 February 1975.

Steiner, George. 'Sermon for Prophets.' Review of *Fellow Teachers/Of Culture and Its Second Death,* by Philip Rieff. *Sunday Times,* 29 March 1975.

Toynbee, Philip. 'Critique of Freud.' Review of *Freud: The Mind of the Moralist,* by Philip Rieff. *Encounter,* April 1960, pp. 73–6.

Vandermeersch, Patrick G.M. *Ethiek tussen wetenschap en ideologie* (*Ethics between Science and Ideology*), Leuven: Peeters, 1987.

– *Unresolved Questions in the Freud–Jung Debate: On Psychosis, Sexual Identiy and Religion.* Louvain Philosophical Studies. Leuven: Leuven University Press, 1991.

– *La chair de la passion – Une histoire de foi: la flagellation.* Paris: Cerf, 2002.

Voegelin, Eric. *Order and History,* vol. 4, *The Ecumenic Age.* Baton Rouge and London: Louisiana State University Press, 1974.

Watson, Gerry. 'The Impossible Culture of the Therapeutic: An Essay on the Sociology of Philip Rieff.' *Compass: A Provincial Review* 5 (1979), pp. 39–62.

Wilson, Bryan. 'The Return of the Sacred?' *Journal for the Scientific Study of Religion* 18(3) (1979), pp. 268–80.

Woodhead, Linda, Paul Heelas, and David Martin (eds.). *Peter Berger and the Study of Religion.* New York: Routledge, 2001.

Woolfolk, Alan. 'The Therapeutic Ideology of Moral Freedom.' *Journal of Classical Sociology* 3(3) (2003), pp. 247–62.

Wright, Gordon, and Arthur, Mejia Jr. *An Age of Controversy: Discussion Problems in Twentieth Century European History.* New York: Dodd, Mead, 1964, pp. 417–21.

Index

aesthetic(s). *See* authority; form
ambivalence: in Freud's theory, 7, 31, 33–42, 58, 61, 94; of Rieff towards Freud, 61
anti-Judaism, 115–16, 135, 188n55
art: as substitute for religion, 161; function(s) of, 6, 94, 96, 99–100; modern, 83, 105–7; Rieff as art collector, 22; works of art, 98, 133
Augustine, Saint, 188n64
authority: aesthetic(s) of, 125–6, 165; crisis of, 120, 123, 136–8, 159; cultural role of, 9–10, 32, 52–3, 57, 65, 71, 75, 90–7, 128, 144, 161; Freud's theory of, 7–8, 15, 49–52, 61–2, 75, 100; and identity, 137–9; operation of, 102–3, 105–8, 119–22; release of, 109, 114, 156; and religion, 72, 86, 161; and sacred order, 90, 122–5, 133–4, 141; and sublimation, 56, 102–3; Weber's theory of, 106, 192n46
autonomy of individual, 30, 32, 50–1, 70, 131, 164

Bellah, Robert N., 147, 158, 163
Berger, Peter L., 144–7, 154, 162
Borges, Jorge L., 138
Brown, Norman O., 15, 53–6, 110–12, 161

character, 27, 36, 38; character-ideal, 43–66, 67–89, 104, 121, 124, 156; Jewish character, 58
Christianity, 44; decline of, 7, 41, 68, 84; and morality, 31; relation to Judaism, 59, 115–16, 135
church, 45, 79, 115, 127, 134, 135, 157, 162–3
civilization, 78, 88, 115, 127, 134; Western, 44–5, 59, 142; origins of, 75; transformation of, 22
commitment, 67–89
communism, 13, 22
community: participation in, 79–80, 84; interaction between individual and, 6, 32, 50
Comte, Auguste, 4, 32, 113
Conrad, Joseph, 181n23, 187n53
counterculture, 19–20, 104, 145
culture: anti-culture(s), 5, 83, 117, 130, 141; crisis of, 6, 9; criticism, 120, 122, 130, 143; and cultus, 68–70, 156; dynamic(s) of, 46, 133;

elite of, 14, 70, 92, 192n44; function of, 74; high, 96, 117; Jewish, 114–15; modern, 4, 71, 80, 97; and morality, 108; late modern, 68, 74, 82–9, 90, 97, 100, 138, 141, 143, 156, 160; pluralism of, 161; post-modern, 147, 156; pre-modern, 68, 71, 72, 74, 80; psychoanalytic theory of, 10, 17–18, 25, 40–2, 142; and religion, 4, 5, 48, 73, 82–9, 147–63; Rieff's definitions of, 95, 126–8; second culture camp, 9, 119, 134–5, 141, 150; theory of, 5–6, 8–10, 62–6, 96, 114, 147; transcendence and, 5, 8, 143; and the sacred, 5, 90, 119–39

Davie, Grace, 194n70
death: of God / the gods, 3, 30, 123; as limit, 105; second death of Western culture, 188n64
Derrida, Jacques, 125, 176n50, 186n21
desecularization, 4; theory, 148, 150–65
Dewey, John, 34, 36, 38
Deuteronomy, 127
dogma(s), 47, 91, 134
Durkheim, Emile, 5, 114, 163, 172n21, 181n29, 192n46

education, 85; academic, 20, 91–3, 113
Enlightenment, 44, 124, 125, 141, 189n4
Elias, Norbert, 48
eros, 10, 52, 65, 94, 102–3
Exodus, 99, 104, 131–3

faith(s), 30, 44, 45, 67, 70, 72–4, 82, 113, 138, 149, 153–65; negational, 121
form(s), interdictory, 100, 103, 105–10, 114, 116–17, 119–22
Freud, Sigmund: *The Ego and the Id*, 95, 181n17; *History of the Psychoanalytic Movement*, 26–32; *The Interpretation of Dreams*, 38, 175n39, 176n40; *Moses and Monotheism*, 57–62, 82, 116–17, 175n33; *Totem and Taboo*, 58, 82, 172n39, 178n23
Freudianism, 14–18

Gauchet, Marcel, 171n13
Geertz, Clifford, 148
Genesis, 49, 131–3, 137–8
God-term(s), 36, 47, 81, 104, 106
guilt, 70, 75, 105–8, 124

Hamlet, 117, 125
Hegel, G.W.F., 37, 58, 60, 112
Hervieu-Léger, Danièle, 161–3
history, 22, 34, 40, 57, 109–12, 149; Jewish, 104, 114, 116; psycho-, 45–6, 58, 61, 110; Western cultural, 9, 44–5, 116
Hitler, 117, 135, 186n16

identity: collective, 71; communist, 80; gender, 50; individual, 37, 112; Jewish, 58, 116, 135–9; quest for, 107
identification: and authority, 7–8, 51–2, 137; and guilt, 75; with ideal-figures, 7–8, 50, 67, 75–6, 81, 88, 100, 156; and neurosis, 7–8; upward, 124
imagination, 9, 63, 76, 126–35, 138, 162
Imber, Jonathan, vii, 19, 21, 170n23

instinct: theory, 36; Rieff on, 62–6, 111, 173n6
institution(s), 14, 64, 82, 108, 110–11, 128, 136, 162; academic, 16, 112, 157; religious, 82, 85, 157, 161
institutional form of authority, 165
intellectual(s), 14, 18
interdict(s), 96–100, 105–8; and culture, 96–100, 104, 114, 127–8, 157, 164–5; Freud and, 96, 116, 123; of interdicts (death), 105; and Jewish law, 110, 116 (*see also* Deuteronomy; Exodus); and sublimation, 100–1, 104. *See also* form
interdictory figure(s), 101, 116
interpretation(s), 47, 93, 114, 127, 176n50
irony, 18, 143

Jew(s) of culture, 114–18
Joyce, James, 125, 138, 187n53
Jung, C.G., 82–5, 93, 128; and Freud, 26–8

Kafka, Franz, 125, 181n38, 187n53
Kant, Immanuel, 30–1, 62, 157
Kierkegaard, Søren, 20, 177n20
knowledge, 31, 47, 91, 108, 153; and faith, 30, 127; of guilt, 107

Lasch, Christopher, 15, 21, 23–4, 157
law, 106–8, 135–6; therapeutic dissolution of, 111; Mosaic (Jewish), 59, 110, 116
Lawrence, D.H., 82–3, 87–9, 93, 128, 143–4
liberal revisors of Freud, 36
libido. *See* instinct
liturgy, 156, 174n16
Luckmann, Thomas, 184n95
Luther, Martin, 183n60

MacIntyre, Alisdair, 24
Madonna, 50, 178n44
man: economic, 44–5, 68–9; political, 44, 69, 105–6; psychological, 4, 15, 42, 43–5, 49, 53, 68, 144; religious, 44, 68–9, 105
Marcuse, Herbert, 15, 17, 53–6, 102–3, 173n6; one-dimensional man, 15
Marx, Karl, 4, 8, 116
Marxism, 6, 13, 14, 17–18, 60, 80; Freudo-, 17, 55; Wilhelm Reich and, 85–7
Marxist analysis of modernity, 79
metaphor, Rieff's use of, 143
Milbank, John, 148–50
modernity. *See* culture, modern
motif, interdictory, 114
myth(s), 46–54, 68, 84, 129, 159; of man, 45

negation, 94, 95, 121
neurosis, 7, 17, 31, 34, 38, 51, 96; Freud's etiology of, 39–40, 48
Nietzsche, Friedrich, 3, 19, 37, 125, 138

Oedipus, 117; complex, 40, 49–53, 57
order: political, 44; sacred, 4–11, 119–39, 152–65

Plato, 44, 54, 69, 78, 92, 129
political science, Rieff and, 12, 14
politics, 17, 43, 149. *See also* man, political
possibility, primacy of, 122–30, 160
postmodernity, Rieff's theory of, 20

power: and aesthetics, 117; and authority, 107; of the past, 40
psychoanalysis: aim of, 29, 32; and authority, 51, 94, 100; cultural influence of, 9–10, 16; Rieff's interpretation of, 41–2, 43–66, 96; as scientific discipline, 28–9, 33–6; as theory of culture, 6–11, 25, 31, 41–2, 75
psychoanalytic movement, 25–8
psychology: cultural influence of, 25, 43; Jungian, 83–5; psychoanalysis as, 27–8, 33–6

rationality, 105, 159; Freud on, 31
rationalism, 144, 179n49
reality, 5, 29–31, 46, 65, 92, 102–3, 132, 153
reason, 44, 54, 84, 87, 103, 155
Reich, Wilhelm, 17, 82–3, 85–7, 128
religion: crisis of, 3; and culture (*see* culture); Freud on, 27–8, 31, 57–62, 116; 'new,' 4, 161–3; of psychological man, 45; pseudo-, 82–9; Rieff on, 72–4, 147–65; sociological analysis of, 4–5, 48
remission(s), 69, 87, 89, 106, 123–5
repression: dynamic of, 50–3, 57–65, 85–7, 90, 94–6, 126, 141–2, 152, 165; Freud's theory of, 27, 38–42; primal, 95, 123; and sacred order, 119–23; and sublimation, 100–2
revelation, 131, 152
Romanticism, 37
Rousseau, Jean-Jacques, 69, 79, 189n4

sacred order. *See* order
Saint-Simon, Comte de, 32
salvation, 70–80, 84–6, 156
science of limits, 105–6, 114, 142
secularization, 110, 116; thesis, 4, 153–4, 160–3
sexuality, 54–7, 63; homo-, 145
sociology, 83, 96, 113, 147; task of, 43, 112–14, 149; of religion, 4–5, 62, 113, 160–3; therapeutic, 113
Stevens, Wallace, 125, 132
sublimation, 8, 10, 53–7, 100–4, 120, 141–2
super ego symbolism, manipulation of, 93–4, 120
symbol: saving, 81; system, 28, 68, 79, 137; system of Western culture, 9, 75, 78, 81–2, 138
symbolic(s), 97, 109, 128; impoverishment, 77; of communal purpose, 69; of creation, 131; cultural, 68, 69–87, 155–6; sacred order and, 122, 128; worlds, 6, 128

theory of theory, 28–32
therapeutic(s), 76–7, 80, 81, 97, 98, 105–8; as cultural type, 109–10
therapy: and faith, 153, 154, 158; origin of, 109–10: premodern and modern, 72–82; psychoanalytic, 9, 41, 51, 55, 101, 121; Rieff's definition of, 32, 67, 69–70, 148
theology, 4, 112, 147–50, 155; psychoanalysis and, 15; Rieff's use of, 22, 47; sociology and, 149–50, 153–5
tradition(s), 32, 52, 112, 159; Jewish, 58, 114–18, 137–9; Freud and, 40, 41, 59; liberation from, 122; religious, 76, 79, 84, 127, 159
transference, 39–40, 52, 74, 100

transgression(s), 20, 97, 106, 108, 112, 117; remission and, 124–5

unconscious: collective, 84; controversies over, 27–8, 53–7; Freud's theory of, 36–8, 51–2, 94–6, 122–3; Rieff on, 62–6, 94–6, 108

Weber, Max, 5, 92, 106, 112, 114, 153, 192n46
Weltanschauung(en), 4, 17, 49, 119, 160
Wilde, Oscar, 22
Wilson, Bryan, 4–5, 158